DISRUPTION PROOF

ALSO BY BRANT COOPER

The Lean Entrepreneur

DISRUPTION PROOF

Empower People,
Create Value,
Drive Change

BRANT COOPER

GRAND CENTRAL
PUBLISHING

NEW YORK   BOSTON

Grand Central Publishing
Hachette Book Group
1290 Avenue of the Americas, New York, NY 10104
grandcentralpublishing.com
twitter.com/grandcentralpub

First Edition: October 2021

Grand Central Publishing is a division of Hachette Book Group, Inc. The Grand Central Publishing name and logo is a trademark of Hachette Book Group, Inc.

The publisher is not responsible for websites (or their content) that are not owned by the publisher.

The Hachette Speakers Bureau provides a wide range of authors for speaking events. To find out more, go to www.hachettespeakersbureau.com or call (866) 376-6591.

Print book interior design by Tom Louie.

Library of Congress Cataloging-in-Publication Data

Names: Cooper, Brant, author.
Title: Disruption proof : empower people, create value, drive change / Brant Cooper.
Description: First Edition. | New York, NY : Grand Central Publishing, 2021. | Includes bibliographical references and index. | Summary: "One thing in life is certain: change is constant. Thanks to the rapid pace of technological innovation in the digital age-and further accelerated by the global COVID-19 pandemic-massive structural change is happening more frequently and on a greater scale than ever before. Faced with unprecedented complexity and uncertainty, most business leaders struggle to see the way forward. Yet company organization, systems, and management are still largely based on what was most effective in the Industrial Age. Disruption Proof offers a new approach that addresses our current needs. Through powerful case studies of Moves the Needle's notable corporate clients like Intuit, General Mills, Proctor & Gamble, and more, Cooper demonstrates how, with the right tools, anyone can weather turmoil and protect future profits. Disruption Proof provides readers with detailed instructions on for progressing through four stages of implementation in order to embrace a new way of working company-wide, including how to: develop an understanding of customers and colleagues that lead to insights (empathy) run tests to challenge assumptions (exploration) leverage data and insights to breakthrough biases (evidence) balance operational execution with learning (equilibrium) manage behavior to match corporate values (ethics) By adopting these "5E"s, all employees can ensure their company's ability to navigate moments of crisis and find transformative opportunities. Cooper explains how innovation at every level is the key to organic and sustainable growth, and guides leaders to create lasting value in the world. With Cooper's action-oriented advice and tools, anyone can help steer their company toward durable success"-- Provided by publisher.
Identifiers: LCCN 2021023043 | ISBN 9781538720196 (hardcover) | ISBN 9781538705995 (ebook)
Subjects: LCSH: Organizational change. | Organizational learning. | Industrial management--Technological innovations. | Business enterprises--Technological innovations.
Classification: LCC HD58.8 .C65656 2021 | DDC 658.4/06--dc23
LC record available at https://lccn.loc.gov/2021023043

ISBNs: 978-1-5387-2019-6 (hardcover), 978-1-5387-0599-5 (ebook)

Printed in the United States of America

LSC-C

Printing 1, 2021

In memory of my dad, Ross Ellston Cooper

CONTENTS

AUTHOR'S NOTE

The creation of *Disruption Proof* was begun before the COVID-19 pandemic, not as a response to the challenges societal institutions face in the wake of its global disruption, but as a recognition that we live in an era of continuous disruption. This recognition came from my career in startups, where we earnestly sought to use technology to disrupt markets in order to change the world for the better. It came from a decade of working with some of the largest organizations in the world that were grappling with "innovation" and "digital transformation." It came from helping cities establish startup ecosystems, in order to create jobs and maintain their communities.

And then, well, boom! The pandemic hits. Rome is burning.

The pandemic was a hot mess. All the components of the disruption story are here: the incredible wins of capitalism in creating vaccines; the failure in bailouts going to executive compensation and stock buybacks; the accelerated inequity of the economy; the struggle of some businesses versus the rapid growth of others; the failures, challenges, and successes of various governmental institutions. The list goes on.

In the end, we should not lose the bigger picture here. The pandemic is a microcosm of the larger disruption at play. Business cannot return to the way things were before. The pandemic is a lesson we mustn't miss. Continuous disruption is the new norm. The question we must answer is: How do we ensure that disruption benefits us all? How do we protect those that are disrupted? And moreover, how do we create radically resilient organizations?

Introduction

BRAVE NEW DISRUPTION

One of my professors in college was a wise and weathered Polish émigré. He wore thick glasses and spoke with an equally thick accent, in a late-afternoon, nap-inducing monotone. Through his lectures one got a sense of the intensity of a life constrained behind the Iron Curtain, of a time before he and countless others made their way West, to democracy and the freedom and fulfillment it provided.

The class was Comparative Economics, which detailed the differences between economic systems, primarily Western capitalism and Soviet-style communism. This was before the Solidarity trade union led the movement that ended the communist rule in Poland. My professor had spent much of his life under the Soviet system. I can still hear him telling us, "In the Soviet Union, when the five-year plan called for five tons of screws, manufacturers would produce five 1-ton screws." My professor may have even got a laugh out of the class, but I'm pretty sure I took it literally to mean five metal screws, each one the size of a small Chevy.

The Soviet system was fixed and predictable, the outcomes rigid and predetermined. It utterly lacked any of the dynamism we enjoy in the West. It collapsed for a variety of reasons, financial and human aspirations key among them.

Today it's widely accepted around most of the world that, generally, market forces will create a more efficient economic system than the government can through top-down management. A laissez-faire government works best. The extreme opposite to the laissez-faire–style government, the Soviet economy was a brute-force, execute-the-plan system. More, bigger, faster. The metric that mattered was quantity of output. The state enforced output via its power. *It was a dull, dehumanizing approach.*

As a contrast, it's not difficult to look across the broad spectrum of goods and services that comprise markets today to recognize the extraordinary success of capitalism. Take the astonishing number of jobs created. In 2019 alone, the United States logged more than 2.09 million jobs, according to the U.S. Bureau of Labor Statistics. That's about 239 jobs for every hour of every day. The number of small businesses (those with fewer than 500 employees) is equally jaw-dropping, at 30.7 million, accounting for *99 percent of all businesses*, per the U.S. Small Business Administration (SBA).[i] Granted, these numbers are robust by any measure, and while the COVID-19 pandemic resulted in a dramatic shift in these stats for 2020, they nonetheless speak to the power of American hard work, innovation, entrepreneurship, and value creation. *All qualities our system rewards.*

I lived through the dot-com boom and bust of the late 1990s and early 2000s, and back in my startup days, I remember getting a tour of a manufacturing facility. I was amazed by the sheer size and sophistication of the machines used to…make other machines. Skynet from James Cameron's *Terminator* movies came to mind, but nonetheless, it was awe-inspiring. When I travel to great port cities around the globe, I'm easily mesmerized by the automated cranes moving shipping crates from ship to stacks to trucks and vice versa, with extraordinary precision. It's speed, it's progress, it's the potential for fulfilling needs and wants on a massive scale.

I get a particular feeling of joy when I'm driving through a city, and see a business like Big Lebowski's Bowling Pin Supply company, and think, "Who the heck ever knew that such a business needed to exist?" Capitalism does that, naturally. No intervention required. It's not part of any government's five-year plan, but instead is a reflection of the owners' dream, the employees' service, and the customers' loyalty.

The crux to all of this is a freedom of choice my professor lacked prior to arriving in the United States. It is the freedom for people to create and sell a product or service, the freedom to choose where and for whom to work, the freedom to choose among providers when looking to address a need. It also offers the freedom for people to invest in a company, its leadership, its employees, and its mission. The outcome of all this freedom is value for customers, jobs, tax revenue, and potentially other goodwill initiatives for the community.

These freedoms, though, are often competing. The relationship between economic entities is symbiotic, both supplying and receiving value. Entrepreneurs or business owners who create and sell products naturally wish to be the *only* seller within some context, to achieve some minimal ends. Exceptions exist, but sellers strive for some level of market exclusivity in order to meet their own needs and desires. "It is not from the benevolence of the butcher, the brewer, or the baker that we expect our dinner," wrote Adam Smith in *The Wealth of Nations*, "but from their regard to their own self-interest." Every company, regardless of size, wishes for profitability, growth opportunities, and, most important, longevity.

The professional worker sells her own services and wants the highest price she can get, and so does not welcome competition. Just as with the business owner, the person who sells the product of their labor must be able to achieve some minimal ends. Tension exists, therefore, between employer and employee for the price of labor, and this contributes to tension between owner and consumer as well.

The consumer wants choices in order to find the best value. Value in this context is not simply lower price, but a balance between quality of the job performed and affordability. Choice means competition, which runs directly counter to the wishes of the business owner. It's obvious, but worth pointing out, that both owner and worker are also consumers.

The tension among these three stakeholders (owner, worker, and consumer) is a good thing. A system becomes stable when opposing forces achieve equilibrium. The forces do not have to be equal, as long as a balance is achieved. The power of the forces determines the characteristics of the state of equilibrium. The state of the equilibrium, for example, will vary widely among scenarios where workers don't have options for finding work or consumers have no product choices or owners cannot find enough skilled workers, or have hundreds of competitors.

There is a paradox here that is unique to human beings: People can perceive the desired need to exercise their own power, while also understanding the need to keep the system stable. If one stakeholder overpowers another, the system collapses. The power desired by any one stakeholder runs counter to the interest in system stability. In contrast to the wolves in Yellowstone that do not care how the beavers are doing, the different players in the economic system recognize the need for the other players.

While aware of others at some level, human beings are inherently biased. That they will naturally seek to benefit themselves is an immutable fact. However, they're not always right. In other words, they don't always make the choices that will best serve their interests. They also are not always rational. So the system itself must achieve a balance such that everyone benefits, though not likely to the extent each desires. The system needs to be as sturdy as possible against the whims of human behavior, which will inexorably lead it to attempt to tip the balance in its own favor.

Notorious billionaire entrepreneur Peter Thiel put the bias to push toward imbalance for self-benefit more bluntly: "Competition is for losers."[ii]

Of course, not all capitalists believe exactly that, but it's hard to argue that sentiment isn't a part of the natural state of running a business. There are numerous examples of erstwhile competitors co-operating in order to solve wicked problems, such as delivering a vaccine for a novel coronavirus, or to create new markets like space exploration or electronic warfare technology in World War II. But there's enough truth in the statement to believe that the striving-for-monopoly ethos is present, if not paramount, and ironically risks collapsing the system.

In order to establish and maintain stability, the system needs an outside party to manage it. This is the role of government. In a democracy, society chooses the state of economic equilibrium through governmental policy. The government manages the power of the forces. Each of the players—business owner, worker, customer—belongs to the society and has a say in the creation of the system's rules. Easy as pie, right?

In our ongoing quest for more civility in society, we often strive toward consensus and bipartisanship. Civility—or the appearance of civility—becomes more important than the real-world consequences of policy. As Jack Nicholson's President Dale says to the Martians in *Mars Attacks!* "Why can't we all just get along?"

We can, as long as "getting along" means that we strive for a stable, equitable system, while also understanding that it's okay for us to have opposing interests. In a widely heterogeneous society, it's not a surprise that people differ on what a stable system looks like, what the right power level for the economic players should be, and how we establish that. But such is democracy. It's messy. We don't need to agree on the results, but we do need to ensure fair and equal participation and to live with the outcomes, while striving for change. It requires us, like the Dude in *The Big Lebowski*, to simply abide.

The rules exist to bring fairness, order, and some amount of pre-dictability to the broader economic system. We *choose* capitalism. But we also *choose* the rules of capitalism in order to create the world we want to live in. As it stands today, the output of the system is broadly viewed as off target.

The problem is that the system is not only becoming increasingly complex, it is also being continuously disrupted, yet managed in anachronistic ways.

The COVID pandemic of 2020 was a massive wave of disruption. The Black Lives Matter protest was disruption. The insurrection at the U.S. Capitol was disruption. The power infrastructure collapse in Texas was disruption. Waves of technological innovation, big and small, have transformed industries continuously throughout the twen-tieth century. But two decades into the twenty-first, we are in the midst of something bigger.

The disruption we face today no longer resembles the periodic crashes of impressively sized waves. Instead, it resembles a killer tsunami that has made landfall, and we don't quite know what to do about it.

Make no mistake about it: You, we, all of us, are being disrupted on a scale unforeseen until now.

We are in the midst of the transformation of all society, caused by the shift from the industrial to the digital age. It's not just about startups disrupting markets, or robots replacing workers, or hailing cabs with an app, but life at the speed of digital. It's the pace of invention. It's globalization. It's the diffusion of information and knowledge. It's a meshed network of instant communications. It's workers becoming owners and owners becoming workers and consumers becoming owners. It's an information shift from centralized control to the masses.

The way we manage the various aspects of society has not kept pace with the change. Mostly, we manage business, government, education, and so forth the same way today, in the digital age, as we did through the industrial age. This failure to adapt exasperates an already out-of-balance economic system.

Recognizing the power of the digital-revolution tsunami, the forces at work on our systems, the immense challenges and opportunities that confront us, and the new balance of economic forces we must attempt to achieve are the focus of this book. It is my belief that focusing primarily on the business side of the equation will have the greatest near-term impact. In other words, in our we-choose-capitalism society, it is likely that business will lead the way in figuring out how to manage organizations faced with the massive uncertainty caused by increased complexity and continuous disruption.

Like a wave, power moves from core to edge.

The earthquake at the bottom of the sea, the origin of the tsunami, is easy enough to understand; we can even measure its enormous energy. However, its impact as it reaches miles of shoreline is complex and impossible to predict.

Take taxi drivers across Europe. In 2014, they went on strike to protest the proliferation of ride-sharing apps like Uber and Lyft. The protests backfired, ironically resulting in nine times the number of app downloads. A big wave, but the disruption of one industry. Now multiply that figure by ten thousand industries simultaneously. That's a tsunami.

This is disruption by revolution—an end to the execution-oriented, efficiency-of-output, assembly line–driven industrial age. It has been replaced by the momentum-grabbing new age characterized by: global reach, networked information moving at the speed of light, complex computing platforms and algorithms, rapidly shifting demographics and tastes, increased consumer knowledge, and transient economic system power dynamics.

The digital revolution, the promise of which was, for some, increased democratization and equality, has instead created deepening inequity. Even the stalwarts of unapologetic capitalism have taken notice.[iii] But has the root cause been identified? It's not obvious that business leaders understand the implication of the revolution on their own companies, let alone society. Nor is it obvious that other players in the economic system understand the role of the revolution in their current situations. The tsunami of disruption brought on by the digital revolution is happening whether or not one chooses to understand, accept, and consciously participate in it.

The challenge for all of us, in the face of the massive turmoil, is to accept that we must be intentional about our response. In other words: *We have to own the disruption.* We must create institutions that are designed and managed such that they not only survive disruption, but can continue to create value for all stakeholders. How we as business leaders, as professionals, and as humans who participate in many different aspects of society, seize upon owning the disruption is a key through line in this book.

Here in the United States, as well as in many other countries, we have chosen capitalism. We choose this economic system because we believe it's the best at solving problems. In order for this to continue to be true, business leaders must reinvent their organizations for the twenty-first century. Most organizations today are still structured and managed as though they are extended assembly lines. We're not in the industrial age anymore. We must reimagine what twenty-first-century businesses look like. And that's the path this book lays out for you.

The first part of this book offers a deep dive into the nature and magnitude of the disruption we are in the midst of, makes the case for fundamentally changing how leaders and professionals of various ranks organize and manage their businesses, and also describes how we all can set forth to adapt and own the desired outcomes of disruption.

The second part of the book describes how to make that change happen. While it's optimistic to imagine that there's a one-size-fits-all scheme for this, that is not a practical approach. The desired outcome of change is the creation of an organization that is Resilient to disruption, Aware of its environment, and Dynamic. In other words, a "RAD" organization that knows change is occurring and can react quickly is an organization built to last.

I've distilled the necessary change into the Five Elements, or "5Es," which describe the desired behaviors or states of being required for a RAD organization. The 5Es are Empathy, Exploration, Evidence, Equilibrium, and Ethics. I make the case that decades of research and real-world experience support the promise that some combination of these attributes, implemented and propagated throughout an organization, will produce a business that is able to deal with the accelerated world and massive change we're all a part of.

One challenge, of course, is to navigate the intentional evolution of the business, while the business must continue its current execution. The flow of my proposed evolution is such that the new business emerges from within the old. It reveals itself from the ground up, while being sculpted by the very organization it is replacing. This is a departure from the external disruption paradigm peddled by the Innovation Industry. It's different from the typical mandate-driven change programs offered by the Management Consultant Industry, dominated by companies suffering from the same twentieth-century anachronisms as those they counsel.

It bears repeating: Your new businesses emerge from within the existing.

I propose ways to kickstart the change, intentionally urging behavior change until momentum takes over, change then accelerates based on need and driving impact, scale is created as change is pulled in by core groups, and eventually the very structure creates the desired behavior so that RAD organization will endure.

The third part of the book looks at fulfilling the broader promise of capitalism. The newly emerged businesses, in combination with the purposeful reinvention of other economic and societal entities, provide a powerful opportunity to create the world we would like to live in. Societal transformation depends on how we all apply a RAD mindset, methods, and models to drive initiatives designed for impact on and benefit to various institutions, like government, education, NGOs, small businesses, and others.

We often tinker with outcomes. Our economic system creates inequities, and so we try to correct those, which inevitably are politically charged. Whether or not actually the case, tinkering feels like a zero-sum game, where fixing one area breaks another. I make the case for a reimagined role for capitalism, which protects the fundamental purpose of business but contributes to a more balanced economic system, such that the vast majority of stakeholders benefit as opposed to the few. Instead of trickle-down, it's value flowing up.

The book is primarily geared for members and leaders of the management teams of large, well-established businesses. But it is also for the organizational layers below the board and C-suite who must define, teach, mentor, and ultimately put into practice the new desired practices. The bulk of the difficult work of change must be demonstrated and spearheaded from the ground up.

As the dominant force in society, business will lead the way in reshaping and reimagining our future. But similar, conscious disruption must occur in other organizations as well. The leadership in all levels of education, government, NGOs, and so on will see themselves in these pages, and can follow the same program.

Entrepreneurs, startup founders, and employees will recognize many of the behaviors described in the book. Indeed, people at all levels can embody what I consider to be the "entrepreneurial spirit." It is important, however, to understand how to maintain that spirit and what the final outcome of what a scaled business should look like in the twenty-first century. It's not likely to be the same as the vision advisors, mentors, and investors have in mind.

Finally, we all wear multiple hats in our lives, whether as business leaders, students, parents, siblings, volunteers, and so on. The Five Elements can play a part in helping us navigate many of our different hats. By learning how to apply the 5Es to other organizations we are a part of, we can help make them RAD as well.

For those of you who enjoy the view through a broad lens, the history of change and complexity offered in Chapters 1–3 is my take on where we came from, where we are, and the opportunity at hand. If you're more interested in diving right in to empowering people, creating value, and driving change in service to creating resilient, aware, dynamic organizations, Chapters 4–8 are where the phases of change begin. Chapter 9 offers a perspective, as well as system changes to pursue, in service to more equitable outcomes, and Chapter 10 provides examples of the work already under way and hopefully some inspiration on where you might contribute beyond helping businesses change.

Transforming your organization requires strong top-down leadership with equally strong ground-up behavior change. Gone are the days of hierarchical, command-and-control, execution-minded, output-driven management. Here are the days of working with speed and agility, with empathy, vulnerability, and the empowerment of people. Here, too, are the days of less hierarchy while still maintaining some hierarchy; accountability, but with new metrics; and leadership that rallies people, both for their own benefit and that of the world.

The promise of capitalism has always been about raising the standard of living for all people. It's not a zero-sum system. For much of the twentieth century, capitalism made the middle class. Capitalism solves problems. We celebrate that. But it doesn't do so perfectly. It is sometimes ugly, brutal, and systemically discriminatory toward people who have had as much to do with its success as anyone.

In a world filled with invention, value creation, and entrepreneurial spirit, there's absolutely no reason why we cannot apply this spirit to fixing problems in the system itself. We will continue to succeed through capitalism by reinventing how it works for the twenty-first century, leveraging the revolution from the industrial to the digital age by purposefully making disruption work for all. Let's get started.

DISRUPTION PROOF

PART I

THE SETUP

CHANGE IS EVERYWHERE

"The coffee is free, but now we rent the tables."

Illustration courtesy of CartoonStock.com

Chapter 1

BIG WAVES AND A WORLD OF DISRUPTION

While I've never been called the world's greatest surfer—far from it, to be honest—I have always admired the enduring freedom and spirit of the sport. It's at once exhilarating and calming, physically intense and intellectually challenging. It truly can be a unique experience wherein we seek harmony with the laws of the universe and simultaneously avoid being rolled onto a jagged reef or, worse, getting devoured by a shark.

For the better part of a decade, the "endless summer" for us Cooper brothers meant dawn patrol driving up and down the San Diego coast at six o'clock in the morning searching for the perfect wave. My younger brothers, Craig and Todd, chose the break while I tagged along. I was happy to be a part of the experience, whenever and wherever. Or at least wherever there wasn't too much of a crowd and I had space to watch, wait, and immerse myself.

From shore the swell was mesmerizing: Neatly arranged horizontal lines, spaced like furrows in a vast liquid farm, sometimes stretched out to the horizon. I found observing the raw power of the ocean often intrigued me more than competing with others for a takeoff spot close to the peak. I liked to see how the waves would form seemingly out of nowhere. The waves appear to be moving, but the water actually doesn't move much. The lines are undulating energy pulled by invisible forces of physics.

Depending on the contours of the land beneath the water and the energy of the swell, the wave might ease into its break, as if the white water was revealed by an invisible hand pulling back the peel. Other waves, when the Santa Ana winds blow in from the eastern desert, are held upright like a rearing mare, her white mane flowing back, before crashing down in an emphatic statement of might.

The force of a wave can be deceiving, too. No matter the size, sitting on your board in the cool ocean water, rolling up and down with the swell, you can feel its subtle power.

Swells travel great distances during which waves group together into sets, such that the bigger waves form in the middle and smaller waves arrive at the beginning or end. People who spend time in the ocean understand this without needing to know the science. Much about swells, however, can be measured and their travel time predicted. It's a normal part of coastal weather forecasting you can find in a tide table.

Surfers know where a wave will break before getting a good look at it. The glimpse of a rising swell on the horizon will set off a paddling frenzy to deeper waters. The shape and shadows of its contours indicate which part of the wave will peak first. One remembers the patterns of the waves crashing from experience—and usually from getting pitched off your board into the saltwater. This is the sport of surfing. And while waves are never fully 100 percent predictable, they do present a certain, observable pattern.

Innovation—the real thing, the creation and adoption of new value for people, not the meaningless buzzword—comes in sets of regularly repeating waves, much like surfing. Most of these waves appear as relatively small ripples, which have a small impact on business and society. On occasion, some of these waves are far bigger, producing far-reaching effects and lasting impact—reinventing whole industries, destroying old jobs, and birthing new professions.

INNOVATION FROM WAVES TO TSUNAMIS

Sets of waves, be they in water or innovation, tell us nothing about tsunamis.

A tsunami is a different type of wave altogether. The normal swells we experience at the beach are wind waves. A tsunami is a series of waves caused by a massive displacement of water from an underwater earthquake, a volcanic eruption, or some other major seismic disturbance. Its devastating impact on the shores it reaches may permanently alter the ocean basin, the marine ecosystem, and the human-built environment close to shore. Think of the tragic 2011 Fukushima disaster in Japan as a nightmarish example.

To further stretch the analogy, while an innovation wave may have lasting impact on an industry, *an innovation tsunami disrupts* all *industries to some degree over time, affects* all *areas of the economy, and* permanently *alters the structure and organization of society*. Consider where the world is presently and what society faces in terms of unprecedented speed of change and continuous uncertainty. I wonder what it was like when fire or the wheel went mainstream.

When it comes to the fundamental changes under way today, we are not surfing or observing "normal" wave patterns. Instead, we are in the midst of an innovation tsunami. Digital technology is the volcanic force upending nearly every aspect of our lives. By 2050, the very structures of government, education, and business will look drastically different than they did in the early 2000s, let alone the twentieth century. It's been said by many, "We don't know where we're going, but we'll know when we get there." That's a truism. And by 2100, it's anyone's guess what the forces of change will have shaped.

To understand this tsunamic transformation, it helps to recap a recent history of digital innovations, which traversed from the core of the economy to the edge.

In 1939, Bell Telephone Laboratories completed the Complex Number Calculator, designed by scientist George Stibitz. In 1946, the one-thousand-square-foot ENIAC, built by John Mauchly and J. Presper Eckert, was unveiled at the University of Pennsylvania; it used switches for programming. In 1948, Frederic Williams, Tom Kilburn, and Geoff Tootill, researchers from the University of Manchester, ran the first computer program in history on their Small-Scale Experimental Machine.[iv]

Fifty years later, the internet was all the rage, affecting the work of all businesses big and small. Anything seemed possible. Today it's hard to imagine that there was a time when buying books online was new and great, but buying pet food from a website was considered an unworkable business model. People actually predicted that the ups and downs of the business cycle were gone forever.

In 1994, Wired.com (then Hotwire.com) sold this new thing called a "banner ad" to AT&T for $30,000.[v] I'm proud to say that to this day, I have more teeth than banner ads I've clicked in my lifetime. By 1997, internet advertising revenue rose to roughly $900 million, and by 2008, it was $23.4 billion; mobile advertising was just beginning.[vi]

In 2008, software helped bring the global financial economy to its knees. The causes of the collapse run deep, including the housing bubble and deregulation of the financial industry, which allowed banks to take on too much risk. But it's also true that literal rocket scientists created multilayered bundles of financial assets that were too complex for humans to grasp, and software engineers built systems that, according to *Scientific American*, "permitted traders to enter over-optimistic assumptions and faulty data into their models, jiggering the software to avoid setting off alarm bells."[vii]

At the very same time, Apple opened up the one-year-old iPhone App Store to independent developers, creating the first smartphone that was actually a computing platform. Apple sold 11.63 million phones that year, up 800 percent over the previous year. While the economic market collapsed, mobile computing became the new rage.

By 2016, mobile revenue had surpassed nonmobile digital ads. Three years later, digital had surpassed all nondigital media advertising revenue.[viii]

In 2019, approximately 1.52 billion smartphones were sold worldwide. Pew Research estimates "more than 5 billion people have mobile devices today, and over half of these are smartphones."[ix] That means 2.5 billion people carry in their pockets computers thousands of times more powerful than the old ballroom-sized ENIAC computer.

Ten years after the dot-com bust of 2000, Marc Andreessen, founder of boom-era darling Netscape, coined the phrase "software eating the world" to describe how software had become an integral part of society. His point was not that software companies would necessarily rule the world (although they're doing pretty well), but rather that software would be a part of everything.[x]

He wrote that we buy books from software companies. We buy movies and music from software companies. We buy toilet paper (and pet food) from software companies. The companies that produce and digitally distribute books, music, and movies all rely on software, and that's largely how we interface with them. Whether it's downloading MP3s or listening through a streaming service, reading a pdf on our iPad or an ebook on Kindle, or putting in our grocery order via an app on our iPhone, we have turned all these experiences into software-dependent transactions. People can purchase their products using voice recognition software and hardware gadgets running software.

Home entertainment has evolved from the radio, to antenna-based TV, to cable TV, and now streaming via software. The devices we use are TVs without tubes and mobile devices, running different versions of the same software operating systems.

Even John Deere—the tractor maker—calls itself a software company. Does that make the tractor the largest "internet of things"? Beyond the dominant high-technology companies—Amazon, Google, Facebook, Apple, Microsoft—software is a fundamental component to all aspects of major corporations. ERP systems manage complex operational systems and processes. Office workers use software all day long: internal communication platforms, sales and marketing automation, product development systems, human resources management, accounting, document management, contracts, vendors, customers managed by software, software, and more software.

Manufacturing floors are run by automation software. Supply chains are managed and visualized with software. Robots, run by software, manufacture products and manage inventory. I once sold software to a world-famous brewery, whose top-tier guzzling-football-fan brand slowly turned into its low-rent, college-fraternity-brother brand, as vats of beer sat with their ingredients aging longer on crashed factory lines due to the infamous Windows NT "blue screen of death."

Think of the behavior behind the numbers. The ubiquity of information, the speed of communication, both the benefit and curse of instantaneous knowledge sharing. Back in the "good old days," people we know would call us on our landline phones. Randomly. Without warning. Dang, that was annoying. But we would always answer, because, I don't know, maybe it was Ed McMahon from Publishers Clearing House. Every once in a while, I still get a phone call from someone I know out of the blue. But now I can see who is calling. And now I *choose* not to answer. All this crazy digital technology allows me to prioritize my work.

Digitalization is so pervasive, you don't even think about it anymore. Your car is more likely to break down due to a software problem than a mechanical one. Maybe some people love that their coffeemaker can tell them they're out of milk, but others couldn't care less. And speaking of coffee, credit card companies are testing technology to read your card as you stroll past the coffee shop you *thought* about stopping at for a butter-infused, collagen-enriched $12 cup of coffee. (Just kidding. I hope.)

Consider how you bank now versus the recent past. Consider how my twentysomething daughters bank. I'm not sure they know what a bank branch is, but they know how to send money to each other (read: receive money from me) in milliseconds with a phone app. The last time I went to a physical branch, my former car mechanic was the manager. He said he was relatively new to computers, and compared to the head-scratching, sophisticated technology in cars, he had little trouble transitioning into banking. I'm so old I remember when software-enabled "Automated Teller Machines" existed only on *Star Trek*. Now, I'm annoyed when I have to visit one of those IRL ATMs. My mom still balances her checkbook every month.

Before they turned eighteen, my daughters had conversed live with human beings on the other side of the world whom they had never met in person. My friend, Lean Startup consultant Mthetheleli Ngxeke, reached out to me after reading my first book, *The Lean Entrepreneur*, as an "entrepreneur in training" at a juvenile prison in Cape Town, South Africa. My mom found long-lost cousins on Facebook. Every week I delete voice mails from my iPhone that are poorly translated Chinese-language messages. I've been offered large quantities of money by Nigerian princes. It's nice to be so popular.

What else have mobile devices brought on? Riding in cars with strangers. Digital photography. Yes, I know, selfies (rolling-eyes emoji here), but it's been suggested by my always prescient, digital-artist neighbor that by 2050, every conceivable type of picture will have already been taken. Emojis. Text messages that self-destruct. Five hundred thirty-two different applications to share cat memes. Twenty-four/seven biorhythms, I mean fitness data. Addictive games. Mobile Addiction Algorithms™.

As if the sets are coming faster, the waves of disruptive events are relentless. The wavelength of change grows shorter. Pending technological developments ensure the pace of change will not slow:

- Artificial intelligence, machine learning, robots, software-writing software: Systems have the ability to learn and improve from their own experience without being explicitly programmed, accessing data and using it to learn for themselves.
- Nanotechnology: The branch of technology that deals with dimensions and tolerances of less than 100 nanometers, especially the manipulation of individual atoms and molecules.
- Genetic engineering: The deliberate modification of the characteristics of an organism by manipulating its genetic material.
- Quantum computing: An area of computing focused on developing computer technology based on the principles of quantum theory.
- Big Data: Trillions of bits of structured and unstructured data are produced every day. Powerful new technologies, including distributed processing and complex mathematics, are used to extract trends, detect anomalies, answer questions, and solve complex problems, allowing researchers and businesses to advance their efforts to create new value.[xi]

And, of course, the greatest innovations often come from combining technologies and responsive adaptations accelerated by unforeseen events, portending more changes and other new ways of living or working.

A GAGGLE OF BLACK SWANS

One wonders, if a global economic catastrophe happens at least once a decade, *are they truly black swans?*[xii] Is this the new normal? It would seem to me that the nature of such events has more to do with the fact that the global economy is inherently a complex system, has become more so in the digital age, and yet is being "managed" by a rigid, albeit fragile, structure from a simpler time.

Since the twenty-first century began, a rapid, staggering economic decline has happened three times in two decades:

The dot-com bust of 2000, in conjunction with 9/11, marked the digital revolution's first economic disruption. Years of growth, an ebullient mindset bordering on naivete, and stock market froth completely divorced from economic value came crashing down. Ring a bell?

Following roughly eight months of recession after 9/11, an economic recovery ensued, but manufacturing jobs never fully recovered for the first time in history. The airline industry received government bailouts to survive.

"The [U.S.] economy's performance between 2001 and 2007 was weaker, overall, than its performance in the equivalent years of the 1990s.... The Gross Domestic Product, consumption, net worth, non-residential investment, wages and salaries, and employment all grew less rapidly than during other comparable expansionary periods." Corporate profits, however, fared well, experiencing an average annual growth of 10.8 percent.[xiii]

Ultimately, the subprime real estate bubble that began pre–dot-com bust, plus increased volatility in the financial system due to deregulation, brought the global economic system crashing down again.[xiv]

A long, slow economic expansion began in 2010, yet was unevenly distributed; roughly half of GDP growth from 2009 to 2015 went to the top 1 percent of households.[xv] Unlike every previous postwar expansion, GDP growth remained under 3 percent for every calendar year.[xvi] In the United States, approximately 22.2 million jobs were added to the economy from 2010 to 2019. All of that gain was eliminated in the first two months of the pandemic, March and April 2020. Roughly six months later, fewer than half of the jobs had come back.[xvii]

MORE UNPREDICTABLE, COMPLEX, AND CHAOTIC, NOT LESS

The COVID-19 pandemic was another disruptive force, with its first wave striking the United States in the late winter of 2020. Sickness, death, people sheltered in their homes, and a closed economy wreaking havoc on businesses and individuals around the world. Beyond the obvious turmoil and devastation it brought with it, a new wave of change accelerated through society:

- In June 2020, the stock valuation of nine-year-old Zoom increased to $67 billion, more than 85 percent of the Standard & Poor's 500, due to remote work and homeschooling.[xviii]
- By April 2020, 48 percent of physicians were seeing patients remotely, up from 18 percent in 2018.[xix]
- What was once considered risky to businesses—working from home—became a requirement for many companies and a safety feature for professionals.
- The collapse of malls and retail led to even more market share for the big five tech companies, Google, Apple, Facebook, Microsoft, and especially Amazon.
- Real estate prices dropped substantially in big markets (New York and San Francisco) while rising in other suburban or emerging markets (Austin and Miami).[xx]

The COVID-19 pandemic accelerated the already rapid digital revolution, and what we experienced is not only ubiquitous but subjective and idiosyncratic, impacting individuals differently across geographies, cultures, and generations. It was hugely beneficial to some and devastating to others. It somehow simultaneously portended both utopian and dystopian futures.

The pandemic also exacerbated long-standing class, racial, and gender divides. According to an Institute for Policy Studies analysis of *Forbes* data, "the total wealth of the more than 600 U.S. billionaires has grown significantly under Covid, the fortunes of the richest five have grown even faster.... According to University of Chicago researchers, the lowest-income workers were the most likely to lose their jobs between February 1, 2020, and the end of June [2020]."[xxi]

The expected result of chaos in such a system is the strong get stronger and the weak get weaker. Consider the following:

- Income inequality—in the United States it's at the highest level in five decades, with scant upward mobility and a stubbornly slow wage growth since the 1970s. "78% of Americans are at least somewhat concerned about the rising level of inequality in the U.S. and 48% are very concerned."[xxii]
- Wealth inequality—The worst it's been in one hundred years, according to Federal Reserve data: "The top 1% of Americans have a combined net worth of $34.2 trillion (or 30.4% of all household wealth in the U.S.), while the bottom 50% of the population holds just $2.1 trillion combined (or 1.9% of all wealth)."[xxiii]
- Growth in consumer debt—"[U.S.] consumer debt has increased nearly $2.3 trillion since the height of the Great Recession in 2009—growing across almost all debt products to top $14 trillion in 2019."[xxiv]
- Longevity—U.S. life expectancy is declining for the first time in

seven decades, due to the pandemic and an increased number of suicides, as well as the growth of diseases related to unhealthy diet and lifestyle, such as diabetes, obesity, and alcohol.[xxv]

- Digital divide—"21.3 million Americans lacked a broadband internet connection at the end of 2017....Millions of people in rural America still have to go to extraordinary lengths to find the kind of internet access that most Americans take for granted."[xxvi]

- Big business profitability and layoffs—"Between April and September [2020], one of the most tumultuous economic stretches in modern history, 45 of the 50 most valuable publicly traded U.S. companies turned a profit....Despite their success, at least 27 of the 50 largest firms held layoffs...collectively cutting more than 100,000 workers."[xxvii]

- Access to health care—In 2018, 67.3 percent of the population had some type of private health insurance coverage and 34.4 percent of the population had public coverage, including Medicare. As evident from the numbers, a small percentage had a mix of both private and public coverage.[xxviii]

The devastation of disruptions over the decades has destroyed cities. Places like Cairo, Illinois, have been left behind. "We used to make things in this town, like shoes and rubber," a local told Chris Arnade, ex–bond trader turned photographer and author of *Dignity: Seeking Respect in Back Row America.* "Our national government allowed factories to leave."

Arnade captured the poetic thoughts of a woman he met:

"We are a town with a lot of hopelessness, lot of sorrow, lot of despair, lot of pain. But we are good people, smart people, who could show that if we had opportunity. We can be productive, but there is no grocery store, no gas station, no resource center. Nothing is here."

Think of a roaring Detroit, Michigan, of the midtwentieth century, with a population approaching a million people, and the center of the world's automobile industry. It was a place where tens of thousands of people flocked to good jobs each year, and the promise of joining a burgeoning middle-class lifestyle marked by home ownership, decent schools, and college education for your kids, access to arts and culture, summer vacations and retirement. Contrast this to the Detroit of the early twenty-first century: a collapsed auto industry, thousands of unemployed workers, crumbling infrastructure, a population of fewer than five hundred thousand, and the largest municipal bankruptcy in history.[xxix]

The digital revolution in and of itself didn't cause the above collapses, though it certainly contributed to them. Given the right triggers, the interconnectedness of systems, the speed of information, the sensitivity of monitoring, and automated processes cause large and small fluctuations that crash the system. These are not only unpredictable, but often unobservable in real time.

Significantly, if this is our new world, it's the system management that needs to adapt. The chaos is the result of an anachronistic economic system that lacks a balance of forces, adaptability, and resiliency such that it maintains its integrity.

Similarly, the pandemic wasn't the cause of the uncertainty in business, but it exacerbated what the digital revolution has wrought. Leaders who respond to disruptions by looking forward to a "return to normalcy" are inevitably disappointed that the turmoil and uncertainty continue.

In times of crises, and for practical reasons, the type of leadership that emerges tends to be a command-and-control, execute-what-we-know type of leadership. They repeat what used to work, resulting in small victories and defeats, but ignoring the difficult work required to establish the root causes and create lasting solutions.

Despite the (sometimes true) rhetoric regarding big businesses behaving badly, it's worth noting that most business leaders themselves are perplexed by the digital revolution:

- Struggling to innovate—A 2019 McKinsey survey says 94 percent of executives are dissatisfied with their firms' innovation performance.[xxx]
- Struggling with digital transformation—From failed programs to reluctant employees to lack of digital skills, many leaders know they must change, but not how.[xxxi]
- Struggling with retention or engagement—Even during the pandemic—and perhaps associated with digital transformation—attracting and keeping talent was listed as the most significant issue to their respondents' businesses in a KPMG survey.[xxxii]
- Struggling to grow—Markets have fundamentally changed. Product, marketing, and sales teams must orient to shifting value equations in local, national, and global markets. And what to do about trade wars?[xxxiii]
- Struggling with their ethos—Shareholders are voicing their concerns about sustainability and human capital management. "According to a 2018 global survey by FTSE Russell, more than half of global asset owners are currently implementing or evaluating environmental, social, and corporate governance (ESG) considerations in their investment strategy."[xxxiv]

THE AXIS OF EXHAUSTION

Beyond the business challenges, economic recalibration, and leadership development needed, for most of us, this disruption produces a feeling of anxiety. We are uncertain and uneasy, and we have difficulty attributing it to a particular cause. At work, it affects leaders, team members, job candidates, new hires, and customers. Away from work, more broadly, it affects all human beings. In truth, the unease is caused by the fear of the unknown, fear of change, fear of the future. Fear that what worked yesterday isn't working anymore. Often, people are not conscious of the cause. Individuals think about the pandemic, the economy, their jobs; they worry about a reorganization occurring at work, about their performance review, about the volatility of the stock market (even when they're not in the market). People worry about elections and their effect on their livelihood.

They worry about relationships, too: family, friends, children—kids who are in college or looking for a job, parents and grandparents who may need assistance, or may need to move into residential care. These are deep and acute but common worries. They have always been in place at some level. Every generation worries about such things. Is it different today? To some degree, yes, as these worries are only exacerbated by the sheer speed of disruptions; as population grows, the sheer volume of people experiencing these worries increases.

Marginalized groups suffer more, obviously, but significantly during downturns. Black people in America have been systemically excluded from many aspects of economic activity, from denial of access to workplace promotions to housing assistance or new business loans.[xxxv] And historically they have been denied basic rights many non-Black U.S. citizens enjoyed, for example, voting in elections, which was finally granted with the passage of the Voting Rights Act in 1965, but which is threatened once again. Black Lives Matter and other movements represent real levels of anxiety that include all the economic stress, but also stress from threats, exclusion, and other forms of discrimination and prejudice.[xxxvi]

Take the wage gap, for instance. Women in America have suffered from economic inequality, earning far less than their male counterparts. "Analyzing the most recent Census Bureau data from 2018, women of all races earned, on average, just 82 cents for every $1 earned by men of all races."[xxxvii] Female layoffs were 1.8 times higher than men's during the 2020 pandemic.[xxxviii] Serious work remains to foster more inclusion and parity.

To be sure, some of these fears and concerns are representative of the human condition, but they also represent opportunity. The melting pot that has long represented the promise of the United States is becoming a global phenomenon. It adds more variables to the complex system of society, but it also demonstrates that inclusion is a requirement to address complexity. Diversity is a requirement for growth.

Business leaders have a special role in the academy of uncertainty. They share the same anxiousness as individuals, but also bear the burden of responsibility for the well-being of their employees and their organizations. They face uncertainty that is immediate, but also stretches out long-term into the future. They are often called upon to make decisions without the depth of information they would like to have. They are often reactive, constantly fighting new fires, unable to find the time and space to reduce future uncertainty and thereby prevent future fires. A reactive-only modus operandi leads us into the danger zone of self-fulfilling prophecy.

Whether conscious or not, this also produces anxiousness. There's anxiety caused by not understanding where growth is coming from in the future, or not understanding how to reduce costs in order to demonstrate profitability in the short term. Among most corporate leaders, there's anxiety around keeping employees contented and secure, which also has both short-term and long-term elements to it. But again, is it different today?

"In 2019 alone, venture capital (VC) companies invested a record-breaking $637 million in more than 60 different mental health–oriented companies, which is more than 22.8 times the investment in 2013."[xxxix] Add the pandemic to the list of anxiousness triggers, and one can understand why investors see an opportunity for both impact and profit in the arena of mental health and soothing uneasy minds.

ADOPTION OF A WHOLE NEW MINDSET

Managing our organizations, leading groups of people, and even managing ourselves without adopting a new mindset and adapting our approach just doesn't work well in times of acute disruption. We need new approaches and new ways of understanding how we can manage to best effect, while admitting we can't manage the complexity of systems themselves. We also, then, must build or rebuild organizations recognizing this reality, in order to minimize adverse consequences.

Dave Snowden is a pioneer in the research of the field of complexity. He developed the Cynefin® framework to help leaders be aware of uncertainty, understand whether it's due to complexity, and to take the appropriate response. Unfortunately, many business leaders tend to respond to most situations with a single response: execute harder. Efficiency is the hammer that never found a surface that wasn't a nail. One imagines this is because Wall Street tends to reward indications of efficiency. I say "indications of," since what appears to be short-term efficiency is often debilitating long-term.

It's a great mystery that while 10 percent of Americans owned more than 80 percent of stock value in 2016, the coverage of the market on TV and in the media is as if the short-term fluctuations represent something critical to the masses. People are sold on investing in stocks because of unmistakable growth in equity demonstrated over the long haul. And yet businesses respond to the whims of the same body as if the short-term matters.

It's easy to blame Wall Street and corporate managers who seek to appease analysts on a quarterly basis for a lack of more thoughtful approaches to uncertainty and complexity, but it's just an excuse. On any business day of the year, corporate officers can stand up in front of Wall Street and announce long-term plans to do things differently, to adopt an "innovation mindset," to structure an organization more resilient to disruption, to ensure they maintain their values in their daily work. Wall Street can do what it wants on that day, but the contract is laid out for investors: Invest in us for the long haul or don't.

Whether company officers do this or not is a choice they make. Good people do things of questionable ethics. It's as if *trying* but then failing to "do the right thing" is good enough to be considered ethical. Often, leadership wants to do good things and make pledges to do the right thing, but ends up hamstrung by other elements of the organization. The internal "efficiency" people, such as legal or finance, legitimately do their duty: warn leaders on the ramifications of the do-good decisions. The fundamental problem is that the counselors are not aligned to the business mission, but rather use generic definitions of financial efficiency as opposed to actively engaging with the desired outcomes. This is questionable leadership. Leaders must hold internal functions accountable to the business mission, not the functional expert's opinion.

There are no short-term answers to the uncertainties brought on by fluctuations within a complex system. There are simply resilient organizations built to be aware of changes and be dynamically adaptable to them, and those that are not. There are leaders who are capable of admitting what they know and what they don't, and those who are not.

In Snowden's model, a company can drop from the simple, best-practice realm straight into chaos, because the company's dominant market has been disrupted, yet best practices are still applied. But chaos and uncertainty can and often do lead to opportunity, the bright spots of disruption, as we'll cover in more detail in the next chapter.

Chapter 2

AN OPTIMISTIC CASE FOR CHANGE

I've spent a lot of time over the years helping build up the San Diego startup ecosystem, mentoring and advising countless young firms. Like all nascent ecosystems, we have a lot of well-meaning, retired big-company executives who wish to advise and mentor high-tech, digital startup founders. The mentors have valuable experience to share, but they also give a lot of suboptimal advice, and neither they nor the entrepreneurs tend to know the difference.

One day a founder approached me at the local "tech coffee" meetup I started in 2010 in the coastal North County area of San Diego. He was building a fintech startup.

"My EIR [Entrepreneur in Residence] is urging me to pivot my idea, because he's convinced it won't work. But, I mean, this is my whole idea."

"Who is your advisor?" I ask.

"He's a former banking executive. He says he can make a lot of introductions to angel investors and Sand Hill Road investors. He also wants to be on my board of advisors."

"Yeah," I said, shaking my head. "You need to learn how to *not* take people's advice. This guy is well-meaning, but it's likely he's considering what he believes to be true based on his experience and so can't see how your idea fits in. Because it doesn't. You're trying to disrupt the market his experience depends on. The last one to recognize disruption is the industry expert."

LinkedIn founder and venture capitalist Reid Hoffman once remarked about crazy ideas, "If you're laughed out of the room, it might actually be a good sign."[xl]

John Kenneth Galbraith dedicated a whole chapter of *The Affluent Society* to the concept of "Conventional Wisdom." People resist new ideas because of deep personal and social reasons. "Economic and social behavior are complex, and to comprehend their character is mentally tiring. Therefore we adhere, as though to a raft, to those ideas which represent our understanding."[xli]

Everett Rogers's Diffusion of Innovations, better known these days as the lifecycle adoption curve, describes the genesis, mainstreaming, and stickiness of new ideas. It's represented by a familiar bell-shaped curve remodeled, renamed, and revised for various applications since the 1800s. The fundamental idea is that change moves through several phases, each categorized by its predominant human characteristic, from the radical "innovator" attracted to a counternarrative idea, to the small number of "early adopters" who recognize its benefits, to the dense "early majority" cohort who follow early adopter leaders, until it eventually reaches a tipping point—a critical mass—which leads to sustained adoption via the late majority, and then finally laggards, who must be frightened into changing.

Conventional wisdom is the obstacle that must be overcome to capture the early majority of a new idea, after having convinced the early adopter to give it a go. It then must penetrate those who dislike change, no matter its benefits. "Because familiarity is such an important test of acceptability, the acceptable ideas have great stability," Galbraith says.[xlii]

Change is hard.

WINNING AND WARFARE

Remember the movie *Moneyball*? Oakland A's general manager Billy Beane and his assistant Peter Brand brought data science to assembling the baseball team, which was not popular with the old-timers:

Billy Beane: You're unhappy, Grady. Why?

[Scout] Grady Fuson: Wow. May I speak candidly?

Beane: Sure. Go ahead.

Fuson: Major League Baseball and its fans they're going to be more than happy to throw you and Google boy under the bus if you keep doing what you're doing here. You don't put a team together with a computer, Billy.

Beane: No?

Fuson: No. Baseball isn't just numbers, it's not science. If it was, then anybody could do what we're doing, but they can't because they don't know what we know. They don't have our experience and they don't have our intuition.

Beane: Okay.

Fuson: Billy, you got a kid in there that's got a degree in Economics from Yale. You got a scout here with twenty-nine years of baseball experience. You're listening to the wrong one. Now, there are intangibles that only baseball people understand. You're discounting what scouts have done for a hundred and fifty years, even yourself.

Beane: Adapt or die.

If you watched *Moneyball*,[xliii] it likely came as no surprise that traditional baseball people, the seasoned experts in the sport, were skeptical that Beane could field a better team by analyzing vast quantities of data instead of relying on the experience and gut feel of current methods.

Especially so for the scouts, who were about to be disrupted out of their jobs.

Beane was successful. Incredibly, the movie itself actually helped revolutionize sports. It was a catalyst to move the idea of data analysis in sports from early adopters to the mainstream. Similar data analysis is now standard across baseball, the NFL, English Premier League soccer, and the NBA. Pro basketball is particularly interesting, since to a certain degree, the Golden State Warriors not only figured out which kind of players they wanted based on data, but reinvented *how* the game is played, appearing in five straight NBA Finals starting in 2015, and winning three NBA titles.

I'm old enough to remember when basketball pundits lamented the toss-it-to-the-big-guy style of play, which required less classic basketball skills in favor of size and brute strength. The Warriors changed all that, assembling a team of players best suited for a new style of play that the data indicated would be a winning formula. Of course, ironically, the laggard pundits now wonder if raining down three-point balls from absurd distance is "good for the NBA." As if sinking outside shots isn't literally what the game was designed for.

The Warriors leveraged Big Data technology, advanced software algorithms, and even wearables technology to help make sense of the complex system that is basketball. Data in sports is the new conventional wisdom.

It begs the question: If insanity is doing the same thing over and over again, but expecting different results, what is it called when doing the same thing over and over again begins to produce different results? Best practices are by definition conventional wisdom. We use them because they work. But what about when they don't?

In 2003, U.S. Army general Stanley McChrystal led the Joint Special Operations Task Force into Iraq to remove Saddam Hussein from power and establish democracy. While successful at deposing

Hussein using conventional military tactics and overwhelming fire-power, his forces soon found themselves mired in confusing, bloody, asymmetric warfare with an unfamiliar enemy whose tactics defied convention.

On coming to terms with their situation in Iraq in 2003, McChrystal writes: "Although lavishly resourced and exquisitely trained, we found ourselves losing to an enemy that, by traditional calculus, we should have dominated. Over time we came to realize that more than our foe, we were actually struggling to cope with an environment that was fundamentally different from anything we'd planned or trained for."[xliv]

The U.S. military had encountered the new, networked world—a complex system—using an old-style command-and-control structure. It forced a reckoning that eventually produced a force better suited for the new theater of warfare and additionally saved lives.

Complex systems are defined by having many components that interact with one another, as with nodes of a network, for instance. The systems are said to be nonlinear in that small changes may have dramatic effects. The system itself may affect and be affected by its environment and have properties or behavior not exhibited by the individual parts.

Due to their characteristics, complex systems are difficult to model. Output and outcomes of changes are difficult, if not impossible, to predict. Obvious examples include the universe, the human brain, the climate, the economy, and environmental ecosystems like that of Yellowstone National Park, which includes the interdependent species of wolves, elk, and beavers.

For ages, the conventional wisdom in economics has been that federal budget deficit spending is bad. While economists have had a more nuanced view, the wisdom as understood by business lead-ers, politicians, and the populace is that, generally speaking, federal deficits represent a lack of discipline, and are even, in a sort of puritanical sense, immoral. Deficits accumulate debt that eventually will come due, threatening the future subsistence of all politicians' favorite constituents: our children, the next generation, and posterity.

The problem with the conventional wisdom is that deficit spending has persisted for generations. As the proverb says, "Tomorrow never comes." Despite the observable reality that deficits do not affect the economy as conventional wisdom dictates they should, mainstream economists are reluctant to consider updates to their thinking. It was fascinating to watch this unfold as Stony Brook economics professor Stephanie Kelton launched Modern Monetary Theory into the early majority spotlight with her book, *The Deficit Myth*. Many economists remain the laggards.

Business in the twentieth century was surely a complex system. But relatively speaking, businesses understood their markets, and best practices were developed and executed to successfully build, market, sell, and distribute products people wanted. Companies grew and prospered. Fast-forward to today's society, where products are built for individuals with computers in their pockets: Business is many times more complex than before. Like the battlefield faced by McChrystal, companies exist in a system that is networked, fast, and agile, where nodes and groups of nodes are intelligent, knowledgeable, and empowered to change. It's far less hierarchical and increasingly decentralized. The system itself has proven resilient and dynamic, even while some elements within, such as government, education, and business, have sometimes proved fragile.

The formal study of complex systems is relatively young, tracking roughly to the growth in the computational power of the digital age. Digital tools, including artificial intelligence and Big Data, provide us a means to better model them. Just as with the scouts in the movie *Moneyball*, I might surmise that one obstacle to a change in thinking—

what makes conventional wisdom sticky—is when digital tools attempt to replace the wisdom, experience, and intuition of human beings.

Like I said, change is hard.

Dealing with complexity requires leaders to do as Steve Jobs's slogan for Apple (now a trillion-dollar company) exhorts us: Think different. Back in the day, I was once hired to lead a team to build *products* inside of a large, growing *services* startup. Yes, I can see you shaking your head, fully aware of what's coming. But I truly believed I had done my due diligence, confirming the organization was fully committed to actually investing in a product, rather than hoping to pay for product development while earning an immediate return, as it was used to getting with its typical "billable hours" services business model.

My team applied lean innovation techniques, leading to a major product pivot within the first three months, in response to the market. "Lean innovation" is shorthand for empathy work, rapid experimentation, and being diligent about leveraging evidence to inform decisions. In practice, it is a combination of human-centered design, "Lean Startup" techniques, and agile practices. We successfully built a "minimum viable product," or MVP, got the attention of a competitor who threatened a lawsuit over patent violations, and closed our first deal. I was proud of the team. By any Silicon Valley startup measure, this was quite an accomplishment, lawsuit aside. Alas, I was sent packing because I didn't hit my numbers.

To be fair, extenuating circumstances had made revenue and billability vital to the company, but I remember saying to my boss, "We accomplished quite a bit, including earning revenue, and we did an incredible amount of learning, such as the fact that there's no market for the original idea. Yet you're dissatisfied with a 'failure to execute.'"

"Yes," he confirmed.

In retrospect, my diligence wasn't due enough.

THE CULT OF OPERATIONAL EFFICIENCY AND FRIEDMAN

What is the conventional wisdom of the Western capitalist economic system? Good question. I make no claim of being an academic, and I don't have a perfect model to share with you that will explain all of this in one easy pass. I'm instead going to paint the parameters in broad strokes. The main gist of mainstream academia, media, business leaders, Wall Street, and centrist politicians is that *efficiency* is the ultimate goal of business, the holy grail for producing a functional, stable economic system. Here's what that efficient, functional, and stable system looks like:

- A business should be run to optimize its efficiency as measured by various financial metrics, such as return on investment or amount of output per input.
- Workers' rights must be balanced with company efficiency.
- Mergers and acquisitions that show increased efficiency are good.
- Large companies are more efficient than smaller ones.
- Low inflation is an indication of efficiency.
- Millions of unemployed people is less important than efficiency, unless the number gets too big.

In 1949, Hewlett-Packard cofounder David Packard said at a meeting of corporate CEOs: "A company has a responsibility beyond making a profit for stockholders; it has a responsibility to recognize the dignity of its employees as human beings, to the well-being of its customers, and to the community at large."[xlv]

Two decades later, academic and economist (in other words, not a business person) Milton Friedman wrote the famous Friedman Doctrine for the *New York Times*, where he insisted corporations were responsible only to shareholders. While Friedman left room for business managers to interpret how to deliver that, the evolution of the concept of business efficiency has been a steep, slippery slope, influenced heavily by the 1970s-era Chicago School of Economics. Friedman, a Nobel Laureate in 1976, championed the neoclassical economic school of thought that emerged in the 1930s, associated with the work of the faculty at the University of Chicago, where he earned his master's degree.

You optimize what you measure.

Efficiency in itself is, of course, fine and good. An efficient allocation of resources means you're wasting less. But in service to what? Originally, efficiency was in service to discovering, producing, and distributing products that provided some benefit to customers—in other words, value. After all, that was why the business was in business. This was its mission. How one manages the business, including its relationship with employees, determined, in part, the success of delivering on its mission. And if a business is successful at its mission, value, in turn, is wrought upon owners.

The efficiency-in-service-to-shareholders model relies on a trickle-down theory of value. If a business increases profits, value goes to shareholders and officers first, and if there's anything left over, it will share. Maybe. For a simplistic example of this approach, if a business uses cheaper materials and offshores jobs to lower cost of production, while maintaining its price in the market, it has successfully increased its margins, achieving its duty to shareholders at the expense of customers and employees. That this diminishes the value created for customers is a sad artifact the business has no duty to ameliorate.

Taken to its logical extreme, investors could gain control of a company and completely gut the business of the business, in order to maximize the short-term worth of the company, and then sell off the gutted company. At this point, the company itself is no different from the product that has been offshored for manufacturing. This scenario is, in fact, exactly the business model of many private equity companies.

The financialization of capitalism—efficiency for financial efficiency versus efficiency for mission—completely destroys the intent of capitalism. It creates a market of businesses as assets that is disconnected from the purpose of the assets. One might hope that the economic system would naturally prevent this financialization, except the government institutions responsible for managing the system have bought into the efficiency game, too.

A new conventional wisdom emerged that painted the government as inept, nontechnical, and intellectually incapable of managing the economic system. This contributed to several decades of deregulation, anemic antitrust enforcement, and no entity powerful enough to counter the financialization of business.

In his book, *Goliath*, Matt Stoller neatly tracks the rise of this efficiency mindset. In the late 1950s, a new line of thinking emerged that argued *monopolies* earned higher profits not because of concentration but because they were more efficient. By the 1970s, the thinking had gained traction, much in part to future failed Supreme Court nominee Robert Bork. The Sherman Antitrust Act, passed by Congress in 1890 to prohibit monopolization and restraints of trade, was widely misinterpreted, according to Bork.[xlvi]

Stoller writes: "Congress intended the Sherman Act [...] not as a means of protecting democracy, or markets, or the rights of citizens to produce and exchange free from interference by a monopolist. The only thing antitrust was meant to do was get consumers more stuff."

Eventually, the efficiency argument made its way into official antitrust policy. Efficiency emerged as a winning defense against government antitrust action. From the Antitrust Division of the U.S. Department of Justice: "It is efficiency, not competition, that is the ultimate goal of the antitrust laws."[xlvii]

Again, you optimize what you measure. There's nothing inherently wrong about efficiency, of course, but efficiency of what and for whom matters. How does one define efficiency? In truth, measuring efficiency is hard. So in academic modeling, efficiency was simplified to be the amount of output or product per input of resources. This is fine for measuring product-manufacturing efficiency, but not *business* efficiency.

Financial efficiency measures profit margins—in other words, money made versus money spent. This is famously the domain of business management icon and former General Electric CEO Jack Welch: Squeeze the cost out of all company expenses, including product inputs, maximize productivity, optimize execution, charge as much as you can, and voila, maximized returns for shareholders.

But what's missing from this picture? The customer. Value promised to the customer is not part of the equation. It is immaterial to the twentieth-century concept of efficiency.

In antitrust analysis, companies' market share is relatively easy to determine from the outside, but there is no simple, objective way to measure the efficiency of a market. So the government's antitrust position settled on "consumer welfare" as being the standard on which to measure market efficiency, and thereby enforce (or not) antitrust. And even more narrowly, consumer welfare is assumed to be represented by lower prices.

So once again, we're in a race to the bottom. Rather than promote robust competition as the end goal to be measured, which forces companies to best others by creating value for customers, the efficiency argument created a downward spiral. Businesses seek to lower prices, however they can get there, including cheaper resources, cheaper labor, less regulation. Consolidation of power in the market doesn't matter as long as we get this "consumer welfare." The tables completely flipped from companies having to show how an acquisition will not lessen competition to the government needing to prove the acquisition will raise prices.

That higher prices emerge down the road is immaterial, since the cat is out of the bag by that point. Product quality drops. Innovation doesn't happen because established oligopolies buy and kill competing products. Independent, small businesses are trampled without a care, because they're automatically considered "less efficient." Town centers big and small die all across the country due to the need to increase efficiency. Jobs disappear overseas in order for big companies to be, you get it by now, more efficient.

This is all rather arbitrary and certainly a subjective definition of consumer welfare and efficiency. But no matter how you define these, the end of the twentieth century was a perfect storm of efficiency-minded, execution-optimized corporate power and a government satisfied to sit it out, no matter the result. Ironically, this sounds an awful lot like my professor's description of the Soviet economic system, only the roles are reversed. Is it possible that business power owning government is not a heck of a lot better than government power owning business? They're both output driven, not value-creation driven. If business is no longer tethered to *creating value* for customers, is capitalism serving its purpose?

The optimize-efficiency management style fits well with executing in a known market. Consider the life cycle curve for the industrial age. For the first fifty years or so, a core group of very large businesses, one group for every industry, manufactured and sold a handful of products. Often these were the first of these products ever produced. It marked the emergence of consumerism and the middle class. Layers of businesses were created by demand from the core group, such as parts suppliers, technology, specialized components, and raw materials suppliers. A layer below that supplied parts and materials to the suppliers, and business services, such as accounting, marketing, and legal support. Another layer below demanded dry cleaning, office supplies, restaurants, and so on.

One fast-growing company created a pyramid of economic opportunity. It was a world of "if you can build it so they can afford it, they will buy it." It was the age of *Mad Men*. Companies owned the relationships with their consumers and broadcast their "brand" from the mountaintop. It was a one-way communication aimed at creating or expanding the market based on convincing recipients they had a particular need or that the company's way of addressing that need was better than the competition's.

Companies shared only the information about their products they chose to share, but would tell you anything you wanted to hear to sell their story. Consumers didn't have a relationship with the business, but with the brand. As Jon Hamm's character, Don Draper, says in the *Mad Men* episode "Smoke Gets in Your Eyes": "The reason you haven't felt it is because it doesn't exist. What you call love was invented by guys like me...to sell nylons."

By the end of the twentieth century, the economy might be thought of as being in the late-majority and laggard parts of the lifestyle adoption curve. This side of the curve requires even more aggressive marketing and selling, since you must make people feel left behind and fearful of what they're missing out on, in order to get them to buy.

During this period, companies shifted their focus from favoring R&D (research and development) to tight operations, fiscal restraint, and sales growth (represented by Blake's line from *Glengarry Glen Ross*, "Always Be Closing"). All other business side-of-the-house activities aiming to retain and grow market share were on the table, including government lobbying to create barriers to entry (competition), mergers and acquisitions, and retaining market share through legal maneuvers.

New product development, engineering solutions to problems, and human-centered design took a back seat. These groups still existed but were hidden away in silos or organized in ways to increase efficiencies in existing markets rather than discovering new value that might open new markets. "Innovation" was owned by the marketing team; R&D tinkered in sandboxes with skunkworks.

Conceptually, big business was pro-innovation. The success they achieved in execution mode, as well as the financialization of capitalism, just lessened its significance or, more accurate, changed its role. If your primary purpose is to benefit shareholders, and the primary way of accomplishing that is by increasing profits, and with the government looking the other way, wouldn't you double down on execution by lowering costs, squeezing labor, and paying out to investors? Why innovate for real?

DON'T WE NEED TO INNOVATE?

Generally, most businesses do not need to invent anything. They need to leverage the world's past inventions. From a company management point of view, the proper allocation of innovation resources is in service to efficiency. If efficiency is optimizing the allocation of resources for the benefit of market share or profits for shareholders, then innovation is funding new ways to leverage resources for the benefit of that efficiency.

In fact, the Innovation Industry itself defined the blueprint. Based on the heyday of technological invention from the 1950s through the 1990s, companies managed research and development departments to do "innovation." The R&D was part of the main organization but free to invent. Commercialization was another issue.

This is, of course, the story behind Clayton Christensen's "Innovator's Dilemma." Rational corporate managers will double down on executing existing markets in order to maximize returns. Why put a dollar into a risky new endeavor that may never return a dime versus earning the return you are certain to get on an existing endeavor? Therefore, the story goes, companies should spin out new endeavors so they can develop the new market independently of the mother ship's rationale. IBM did this successfully with their laptop division.

This is fine and good for a significant new technology for which there's some indication a new market will develop and that will eventually compete against your existing business. You simply can't do this for all inventions, the vast majority of which will not develop into markets. In other words, most inventions are not innovation. This doesn't change just because some businesses errantly decide to measure their innovation capability by number of patents developed. Yet again, you optimize what you measure.

Unfortunately, the idea that you should split the "innovation" side of the company from the core has created a paradox for today's businesses, which find it difficult to execute their core enterprises in the face of digital revolution. To be more blunt, the "bimodal model," "dual operating system," or ambidextrous organization where "execute" or "exploit" is managed separately from "search" or "explore" doesn't work.

The Innovation Industry is quick to point out the handful of big businesses that failed to capitalize on inventions because the main execution business got in the way: Blockbuster, Kodak, and Xerox remain popular in the catalog of cautionary corporate big-miss stories. The problem with this type of story is that it's only true in hindsight. None of the businesses failed to invent, by the way. Contrary to the story line, Kodak did pursue the digital camera market. It chose the wrong approach. It's true, Blockbuster didn't foresee the value of mailing DVDs to people's homes, but this is hardly an example of disruptive innovation. "Snail mail" was not an obvious business model. Dozens of companies stream movies. Blockbuster could have joined them at any time. Xerox had the first personal computer, which it decided not to pursue. Lots of companies did pursue the personal computer market and failed. Today, Xerox is a $4 billion company. Was that a missed opportunity? Sure. Was it the wrong choice? That's pretty tough to say.

The bimodal system doesn't solve for any of this. The typical story in corporate innovation is that 90+ percent of the company is dedicated to old-style command-and-control execution mode, while the remaining portion is "innovation." The innovation group is underfinanced, lacks resources, and is not a strategic priority. The structure is based on the R&D lab, even though most companies don't need to invent technology. The secret the Innovation Industry doesn't tell you is that most businesses don't need to do "disruptive innovation."

The problem is that the term "innovation" is not defined within the context of company ambitions. Companies do "innovation" because it's what they're supposed to do. It says so on their website. Innovation is for showing off what the future of industry might be. Innovation is about open floor plans, free Red Bull, and Nerf guns; it's used to help recruit young people. But this is not really innovation. It's innovation theater.

Businesses lost their gumption to actually innovate when they lost the ability to create value for customers. Instead of creating value for customers, they maximized the efficiency of bleeding dry existing markets. To show some returns to Wall Street, businesses latch onto acquisitions, lobbying government, squeezing labor, and reducing product quality because they can.

Digital transformation is the new innovation theater. The thinking is akin to creating a new organizational silo in order to build a mobile app. Digitizing products at some level is absolutely required to compete in the market, depending on the nature of the business, of course. But it's insufficient and doesn't solve the root cause of corporate woes.

Real digital transformation should not just be about technology. Digital transformation, which underlies the economic and social revolutions we're experiencing, is also about mindset. I visited with a large, global European bank that has a sexy, state-of-the-art innovation lab. Its team continuously tests and demonstrates new ideas. It has banners with the words "Transformation," "Disruption," "Change the world!" It's connected to the local startup ecosystem. Leaders speak at innovation, digital transformation, and "future of banking" conferences. They can show you how your credit card will be your kitchen's most valuable utensil within ten years.

I also experienced their business-to-business portal as a client. The technology and user interface was circa 2003. Agreements required "wet ink." Legal documents were passed around using Microsoft Word and MS Exchange. Business was conducted in snail mail time. Where is the digital transformation?

This company has a well-funded group that provides an intriguing and elaborate vision of the future, but they struggle to do today's banking.

The imperative to execute harder, buy revenue through acquisition, hide losses in constant reorganizations, eke out profits by offshoring more functions and squeezing workers has run its course. Optimizing efficiency for efficiency's sake as big business modus operandi is done.

THE JETSONS VERSUS THE FLINTSTONES

There's an amusing joke-conspiracy meme promulgated on YouTube where the Flintstones live in a postapocalyptic future, rather than the Neanderthal past. This is the only explanation, so the argument goes, for why the Flintstones and the Rubbles would re-create twentieth-century amenities such as the turntable, laundry machines, showers, and foot-powered automobiles. Also, since dinosaurs didn't coexist with humans, a Jurassic Park–style genetic technology is the only way to explain, albeit not sufficiently, Fred's pet, Dino.

An alternative version has the futuristic Jetsons living in the same time period, only above them in a floating city, which is explained in a couple of ways. The cave people are hippies living off the land (though their exploitive uses of "dinosaur" labor seem at odds with this theory). Or it's a cartoon version of the movie *Elysium* starring Matt Damon and Jodie Foster, where the wealthy live lavishly in the sky above the masses on a ruined Earth.

Imagine overlapping founder and former Intel CEO Gordon Moore's famous law of exponential growth in computational power, which accelerates up and to the right, with the trajectory of the wealth gap in the United States. The chart in Figure 1 illustrates this—and clearly it doesn't suggest causation. In other words, the advancement in computer chips did not cause the wealth gap; likewise, the wealth gap did not create increased computing power. Nevertheless, we like to assume that innovation improves society.

Yet the data paints an alarming picture of where we may end up. As the wealthy get wealthier, they also become more technologically advanced. Further, the gap between the top two tiers of wealth grows exponentially. I might also point out, the more people there are in the have-nots bucket, the less overall consumption there is.

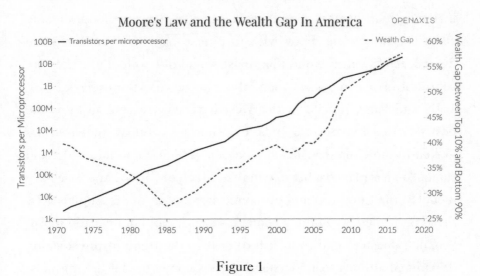

Figure 1

Powered by OpenAxis

Western society has chosen capitalism, and for good reason. But capitalism is not perfect. To dismiss improving capitalism because it's the "best we got" or because "government is inept" is an insult to our ingenuity and entrepreneurial spirit. Capitalism serves by the grace of democracy. Society determines the rules of capitalism. Capitalism needs to change to meet the challenges of the twenty-first century. This shouldn't be a radical idea. What should be considered radical is that we collectively throw up our hands and accept the fate of the horribly unbalanced economic system demonstrated in Chapter 1. We can and must do better.

The vast majority of corporate management wishes to function within the rules of capitalism. (Though I imagine the fewer the rules, the better, as far as they're concerned.) Most people wish to be positive members of society and live meaningful lives. They wish to contribute to the success of the company they work for. They have relatively modest expectations about personal wealth. They want to be with their families and friends, and feel secure in their homes, maintain good health, raise their children, eat quality food, breathe clean air, and so on. They wish to pursue happiness and, to some degree, achieve it. Beyond that, most would like to feel like they are contributing in some way to something bigger than themselves.

By and large, people in the West have chosen capitalism as the best way to achieve those ends. For almost a century, the world has looked to the United States as a beacon of hope for a better life, and capitalism has played a big role in that. Much of Europe and Asia have modeled their political and economic systems on the example set by the U.S. While lazy pundits conflate socialism and democratic socialism, one doesn't need to look further than the trend of privatization of national airlines to understand the economic model driving most European countries is capitalism.

In noncapitalist countries, capitalism never left. A black market is an example of capitalism. China is called communist and yet its economic system is capitalist, managed by a totalitarian government. Throughout Cuba—a stubborn socialist state if there ever was one—you will find private businesses bubbling up on corners and in crumbling old buildings. In Havana, there are "paladares," which are private and often family-run restaurants catering to tourists, offering delicious menus prepared by Le Cordon Bleu–trained chefs. At Paladar La Guarida, where the Robert Redford–backed movie *Strawberry & Chocolate* was filmed, friends tell me the food is almost mythically good, easily offsetting their fears of building collapse. Capitalism thrives anywhere it's given an opportunity to do so.

So let us return to the question: Why did we choose capitalism? Because it's the normal way for us as humans to interact when we want things. A child doesn't set up a lemonade stand because we're a capitalist country. We're a capitalist country because a child sets up a lemonade stand. Capitalism has generally served the West well in creating a strong middle class, but while also systemically denying it to a significant and deserving population. Creating a system that benefits more, which leads to more people being better off, benefits us all.

People who live more contented lives are less likely to commit crime. There's less volatility in the economy. There's more peace globally. It holds that if we create a system that benefits all, then we create a positive loop: a spiral that heads in a harmonious direction, toward more products and services for more people, with far more value created and served in the world, for more contented people.

Think about value creation in the world as a supply-and-demand calculation. If companies focus on creating value for customers, then we generate a surplus of value and it lowers the price so that more and more people can acquire that value. And that raises the standard of living. We all have a part to play in the value equation. It's time we recalibrate and, in spite of the continuous disruptions we face, choose to commit ourselves to creating value, making capitalism work, and building more of what we want in the world.

Chapter 3

THE WAY TO CHANGE

B E MORE AGILE!' Can't I just say, 'BE MORE AGILE!' and people will go be agile?" Moritz Hartmann, head of EMEA & LATAM for Roche Diabetes Care, lamented to me as we sat in his office.[xlviii]

Believe me, if the people in this hierarchical, high-performance organization knew how, surely they would, and not in the least because of his imposing nature. But not knowing is not knowing. Even if they knew what the word "agile" meant, they didn't know what behavior was expected. The leader himself didn't know how to teach what he had in mind. He just knew his team wasn't doing it.

"It was actually very frustrating," Hartmann said. "When I left my last post I felt I had prepared the team. I had given them power and beliefs. But I saw these drift away very quickly after I left. We had established principles that were good, and that we wanted to maintain. That the team should carry forward with their new leader, but it was just all given up much too quickly. At that point, I really began questioning the sustainability of my leadership—had I truly empowered them, or whether I had, in fact, kept the control."

I have run into similar issues myself. In the past I routinely dismissed entrepreneurs who didn't follow up with me after a mentoring session as either not entrepreneurial or secretly not agreeing with my opinions and afraid to voice that. To be clear, these are my failures, not theirs. I own these and benefit from the learning and wisdom they provide me.

Hartmann responded similarly. Although he had worked on himself for a year with leadership coaches, he saw little progress. The introspection was necessary, of course, but the change ultimately came from outside awareness. "I moved from looking at myself into looking at the impact that I had on my environment. It's a very important step to take. As long as you're self-aware, you can change your behavior. But as long as you're not focusing on how your environment also perceives you, you won't get anywhere with it."

In my personal journey, I began showing entrepreneurs explicitly how to be a mentee; for example, how to follow up, how to respectfully receive advice even while dismissing it. After, I saw the expected follow-through. Similarly, more recently and without a lot of success, I tried to empower employees by giving them the authority to make decisions and the resources required to pursue their own ideas. Yet failing to teach how to behave *while* empowered meant they continued to insert me as a bottleneck to achieving their missions. Hartmann says: "That's when I started to act very differently as a leader, and to pay more attention to how my team was actually showing up. What were they doing? Then I started to work with them on reflecting as to what *their* impact on their environment was."

I had a brief meeting with Hartmann right before he was set to speak in front of a team of one hundred or so handpicked employees about to embark on a lean innovation accelerator wherein they would learn and apply empathy, experiments, and agile techniques to improve product commercialization. The audience was nervous. They didn't know exactly what to expect, other than they were going to interact live with customers in order to learn how to better serve them. This was out of their comfort zone, was "against compliance policy," and was "better left to researchers" who knew how to do such things.

"One of my first jobs," he told me, "was dressing up in a dinosaur costume to try to get customers to come into the store."

"Tell that story," I said. "Show them that they can do it."

A natural orator, Hartmann inspired his team to embrace what they were about to learn, develop skills that are useful in life and beneficial to their careers. They would have fun while also realizing that the more they understood customers, payers, and health care providers, the better they could provide products that would benefit them and provide sustainable value. It was a fantastic kickoff to the program and the teams performed exceptionally well, as did most of the other leaders involved.

"There was a lot of discomfort," Hartmann says. "Leaders who have achieved a maturity level where they were already leading people in a different way did much better at this. They didn't have that control mechanism, were more on a creative leadership side. They still had to learn the techniques, but they had a much better experience."

As we learned in the previous chapter, the belief among many for the last five decades has been that a business's sole responsibility was to maximize shareholder value. But that is an incomplete thought. A business operates in order to sell specific types of products or services for particular markets. These products or services represent the company's purpose, or, if you will, its mission. Therefore, in actuality, the belief would be more coherent if instead it stipulated that a business's responsibility is to maximize shareholder value *through its mission*. The shareholder doesn't buy stock in an automobile manufacturer with the assumption that managers will decide to convert the business to a skateboard manufacturer or restaurant delivery service if shareholder value were to increase.

It follows that if the mission of the business is to sell services or products to customers in particular markets, then *customers* are the first priority. Employees must work to accomplish the mission; therefore, *they* are the next priority. If your employees are unable to successfully deliver value to the customers, there is no business and no value for shareholders.

The solution to business woes going forward seems so simple, yet in practice is complex. The straightforward idea is that *business needs to refocus on creating value for customers*. Most companies I interact with believe this to be true. We hear endlessly how companies are "customer focused," "customer-centric," or even "customer obsessed." But it's definitely one of those easy-to-say, hard-to-do concepts.

Perhaps counterintuitively, it has become more difficult because of the digital revolution. It's more difficult because everyone has a computer in their pocket. It's more difficult because of complexity. It's more difficult because twentieth-century methods don't work.

Using twentieth-century conventional wisdom to manage a system of twenty-first-century complexity (such as your business) doesn't work. Facing an unpredictable, unmodeled world that is subject to black swan events requires a different type of organization. With this in mind, and at the risk of exposing my cultural background further, organizations must be something that talented surfers inherently are; that is, they must be RAD: Resilient, Aware, Dynamic.

> **Resilient.** Strong like an oak and flexible like a reed, able to bounce back from adversity, and to remain stable as a whole when parts of the system change or fail.
> **Aware.** People are able to recognize what's not known, to absorb and share new information and data that come from the outside

world, as well as from within the company, and to be present in the moment.

Dynamic. Adaptable, the very structure able to change in response to needs; the organization is fast and nimble.

The mindset change begins at the top. It requires focused self-awareness and vulnerability. In her seminal leadership book, *Dare to Lead*, Brené Brown writes, "The courage to be vulnerable is not about winning or losing, it's about the courage to show up when you can't predict or control the outcome."[xlix] She's exactly right.

Leaders must be able to recognize uncertainty. They must be able to recognize the difference between poor execution of best practices and when they aren't the best practices anymore. They must admit when they don't know the answer. They must be willing to embrace humility quickly. Leaders must understand when to learn first, rather than just execute harder. Ultimately, they balance the efficiency and learning mindsets. Uncertainty has always existed inside of business, of course, but the digital revolution has vastly increased it.

John Chambers, former executive chairman and CEO of Cisco Systems, shared with me a painful story of learning to embrace his own imperfection. "One of the hardest things for me to learn was to admit that I had flaws and there were some areas that I really struggled with."[1]

At a "Bring Your Kids to Work Day" at Cisco, John helped a young girl who was struggling to overcome her dyslexia, onstage in front of an audience of five hundred. In his conversation with her, he admitted his own struggles with the condition—but, little did he know, his lavalier mic was still on.

"I never intended to share with anybody that I was dyslexic because I viewed it as a huge weakness. The audience got really quiet, and I realized everybody had heard me say that I was dyslexic and that I have struggled with reading and writing since I was a young boy. It was crushing because I thought my company and my teams expected me to be a superhuman. Cisco was on its way to becoming the most valuable company in the world, and I thought we needed somebody at the top who didn't make mistakes and didn't have weaknesses. However, I soon realized it actually was the reverse. The fact that I shared with people that I've struggled—and how I dealt with those challenges—built empathy and connection. It was ultimately one of the best things I've ever done as a leader."

The trick to dealing with uncertainty and insecurity is no trick at all: You must actively reduce it. How? You must identify the uncertainties. You must respond to that which you have control over and prepare, proactively, for those areas you don't. To paraphrase former U.S. secretary of defense Donald Rumsfeld, you need to understand your knowns versus your unknowns.

KNOWN KNOWNS

Large, successful businesses become large and successful because they deeply understand their markets. They understand the needs of the market. They understand how to develop, produce, market, sell, distribute, and support products and services that address market needs. A successful company has produced a blueprint on how to do each of those tasks. The company was structured to execute on that blueprint. The company is not large because it is perfect, but because based on industrial-age enterprise business "best practices," it was scaled to optimize the execution of the blueprint. "Efficiency" in this context seeks to increase the effectiveness of the blueprint.

Employees are measured based upon how they are able to execute their components of the company blueprint. They are assigned execution metrics, known typically as Key Performance Indicators (KPIs) or more modernly, perhaps, Objectives and Key Results (OKRs). Layers of management are put in place to ensure that KPIs are completed productively in order to meet predictable revenue numbers. Day in and day out, the vast majority of the company, across the value chain of activities from raw materials to delivered product, work to get products into the hands of customers, to execute on the established blueprint at the lowest possible cost. The proof is in the revenue. These are known knowns.

KNOWN UNKNOWNS

Known unknowns represent a continuum of uncertainty, spanning from minor variances in the blueprint to the need to create new blueprints. The amount of uncertainty varies across time horizons. There is less uncertainty this year than there will be three years from now or ten years from now.

You perhaps have relatively minor variances to existing blueprints that are correctable right away. Employees with the right skills in the right positions make decisions quickly to mitigate the risk of value chain disruptions, for example, so that revenue and cost numbers are not adversely affected. Smart employees add immense value when it comes to navigating the degrees of unknowns and mitigating uncertainty.

Minor productivity enhancements, increased efficiencies, and small changes that improve customer satisfaction might provide an increase in revenues or lower costs but at the very least avoid losses. These items are worked on, on the fly, in the regular course of business. This falls under the continuous improvement umbrella. In *The Alchemy of Growth*, Mehrdad Baghai called these Horizon 1 improvements.[li]

The correcting of small problems or making incremental enhancements to products and processes deals with small amounts of uncertainty. They can occur anywhere across the organization, including functional support teams in human resources, finance, facilities, information technology (IT) teams, and so on. People might need to speak with stakeholders, run tests, collect and incorporate feedback. The work is defined by the creativity and abilities of the individuals responsible for the outcomes.

Bigger unknowns require bigger changes in back-office processes or product-value chains, but still have to do with existing processes, products, and markets. This could include something as simple as redefining sales scripts across the organization to implementing a new payroll system. How to manage the changes is well understood, but the level of uncertainty has increased. These aren't changes that can be made overnight, but they also don't require massive upgrades in systems, architecture, personnel, or organizational structure. The efforts return more tangible cost savings or revenue increases.

If you think expansively into the future, you venture further into the unknown. You may have ideas on how to enter new markets with existing products or break apart existing products to use their components in adjacent or new markets, such as creating a small-business version of an enterprise-software application and selling it online, as Siemens did. Or moving existing "shrink-wrapped" software into a Software as a Service (SaaS) business model, as Adobe did. Or perhaps a developing country is nearly ready for your product or service, and so you take steps to experiment and move into the emerging market, as Roche Diabetes did. Or your IT department must revamp internal systems based on cloud technology. Or you wish to completely reinvent how you do company-performance management.

The complexity and uncertainty are again increased. Generally, you have the abilities inside the company to navigate those uncertainties, but you also may seek external validation. The potential for cost savings or new revenue is significant, but the actual return on the time and capital invested is likely years away. A more concerted effort to learn before executing is required. The existing blueprint is revamped or a new one must be created. Again, you have some people to do the exploration work, but you may need to build more capabilities. These may be Horizon 2 growth initiatives, where the return on investment is several years away. Horizon 2 initiatives have evidence they are worthy of pursuing.

UNKNOWN UNKNOWNS

The final and deeper level of unknowns are the unknown unknowns. There are two types of unknown unknowns. The first are the so-called acts of god. These are events that are largely unpredictable. You may know that they've happened in the past, but you cannot predict when they will occur again. Examples could be global economic catastrophes, stock market crashes, a fire that takes out your headquarters; it could be a global pandemic.

You cannot work these into your blueprint. You cannot take action on them before they happen. That isn't to say there isn't some amount of preparation you can do. You buy insurance, security systems, form disaster-recovery plans, install tornado shelters, create supply-chain redundancy. Interestingly, and as a fallback, fail-safe edge, big business also looks to the government to provide relief, especially in times of unusual stress and immediate demand disruption, as experienced during the COVID-19 pandemic in the spring of 2020. Just ask the airline and hotel industries, among others.

The second type of unknowable unknowns we'll put into the bucket called potential disruption. If you look far enough out into the future, you really cannot predict what a particular industry or market will look like. But that doesn't mean you shouldn't pay attention. These are Horizon 3 growth opportunities. The horizons do not reflect the level, or complexity, of change or innovation required, but rather how far off a solution might be based on its maturity level. Horizon 3 ideas are those that are untested or barely tested.

The Innovation Industry puts too much emphasis on the need to develop disruptive innovation. What are the odds of success when it comes to truly disruptive innovating? Very low. If one looks to the startup world as an example, one thousand startups are needed to get one "unicorn." That's quantitatively nearing impossibility. It does happen, obviously, but it isn't where nontechnical or nonscientific companies need to focus. Despite conventional wisdom, there's no evidence they need to.

Looking far out to Horizon 3, however, is something that companies can and should do. While the outcome is not predictable, the effort to look there can provide tangible benefits. Businesses should periodically do deep exploration, looking to completely reinvent part of the business. Businesses can evaluate predictable demographic changes, scout new technology, look at where government—particularly the Department of Defense—is making technology bets, and establish relationships with startups that are pushing the envelope.

Imagine a continuum of uncertainty: In the near term, there is relatively low uncertainty, and efficient execution on the current business mission is primary. Stretching into the future, there are massive amounts of uncertainty and virtually nothing known to execute upon. But it's important to understand that certainty is highly elastic to volatility. In other words, uncertainty can sweep into the core, known part of the business at any time. One needs to expect to be caught off guard despite best attempts to prepare for it.

Resiliency keeps the company on track toward achieving its mission despite unforeseen circumstances. Fundamental strengths born of mission clarity, the creativity and dedication of its people, and a core quality that distinguishes it from others—such as technology, customer service, or brand—sustain businesses through uncertainty.

Resiliency also speaks to flexibility, the quality of bending but not breaking. Networked systems tend to be resilient, since one part of the network can go down without the entire system failing. Mesh networks are even more so, since communications within the system have no single point of failure.

An aware organization understands the risks of not preparing for unknown unknowns. Back in my IT days, disaster-recovery plans were usually not put in place until after a disaster. Similarly, many businesses began taking a more serious look at supply chain and manufacturing redundancy only in the wake of system interruptions caused by the global COVID-19 pandemic. The pandemic was an "unknown unknown." It was foreseeable and, in fact, foreseen, but not predictable as to when it would happen. Deciding whether or not to build a redundancy supply chain or redundant power equipment in Texas and relying only on a financial-efficiency point of view is using a "known known" frame in an unknown context.

A dynamic system changes based on circumstances. It's active in seeking new information and is able to adapt quickly if necessary. Its very structure is adaptable in response to challenges. A business may spin up a new team or a temporary organization to investigate ways to use existing technology in the face of a pandemic, for example.

Such understanding helped Gerber Technology find not only a new revenue-saving opportunity during the COVID-19 pandemic, but a lifesaving one as well. Gerber is a manufacturing automation company providing software and hardware to client manufacturers operating in the fashion and textile industries. When the company was founded in 1967, "it was all about the iron," says Chief Strategy Officer Karsten Newbury, who also leads their digital effort. Now they have integrated software, cloud, and laser-cutting hardware, enabling manufacturers to automate more of their production lines.

Newbury, a longtime lean innovation believer, has aggressively developed the human-behavior component of participating in the digital edge of the market, where clothing, for example, can be produced on demand. In building the capability, Newbury recognized two fashion business trends: First, an intense effort to minimize the cost of production—"chasing the needle," as Newbury puts it—where apparel manufacturers hop from country to country to reduce labor costs. Second, the emergence of "fast fashion," where the idea is to produce clothes customers like at a rapid rate, but often using cheap materials.

The future, Newbury says, is a combination of those trends: inexpensive, customer-centric, and fast. "We're in an age where companies compete on agility. Being agile and close to the customer made up my mindset when I came to Gerber in 2014. How do we create a solution set that helps companies make clothing better, more efficiently, and closer to their consumers? We had to think about the entire workflow from the consumer to the brand and manufacturer. You are only as agile as the weakest link in that chain."

In the beginning of 2016, they interviewed dozens of their clients, looked at market sizes, talked to startups, tracked industry trends, and so on. They developed a vision of where they needed to be. They created buckets of integrated product sets based on workflows—in other words, based on the way product creation worked from idea to design to production to distribution.

"We have to revamp our customer service experience," Newbury says they determined. "We have to revamp not only product, but sales, professional services, and support. Yet all of these are multiyear projects in addition to all the short-term, pressing items that must be done to keep the business running.

"Before, for example, one of our applications was functionally rich, did a lot of great things our clients wanted, but it was difficult to implement, upgrade, and support, and even required a hardware dongle for licensing. Product versions were released and implemented every eighteen months. But now it's a cloud application that's updated every eight weeks without the client having to go through a difficult implementation project. This gives our clients a lot of time and resources back that they can use to be more responsive to their customers."

This is the backdrop of six years of effort Gerber Tech went through in order to be RAD. "In January 2020," Newbury says, "COVID hit. Our customers' plants in China were closed. Then Italy was hit and then New York. By the end of March, we could see our customers' production was down 70 percent." Production trends reflect retail trends. Gerber consumables orders lag production changes by two to three weeks.

"At the same time, the World Health Organization is saying they need hundreds of millions of masks and PPE [personal protective equipment] articles that just can't be made fast enough." On March 19, 2020, Gerber Tech executives spun up a PPE task force, whose ambition was to get their apparel manufacturing customers switched over to PPE products, pull Gerber revenues out of a hat and keep their people employed, and produce lifesaving products to benefit the world. Not too shabby as missions go.

"I'm never going to forget March nineteenth of 2020," Newbury says. "For the next five weeks, myself and core team members worked crazy hours out of passion for the change we were making. It was just insane. We had seventeen hundred companies around the world contact us, wanting help on how to switch over their operations."

They started with a simple contact form web page. That's day one. Kickstart it. Then they fleshed out a separate, dedicated site. They updated the information, patterns, technical files to download, detailed information on how to switch over, and provided it all for free.

Extraordinarily, a community developed. "A neighbor of a team member is a doctor, and so we were able to digitize surgical gowns. Third parties began uploading their patterns. I went to a guy who was making hospital scrubs and he put his pattern and production files up." Gerber learned to deal with FDA regulations. They reached out to DuPont, Dow, Alstom, and a number of companies to help customers source materials. They worked with the city governments of New York and Los Angeles, state governments in Arizona and Oregon.

"We had companies come to us that did not own a single Gerber product. They were using all competitive gear. They asked, 'Can you help us? You're the only ones who have pulled this all together.' And we said, 'Sure. Here you go.'"

As production bounced back to 85 percent of pre-COVID levels, Gerber Tech added, in less than twelve months, a new segment called Gerber Health Services, a successful PPE consulting service for customers who want more in-depth help, and millions of dollars in new equipment sales. All told, hundreds of customers produced hundreds of millions of PPE items during the height of the global pandemic.

I cannot think of a better example of the new way of working, the new mindset proliferating throughout the organization and making it more resilient, aware, and dynamic. "The success of the PPE initiative," Newbury says, "inspires the rest of the business and employees to have a greater sense of pride and confidence that anything is possible."

The RAD frame is how we adapt to disruption and uncertainty as companies. As leaders, there's more work ahead to ready ourselves for implementation. The brain-bending we need to do is wrapped around the disruption mindset, which is based on five key elements, the pillars on which we build our attack plan for changing how we do business in this new environment.

FIVE ELEMENTS OF DISRUPTION MINDSET

Based on my work with more than sixty enterprises around the globe, working with people on the front lines and in the C-suite, from all corners of organization, I've come up with the 5Es of Disruption, five characteristics of RAD organizations. Dude.

Empathy

Empathy is about understanding people deeply. It requires us to temporarily get out of our own skin and try on someone else's. It's being fully present and respectful of that person's take in the moment. How you use the information and understanding you experience is something else.

Exploration

Exploration is what we do when we don't know. Uncertainty exists everywhere to varying degrees. We can't execute through uncertainty, which typically leads to failure. Humans are learning machines. We learn to walk, run, ride a bike. We fail, learn, iterate, until we succeed. The faster we iterate, the sooner we can execute on what we've learned.

Evidence

"Evidence" is short for "evidence-informed decision-making." Evidence comes from the data we receive through experiments, execution results, feedback loops, and insights we glean through customer empathy work. Decisions should not be made purely by data, except in rock-solid, known-known circumstances. Evidence is a key to forming consensus.

Equilibrium

Equilibrium is established when you have opposing forces that result in a stable system. When one force becomes too strong, the system becomes unstable. Equilibrium inside the business requires balancing efficient execution with exploration. Strategy determines what the stable system should look like based on priorities and gaps in progress toward desired outcomes. Leaders and employees also must achieve a stable equilibrium in their lives. Many forces are at play, including family, security, health, and work.

Ethics

Ethics determines the values a company seeks to maintain in pursuit of its mission. Ethics includes how businesses interact with customers, manage data, including behavior tracking, and privacy. Ultimately, companies need to define expected behaviors, establish guardrails, and enforce accountability. Leaders must model their values. Ethics also establishes the relationship between leadership and employees.

The most common issues I hear are:

- How do we get leadership buy-in?
- How do we get aligned on strategic priorities?
- How do we create an innovation mindset?

While I understand the concerns, these questions are off the mark.

In my experience, leadership *is* bought in. They recognize that the old way of doing things is not working. They see that at the economic level, with the rising inequality, and they see it in their businesses, where growth is difficult to find, while at the same time there's little more opportunity to squeeze more efficiency from the organization.

The 2020 pandemic brought more issues to bear that cost money, time, and resources: issues like employee health and happiness, operational disaster preparation and recovery, and community well-being. Needs, in other words, that aren't compatible with the pure execution mindset of the twentieth century. Leadership is aware of the need for a more "innovative" mindset, but it can't be in service only to "innovation." The question isn't whether change is needed, but what that change will look like and how they can get it.

Traditionally, big consulting firms help with strategy and designing top-down "innovation" programs, or "culture change," or "transformation," all of which start with another reorganization. To beat a dead analogy in the face, it's another plan to rearrange the deck chairs on the *Titanic*.

Additionally, many executives and middle management have spent time with leadership coaches to learn and practice some of the desired behaviors mentioned on the preceding pages, including empathy, vulnerability, and empowerment. But how to apply it to daily challenges is not apparent when there are numbers that need to be hit, fires to fight, more meetings to attend.

Missing is where the rubber hits the road: In the end, it's the behavior change in *the bottom layers* of the organization that drive true organizational change. It can't be just top-down driven. Approaching change from the ground up is an opportunity to equip talented, learning-hungry people with tools for transformation, build shared values and trust, and optimize performance. Your people lead the way.

But not without tension. Once the behavior change occurs on the bottom layers, middle management finds itself in an untenable position: pressure to change in the form of words from the top, change bubbling up from below, yet no modifications to skills, performance measures, or incentives to new behavior. They're caught in a pincer move.

In 2011, ING, the global bank headquartered in Amsterdam, appointed Pinar Abay, a thirty-four-year-old professional who had never managed more than a handful of people, as country manager for ING in Turkey. She took over a bank of six thousand people, which was a military-owned bank serving members of the military before being acquired. "As you can imagine," Abay told me, "the culture was quite different than ING. It was located around military bases, was very hierarchical. You don't really think about innovation, but how to better serve the military customer."[lii]

The building was dark with a very closed design, with brown-walled offices without internal windows, matching the culture. Everything was permission based; all the working times and breaks were rigidly scheduled. "I would attend meetings in which people would look at me for all decisions. Ninety-nine-point-nine percent of the time when I asked, 'What do you guys think?' they would just look at me, looking to me to decide."

Abay went to work, with her primary objective to build trust. You hire people based on their talents, but overcontrolling them wastes that talent. "I had pages and pages of expenses I was supposed to approve, and vacation time, and so on. I went in front of our people at our town hall and said you just need to spend as if it's your own money. And they all looked at me blankly, because they were used to ticking the box on every single item. I told my management team that I didn't need to know how many days of vacation they take and I don't want to approve your expense reports. If I trust you to run a couple-of-hundred-million-euro business, I don't need to approve your hundreds-of-euro expenses, right?"

She changed the physical workspace, opening up the floor plan, adding glass everywhere, increasing the visibility and transparency, adding communal tables and movable furniture. "We added signs on every floor, 'Be yourself.' We want people to be whoever they are."

The flip side of building trust, of coming to work as yourself, is that you are expected to be present, mentally engaged, solving problems.

"I always asked the question 'How do you know?' It even became a bit famous in the company," Abay said. "It's a simple question. We hire really bright talented people who just take it for granted that whatever senior people say must be right. So I started asking in meetings this very simple question to the most senior people, saying, 'How do you know?' They would look at me, 'What do you mean, *How do you know*? I run this business. I know.' And I was like, 'But exactly how do you know?' And if you ask the question five times you realize they don't know."

A couple of years later, when ING rolled out their company-wide lean innovation program, PACE, the Turkey office was their early adopter. "It came natural to us. We just embraced it immediately. It was a perfect fit culturally. It put structure around what we were naturally doing. We felt, 'Oh, here we go. This explains what we were doing.'"

Turkey became the go-to group to prototype and test ideas. "We were naturally externally focused. We'd follow fintech startups, track what competitors were doing. In global ING innovation events, teams from different countries would come up with really good ideas. If Australia comes up with something, for instance, we would call that team and say, 'If you want, we will produce and test your idea in Turkey.' Other countries would reach out to us because they would know within a year, we would produce and test their ideas in the market. This was like part of our DNA, to keep exploring."

Building and maintaining a resilient, aware, and dynamic system starts by taking specific action that puts the 5Es into practice. One must do this in such a way that leverages existing capabilities while also incorporating new skills development, as in the leadership traits mentioned previously. Company impact should be built into the action, such that success is demonstrated as quickly as possible.

There is no one-size-fits-all solution. There is no fixed organizational structure, ready-made frameworks, or airport-sold business books that can tell you how to get to the other side of the long, difficult journey in front of you. My hope is by sharing stories of organizations that have successfully figured out components that work for them, ideas regarding what the desired outcome looks like, and specific actions you might adapt and use to get going, you will be prepared to start the adventure.

In my view, the first step is to not plan. In fact, that's mostly what's happened over the last decade. Since the Great Recession, there has been a lot of talking, planning, reorganizing, and digitally transforming, without actually driving the real changes necessary.

To kickstart change, you have to start. You have the people with the right mindset to get started today with a structured program to work in a less structured way. A successful kickstart brings a positive return on investment. To accelerate, you simultaneously expand the program while also putting in place the vision, values, and vector of the program in service to the organization's mission. Successful acceleration results in "product-market fit," meaning the program is creating momentum for change.

Scaling is the long journey, requiring changes to the broader systems, processes, capabilities, and mindset. As with Joseph Campbell's *The Hero's Journey*, the internal obstacles are formidable. But again, you have the allies and champions to get over them. Successfully scaling means that the new mindset becomes the new norm. An enduring system requires an organizational design that is resilient, aware, and dynamic. You no longer have to push the new mindset. Desired behavior comes out of the structure. Ultimately, the system surviving new disruption will be the test of an enduring system.

A business that works to maximize efficiency *in achieving its mission* is a statement everyone can get behind. Corporate values, based on ethics, establish the behavior needed to achieve the mission within the laws of capitalism. Customers become the primary beneficiary to value creation, since they are likely to be a core part of the mission. Empathy and exploration skills help organizations serve them better now and into the future. Empathy, exploration, and equilibrium principles, applied internally, empower employees to execute on the mission. Evidence-informed decision-making provides a means to overcome disagreement, cut through biases, and build consensus on ways forward. Eventually, all this directly results in value for shareholders.

These elements put into practice immediately, iterated upon, fine-tuned, and made part of the company culture are primed to scale. Organizational structures put into place that natively produce desired behaviors ensure the new way of working endures. This is a twenty-first-century system that produces and supports a successful digital-age disruption mindset. Ensuring businesses thrive in the twenty-first century based on creating value for customers, while demonstrating respect for employees and also producing positive returns for investors, is the first step, and a vital one, toward owning disruption such that it works for all of us. And the *how* of making it work will be the focus of the next few chapters. Buckle up.

PART II

HOW TO CHANGE
THE ELEMENTS AND PHASES OF CHANGE

"This really is an innovative approach, but I'm afraid
we can't consider it. It's never been done before."

Chapter 4

THE FIVE ELEMENTS OF
ORGANIZATIONAL DISRUPTION

In my high-tech startup days, I once ran the product management team for a software company that sold utility products to software and network engineers. It was a promising venture with modest ambitions. At some point, the founders decided they wanted to stop playing small ball and instead go big. This meant pursuing corporate customers with multi-million-dollar budgets. For that, they brought me in to help.

The process for developing a new product looked roughly like this:

1. The CEO had a "vision" of what he wanted the business to accomplish within a specific enterprise networking market. The vision was light on details, but he was, you know, the boss.
2. I traveled extensively with our company account managers in order to better understand what customers were trying to accomplish, what their priorities were, and where we stood relative to the competition. The competition was, by the way, the proverbial eight-hundred-pound gorilla in the market.

3. I merged the vision with reality to come up with the product "marketecture," which was what I called the nontechnical version of what the product needed to do.
4. The product management team negotiated with the engineering team to create the product specification and the release date.
5. Engineering built, iterated, and eventually released the negotiated version of the product on the agreed-upon date.
6. Marketing and Product Management managed the launch.
7. Sales prepared customers and then sold the product.

Despite the planning, it took us multiple versions of the product and often years to get it right. In the end, the customer determines what is right. The customer determines when the product is done. We had been in business for many years and had built a strong reputation; we developed a product that was technically superior to the competition's, and one that cost significantly less. We received positive attention from analysts and the media, but had a tough time selling it to the enterprise market. Despite the superiority of the product, there was not a compelling enough reason for IT directors to risk replacing the incumbent product, which was "good enough."

Disruption hit with the tragic events of 9/11. War and economic collapse followed. Crazily, much like many of the digital businesses that benefited from the COVID-19 tragedy, our startup *grew* during this period. The new economic environment meant that enterprise price-for-performance requirements suddenly made us the best choice. Hindsight is 20/20, of course, but it's easy to see that we were operating through the entire process in "execution" mode. In other words, we were light on learning or exploring. Despite our breakthrough, we had done it wrong:

- We failed to truly understand our customers.
- We had no concept of learning from the market, other than getting feature requirements and paying attention to competitors.
- Our strategy was determined by internal strength of personality as opposed to market-based evidence.

We could have benefited from another approach, a better way of thinking. And this is where the Five Elements of Disruption carry massive power and meaningful application for all organizations. Especially in these times of continuous ripples and constant disruptions, we must purposefully address uncertainty.

THE FIVE ELEMENTS OF DISRUPTION

1. Empathy: Understand customers deeply
2. Exploration: Deploy learning
3. Evidence: Make informed decisions
4. Equilibrium: Work toward balance
5. Ethics: Do the right thing

1. Empathy: Understand Customers Deeply

Empathy is vitally important to organizations seeking to succeed in the complex world of the twenty-first century. Yet it is an overused and often misunderstood term. It's easy to get empathy wrong, and many of us do. So what do we mean by developing empathy in a business context?

Trying to be empathetic toward someone is not determining what *you* would do if you were in their shoes. Empathy is accepting and seeking to understand their perspective. It's not drawing conclusions about their view or judging what you hear. In the moment, you don't want to be evaluating what you might do with the information you glean. You're in listening-and-trying-to-understand mode. This is a process, one that requires time and reflection. The goal is to connect with the emotional component of *what* people share. You try to understand how something makes them feel.

But why is this important? Because when operating in uncertainty, there's no one right way to understand a problem, nor is there one right way to address it. When we "know," we can look to best practices to solve a problem. We can teach people how to solve it and we can course-correct as we proceed, if necessary. We can evaluate how well the problem was solved. But if we "don't know," then we need to learn all these things.

Customer empathy is almost a corporate buzzword these days, and while I'm skeptical that millions of corporate employees are actually out developing a deep understanding of their customers, the fact that some are trying to pay attention is meaningful progress. Truly developing empathy for customers—understanding beyond feature requirements—can pay huge dividends across the organization. It's not just useful for core product development, but also for making incremental improvements to all aspects of commercialization, including pricing strategies, marketing messages, and sales objections that must be overcome. Through empathy, unknown issues, such as channel problems, product complaints, partnership opportunities, and customer service needs, come to light.

Future growth is dependent on having an ear to the market, which is not simply reading market research reports. Maybe strategic objectives seek growth through capturing market share? Maybe there are companion products or services you could offer? Maybe a product retooling opens adjacent markets? The possibilities come from insights into customer needs.

In each of these examples, the customers do not necessarily know what they need. Customers often don't understand what the possibilities are. It's your business's responsibility to understand each of these opportunities to serve, satisfy, and solve your customer needs. You may be able to solve bigger, more painful problems by understanding your customer more deeply. And therein lies a key payoff of empathy.

As the axiom goes, you can't win the game if you don't play the game; you can't know your customer if you don't listen to your customer. In a business environment where technical risk is less problematic than market risk, customer insights represent your new and vastly underappreciated intellectual capital. The risk to business is less "Can we build the product?" than "Should we?" For the vast majority of product ideas, we know they technically can be developed. Customer insights represent an important and vastly underappreciated intellectual capital versus, say, patents.

Striving for efficiency alone without incorporating the business mission hurts the empathy development process. You may have a centralized customer research organization, but that isn't the same thing. Customer research primarily seeks to market and sell more efficiently. Traditional customer research answers the question "What is the top gaming platform of fifteen- to twenty-five-year-old white, suburban males?" Surveys and focus groups can help in understanding characteristics of broad market swaths, but aren't great at uncovering insights. Customer research doesn't answer "Why?" It doesn't explore human emotion or the unknown.

It's also important to note what empathy development is not:

- Market research, such as typical surveys, Net Promoter Score, focus groups
- Imagining you are the customer
- Customer journey mapping or agile user story development without customer validation

Good empathy development helps you understand:

- Customer environment or culture
- Why customers make the choices they make
- What customer needs, desires, and aspirations look like
- The priority of customer needs
- Obstacles to implementing product
- Behaviors the customer must change to get value from the product
- Objections to purchase

A leading insurer in Malaysia, we'll call it KL Co, ran a series of weeklong "lean innovation" sprints, where internal teams comprised of individuals pulled from various parts of the organization develop empathy and run experiments to generate evidence for ways to improve business. The then–chief customer experience officer, Troy Barnes, was a great cheerleader to getting his teams out of the building and speaking with customers.

One team, led by innovation coach Van Tran, thought an AI chatbot might help lessen the load on the overburdened call center. Talking to the head of the call center, the first thing the team learned was that the top callers were not customers, but the independent agents that sold and supported KL Co products. Many of these people were a couple hundred feet away, in the building next door to KL Co headquarters. One in particular was a very influential and "difficult" agent.

So they made the walk over to the agent's office. Tran recalls, "She blasted us for a good ten, fifteen minutes. It was incredibly uncomfortable hearing just how difficult we, KL Co, made her work. And she was like, 'I'm one of the highest sellers. I'm sending you all this business and we never see anyone from HQ. You just throw over new apps and we don't know how to use them.' I remember feeling, 'Oh, wow, that's a really difficult way to start a conversation about a new app.'"[liii]

The head of the agency shared that she and her agents, as well as other agencies, worked outside of the KL Co–provided tools. They belonged to a WhatsApp group where they could share tips and other information to answer customer questions. They were on Facebook, not the KL Co website.

Says Tran, "The agent took out her iPad and she's scrolling, saying, 'I've got all these apps. I don't even log in. I don't know what they do. No idea.' Our learning was we need to support these agents by going where they are. They're on Facebook, I'm on Facebook, too, I'm two seconds away from Facebook. So that was a big turning point for us. KL Co interacting with Facebook or a platform that was already established with the agents was, I think, a radical idea for us."

The minimum result one gets with developing customer empathy work is a feature set. The ultimate result? To get insights that act as a competitive advantage for your business. The practice of developing empathy can be learned by anyone. Democratizing the ability means that everyone in the organization is capable of discovering insights from their stakeholders. It means that empathy skills can be employed internally as well.

Back-office-support functions benefit from understanding their colleagues better when they are launching internal initiatives. With empathy practices, departments can share information better and build new processes to improve efficiency. Employees work better when they are heard and understood. Leaders manage their people more effectively when they understand those people's situations better. All this is more important in remote work situations.

Dr. Brené Brown's work on empathy is focused on internal application; specifically, on how executives become better leaders through empathy. In her book *Dare to Lead*, Brown identified ten common issues leaders face in their organizations, most of which are resolved through a greater understanding of employees, colleagues, and leaders (empathy flows both ways) and a willingness to speak directly. The common issues include, for example, that people are scared to look wrong or not in the know, that they are unwilling to take the time to identify problems or shift away from ineffective solutions, and diminished trust among colleagues.[liv]

The work of developing empathy drives real value across the organization and positively affects all teams, but even more so in situations of uncertainty. I often get a raised eyebrow when I suggest the idea that employees develop empathy for leadership. But one of the biggest obstacles to reinventing old-school business management is that to effectively work within a complex system, decision-making must be *pushed down* the hierarchy. Leaders must recognize that the smart people they've hired, those employees who are closer to the problems, can make better, more timely decisions to solve them, without running everything up the stack for approval. For this to work, however, empathy needs to go both ways.

It's rather obvious that a leader better understanding their people will help empower them. Perhaps less intuitively, if people understand more about managers and leadership, their backgrounds, the experiences that shape their worldviews, their philosophies, what keeps them up at night, their business fears, and so on, they will better learn how to make the most of that empowerment. They will learn how best to ask for and accept guidance, when and how to push back, what evidence to bring to conversations, and when to seek help for a key decision. This requires openness, awareness, and vulnerability on both sides.

A former innovation leader at GE—we'll call him Samuel—shared a story with me that demonstrates the type of learning that can lead to internal changes in the way people work, while directly benefiting the organization. Samuel's team struggled to receive adequate funding for their innovation projects. As is the case in many companies, his team was funded as a program or project, with an annual operational budget that is scrutinized each year based on how the money was spent and its "return on investment." This term (also known as ROI) is in scare quotes, since it's next to impossible for an innovation group to get a return each year. It was one of these flawed, Dilbertish management-by-efficiency moments where a program designed to find future growth is funded according to the requirement of an immediate return.

Samuel went about changing the funding mindset through a series of friendly lunch meetings with the head of finance. Samuel's goal was to learn about her mindset:

- What sort of accounting background did the CFO have? Was she a CPA? Did she work for any of the industry titan consulting firms? Had she ever worked at a startup?
- What kept her up at night with respect to the current state of the business?
- Outside of the normal operational budget process, what sources of funds did she have at her disposal to fund multiyear initiatives?

Samuel sought insights that would inform him of how she thought about being a steward of the complex finances of a massive corporation. Next, Samuel wanted to get her thinking on certain hypotheticals that affected his team, but also would benefit the future of the company. These had to do with philosophy:

- If she had her druthers, where would the company focus its growth efforts?
- If Finance was administering the company's innovation, what data would she expect reported back to her and at what cadence?
- How might she alter financial practices if unspent funds were immediately returned?

Samuel looked for insights that would instruct how he could demonstrate that he, too, would serve as a good steward of company money, and that he would be more transparent than in typical budgeting scenarios. Finally, the concept of returning unspent funds before the year was up was so mind-blowing that he knew he would have to ease the finance group into that. But, in a sense, he was "training up." He was teaching the CFO and other leaders how investments in innovation require a different approach (one that funds based on learning metrics) from execution-minded programs where immediate ROI might be more appropriate.

This was not a one-and-done conversation. They designed a plan to ease into funding innovation teams as investments using funds from a multiyear capital expenditure bucket versus an annual operational one. A deep understanding of each other and the subsequent alignment between the innovation group work and company priorities changed long-held beliefs and practices.

This gets to a broader point about empathy work. There are two sides of the empathy coin:

- Understanding people better
- Doing something with the information learned

As human beings—workers, parents, students, patients, constituents, consumers, and so on—we wish we were better understood. We are confident we could do better in those roles if those on the other side of the relationship would take the time to know our needs, desires, and aspirations better.

Of course, we are also those people on the other side. As employers, doctors, care providers, teachers, politicians, and policy makers we can seek to understand our stakeholders better. *It flows both ways*. Only good can come from it. It doesn't mean we all need to hug it out. It simply means deeper understanding.

After you have built an understanding, you get to do what you want with the knowledge you gain. To some degree, Samuel was using empathy development for his own advantage. He was looking for how he might apply what he learned in order to get what he wants. There are ethical limits to how one can and should use the information, of course, and in this case Samuel was using it to better the company.

I almost hate to say it, but there may be a selfish aspect to developing empathy. One could develop empathy for whole swaths of customers and choose not to build a product that serves them. Or to ignore features for one group in order to concentrate on another. While economic or industry policy makers benefit from understanding the impact of their actions on constituents, they have a variety of points of view they must consider and multiple variables to weigh when developing policy.

2. Exploration: Deploy Learning

Exploration is the new innovation. Exploration better captures the spirit required to both continuously improve existing business as well as discover, test, and validate new opportunities for growth. The term "innovation" means too many things to different people. Most often, the term conjures technology, even when new technology might not be what drives value to customers at all.

3M makes for an interesting example, not least of all because it is a diversified technology company. The company relies on invention. And yet their history is replete with stories of turning what look like failures into wins. In other words, they succeed at inventing, but if no market is found, invention doesn't matter. Even their very founding was a failure. Starting off as the Minnesota Mining and Manufacturing Company, they sought to mine corundum to make sandpaper and tools for grinding. However, underground was anorthosite, not corundum, which is completely unsuitable for sandpaper, and this forced the company to creatively explore other applications. More than one hundred years later, 3M is a multi-billion-dollar company serving multiple industries and billions of customers around the world.

Ideas truly are a dime a dozen. Most companies do not have an "idea" problem. Choosing *which idea* to work on is the real problem. The command-and-control era dictated for ideas to be chosen by rank. Idea competitions and clichéd corporate shark tanks are a low-cost effort to reward employee input and creativity. But the ideas typically go nowhere, since it's impossible to justify funding idea development based on the old-school, business case PowerPoint presentation. They are designed to fail.

The subjective quality of the idea is immaterial. If instead of encouraging people to come up with ideas, we empower people to test ideas and teach them how to do so, the impact on businesses will be immediate. Similar to how scientists use the scientific method to achieve technological invention, people can run experiments to test and observe whether ideas will work in practice, without fully investing in developing the idea. This is true, whether exploring ideas to improve a process, such as lean manufacturing does on the factory floor, or exploring a new business model, like using an app to immediately transfer money person to person. The savings of resources, time, and money in this process are immense compared to the old-school technology invention model.

All new products, services, or internal processes require a change in customer, user, or stakeholder behavior. This is a simple fact. For a new product to succeed, the customer must do something different from what they do today. There are numerous potential obstacles to a new behavior taking hold. In other words, for the new initiative to work, multiple assumptions about behavior must be true. Exploration seeks to answer: "How can we figure out whether customers will change behaviors such that the idea is viable?"

In the example of KL Co described earlier in this chapter, they hoped to resolve the known difficulty of their agents getting timely information to better serve customers. But when the KL Co team spoke with the agents, they uncovered their frustration with KL Co apps. While the idea they had of the chatbot might have resolved the former, many assumptions had to be true for another app to actually solve the problem. The old-school way would be to turn the findings over to the project management group, who, if the project were approved, would build the app like all the other apps, without any customer involvement. The exploration method instead had the team running experiments to test assumptions during the same sprint.

"We found," Tran said, "that 95 percent of agents did not use their KL Co–issued email accounts. Because they said, 'I don't know how to log in.' KL Co was sending 90 percent of their updates via a platform that no one was using. So we decided we'd build the app on Facebook instead."

They quickly built a new Facebook page and hid the chatbot behind an access code. They watched as agents (in their offices) would pull up the page, access the bot, and interact with it. The trick for the experiment was that the bot was actually a teammate back at HQ messaging live with the agents, pretending to be the bot. The team was watching the agent behavior and asking follow-up questions to learn whether the product was viable before building it.

Barnes, KL Co's lean innovation early adopter, urged the five teams forward throughout, exalting them to more than six hundred customer engagements during the one week. KL Co launched their chatbot app on Facebook less than six months later, overcoming old-school resistance about "doing things differently," such as using external cloud-based platforms for customer applications. Going where the customers (or agents, in this case) are is how companies must work in the digital age.

Investors were not interested in the startup I described at the beginning of this chapter, until after we started growing. No one cared about our enterprise strategy, or whatever business case we showed them that was made up out of whole cloth.

What investors want is evidence that proves what startup founders believe to be true is actually the case. Market-based evidence is the output of empathy and exploration. Again, more than intellectual property, insights are the gold nuggets companies seek in order to know where to head next.

3. Evidence: Make Informed Decisions

Evidence-informed decision-making seeks to eliminate the biases we all bring to decision-making. Twentieth-century command-and-control organizational structure supports decision-making by rank. The quality of the decision, the reasoning, or the evidence in support of it doesn't matter, since the structure assumes those with a higher rank have more knowledge or better experience. "The buck stops here" is a valuable ethos in certain situations, especially in times of crises or where decisions must be made despite a lack of information. At other times, rank perhaps properly assumes a greater understanding of the bigger picture. But many other circumstances require specialized expertise or knowledge that are independent of hierarchy. Here, an organization needs to enable the right people to make the call. Evidence-informed decisions are one of the best ways to accomplish this objective.

Insights based upon customer empathy work, and data generated from experiments presented to leadership in support of an idea is a more powerful way to invest in projects versus decisions made by rank, old-market experience, or bias. It also promotes a shift in culture, conferring trust across the rank and file, empowering them to take ownership.

Traditional military hierarchy, for example, determines how, what, and when specific tactics will be undertaken. In special forces, however, the responsibility to lead during portions of a mission depends upon the expertise and knowledge of the individuals, not their rank. In this sense they work as an agile team facing massive uncertainty. Going back to General McChrystal, "We restructured our force from the ground up on principles of extremely transparent information sharing (what we call 'shared consciousness') and decentralized decision-making authority."[lv] The information shared horizontally across services and vertically up the stack is based on the evidence developed by those with "boots on the ground."

Evidence is a powerful way to resolve conflict. Even if not everyone agrees on a course of action, agreeing to rely on evidence to help choose between various courses of action is a powerful way to build consensus.

Using the phrase "research shows" is, however, often an attempt to selectively use evidence to confirm bias. Problems arise when you can't determine whether the research is timely, relevant, and well understood. Without the experts who performed the research, this is difficult to know. Exploration is a good way to create new evidence that should confirm the research.

Dr. Brené Brown's concept of "rumbling with vulnerability" is useful here. The leadership skills she discusses, such as empathy and vulnerability, are in service to driving business impact. When difficult decisions are made in the face of uncertainty, checking egos at the door is vital. But the process of making a difficult decision is not a woo-woo, kumbaya session. It requires participants to show up ready to defend their case. Bring evidence. If leadership decides not to proceed with a team's idea, for example, based on the shared evidence, the team learns the level of proof required for funding.

Optimize What You Measure

An important question regarding evidence is, What data should be considered? Big companies tend to measure the efficiency of execution, which is why it is the focus of optimization. Key Performance Indicators (KPIs) and Outcome and Key Results (OKRs) define execution-oriented metrics. Often what ends up being measured does not have a direct impact on company performance, but rather portends a specific outcome based on historical precedence.

Sales performance is an obvious exception. For existing products in existing markets, sales managers sum up their people's output to report their group's revenue numbers. Sales projections use historical data to predict future numbers, assuming no disruptions occur.

The other end of the spectrum may be the typical innovation metric: number of patents. Technology firms with business models dependent on product commercialization often produce hundreds, if not thousands, of patents annually. Their annual innovations, however, are actually typically zero, since it's highly likely the inventions never see the light of day. But the company achieved its measured objective. Google "most innovative company" awards and you'll likely see patent portfolio as the number one measure.

Most company performance is measured in this disconnected way. Strategic priorities determine the company objectives for the year. The specialization of skills that characterizes particular departments determines what outcome their group needs to accomplish, based on what they've accomplished in the past. Those accomplishments are laid across the calendar to determine what needs to be done by when, creating the milestones. There need not be, and most often is not, an obvious causal relationship between the group's output and the company's performance. These milestones are distributed among members of the group as their KPIs or OKRs.

This method doesn't work very well when facing uncertainty, since, as all prospectuses like to say, "past performance is not an indicator of future results." As a matter of fact, the more uncertainty, the more the guarantee that future results will not be the same. Startup investors, on the other hand, understand learning metrics better than most, since they don't know when they'll see measurable desired outcomes. Startups by their nature understand learning metrics versus execution metrics.

Learning Impact Metrics (LIMs) is a method I introduced in *The Lean Entrepreneur* to determine the learning metrics one might track for a new product, an internal startup, or any initiative faced with uncertainty. As mentioned above, anything that requires behavior change (including culture-change programs) faces uncertainty, and for the initiatives to succeed, certain assumptions must be true. The way to track the progress of a startup, for example, is to measure customers' behavior.

Customers go through seven states from being Aware to being Passionate about a product or service:

- Aware: I am cognizant that a product exists within some meaning-ful context.
- Intrigued: The product seems to address a need I have.
- Trusting: I believe the product will actually work for me.
- Convinced: I am willing to exchange some sort of currency for the product.
- Hopeful: I am waiting until I receive the promised value of the product.
- Satisfied: I receive the promised value.
- Passionate: My experience goes above and beyond my expectations.

For each state, the startup hypothesizes the business action required to induce customers to behave in a particular way that indicates progress to a specific state. The behavior can be measured. Using this method, teams can use exploration techniques to generate evidence that indicates the project is headed in the right direction. Further investment is based on the evidence.

As the team progresses, unknown aspects of the business model convert to known; items that have been learned are now executed upon. Here's a simplistic software-as-a-service video-sharing example:

- When first starting, where the customer, problem, and solution are not well understood, learning metrics might be the number of customers talked to each week, and the results of specific experiments demonstrating potential customer behavior with respect to recording and uploading videos.

- As learning progresses, learning metrics might be the number of users who uploaded a video and a list of their colleagues to share it with (via a form, perhaps, not the actual product, which hasn't been developed).

- The startup team proceeds to fulfill the value proposition by hand, as the metric shifts to the month-over-month growth of people who send one video per week and a list of people to share it with.

- At some point, the numbers indicate a minimum viable product should be built; metrics regarding marketing and conversion funnels are added. For example, the number of unique website hits, the number of account creations, and so on.

- When the MVP is in the field, the number one metric is the month-over-month growth of satisfied users, based on the number of videos sent per week, the number of shares per video, and the number of views per video.

- Perhaps a premium plan is tested to determine what customers might pay for, so metrics that are tracked include conversions to pay, amount of time to convert, and even revenue.

- Revenue, marketing, and conversion execution metrics are now reported alongside continued funnel learning and product learning metrics.

4. Equilibrium: Work Toward Balance

Startups want to execute as soon as possible but are often stuck in mostly exploration mode for years. Achieving an execution-dominated mode means they've figured out much of their business model and they're growing. Big companies, on the other hand, are great at execution and only want to execute, ignoring their need to explore wherever uncertainty exists in the organization. This could be anything from trying to close a sales gap to adding a fallback supply chain, from launching a new Human Resources (HR) recruiting system to reinventing a business model using artificial intelligence.

The amount of time spent executing known practices versus learning new practices depends upon the amount of uncertainty laid out across time horizons. For this reason, everyone in the organization needs to have both skills to some extent. The concept of equilibrium establishes the balance to these two ways of working.

Leadership helps create equilibrium by adding an evaluation of "what's known versus what's unknown" to the decision-making process. KL Co's Troy Barnes shared with me the senior leadership team's frustration that they struggled to get the desired outcomes from major initiatives they undertook.[lvi] I suspected they were going through execution motions on projects that were rife with uncertainty.

To measure this, I had the leadership team work in five teams to lay out on a two-by-two grid the company's top twenty initiatives that were under way or that they were considering funding. The vertical axis measured the predicted impact to strategic priorities, and the horizontal axis measured the teams' level of confidence in their ability to achieve the desired outcome.

Confidence includes internal capabilities, how well they understood the problem they were seeking to solve, the stakeholders' needs, and so on. The five teams distributed the same twenty initiatives on the grid. Two results became instantly clear:

- There was little alignment on the importance of the initiatives or their level of confidence.
- Small clusters existed in the upper right quadrant representing high impact and high confidence; and the upper left, representing high impact and lower confidence.

These projects were both fully funded and assigned to the same Project Management Organization, or PMO group, which in most companies, and certainly in this one, is very execution focused. They receive full funding, so there's not a lot of incentive to use a different mindset just because no one knows whether the project will be successful or not. The hierarchical, command-and-control structure tells you to go and do what you're told—give it the old college try.

This is, of course, not the most efficient process. Instead, those projects should be funded in tranches based upon evidence of progress. They should use a learning mindset at the start and report learning metrics. As they figure things out, producing positive or negative evidence, the leadership team should decide whether to continue to fund the project.

The outcome of the simple workshop was that KL Co decided to split up their initiatives, so that those facing uncertainty went through the lean innovation team, while high-confidence projects continued down the traditional PMO path. The innovation team practiced empathy, ran experiments, and worked as agile teams, launching new products in record time.

Agile is a powerful way to balance execution versus exploration work on any team. The concept of Agile originated with the Manifesto for Agile Software Development, which was published in 2001 on agilemanifesto.org. It has been widely adopted by tech startups in particular, but also by corporations of all types and sizes, and in any company department, not just software development. In addition, an entire industry of frameworks, consultants, and digital tools has emerged to sell and implement the concept.

If possible, ignore all that for the moment. Agile philosophy, principles, and the various tools form an instrumental part of creating a resilient, aware, and dynamic organization. It's ideal for working within a complex system. Without worrying about the specific structure of various agile implementations, which are often anti-agile in practice, flexibility exists in the philosophy such that one can tailor agile principles to fit desired outcomes. Much is left to interpretation and adaptation. With that in mind, I offer my own characterization.

I describe an agile organization as being one which at regular intervals picks its collective head up to take in information from the outside world and decide whether to change its work based on the new information. New information could be relatively minor, such as a change in personnel, or it could be a large, disruptive force reshaping needs and markets, such as emerging technology or a global pandemic.

In complex systems, the further away you are from the source of an issue, the less effective you are at addressing it. Smart companies hire smart, creative people. An agile organization is one that empowers those people to solve problems. They are given a mission they are accountable for, the resources they need to succeed, and the authority to make the decisions on how to achieve their mission, within some defined constraints. Like a startup, teams at this level balance execution and exploration activities based on the needs of their specific mission. Using agile practices provides the means of prioritizing what to work on over a period of time.

Agile organizations share context, show work, and report progress. Human beings fill in gaps of information with fiction. In other words, when we store memories, we complete the "picture" in order to enable better recall. This is why storytelling can be so powerful. If you share points or facts, people essentially invent their own stories with their own assumptions interspersed with the information you shared. But if you tell a story, people will remember the story.

Often running directly contra our tendencies in a command-and-control organization, an agile organization paints as much of the picture as possible so that gaps aren't filled with the human's innate ability to compose fiction. Further, by making the agile teams responsible for this information, leadership is freed up to focus on the things they most need to keep in mind. They perhaps can finally achieve their ideal state of being proactive and pulling together context, rather than managing outcomes at the team level.

Scaling this structure is difficult. The speed and flexibility that make an agile team effective begin to break down if you simply expand the sizes of the teams. More agile teams are great, but there's risk that the larger context gets lost. Information flow becomes critical.

While the best agile organizations are less hierarchical than they were pre–agile transformation, they're not nonhierarchical. Since decisions on what to do on specific items are bottom-up based on knowledge of issues at the source, less management is required at that level. Self-organized teams manage that.

Middle managers become consolidators. They organize the output of teams' work in order to fill in the larger picture. They aggregate teams' progress, steer resources, and ensure the bigger picture remains aligned to group or division priorities. Another layer aggregates the portfolio of products and projects, ensuring they are aligned to company priorities.

The middle management layer doesn't act as a conduit (in other words, a filter or a bottleneck), but rather a coordinator and an organizer of the flow of information—leadership down, teams up, and horizontally across the company. They own the merging of output into the full context, and the structure below necessary to achieve objectives.

General McChrystal ran into a similar "scaling" issue with his "agile" military force. The coordination of the various components of the military operation was vital, but they knew they couldn't return to the top-down, command-and-control operation of the traditional structure.

"It was not possible to make the Task Force one big team, but we also could not stick with our command of teams compromise; stacking our small teams in silos had made us unwieldy. At the same time, we couldn't simply remove the reductionist superstructure and leave each team to its own devices; we needed coordination across the enterprise. Somehow we would have to scale trust and purpose without creating chaos."[lvii]

We must tackle this issue in due order as well.

It's worth noting that the value of Equilibrium can also be applied to employees. To be productive, they need to be able to establish equilibrium within their own lives. The human right described in the Declaration of Independence as the "pursuit of happiness" does not stop at a company's front door. Family, health, wellness, rewarding work, and spirituality are all factors that should be considered in allowing humans to find a balance that works for them.

The 2020 pandemic drove this point home, literally. In the United States, 64 percent of married-couple families saw both parents employed.[lviii] From March 2020 and well into 2021, many of them were working from home. Both those who were and were not at home likely had to deal with their children being home from school. Further, gyms, playgrounds, sports leagues, recreation centers, and other exercise outlets were unavailable. Places of worship were closed, as were numerous other outlets people use to exercise various aspects of their personalities.

All of their "being human" was crammed into their living spaces. Anyone managing people working from home quickly learned that the nine-to-five work era was not only untenable but unnecessary. It was impossible for workers to juggle all of these moving parts while at the same time pretending they were on their work premises. Yet generally, productivity didn't suffer; in fact, for many companies, productivity *increased*.[lix]

Managers feeling comfortable only when they know their workers are at their stations is an artifact of the command-and-control era. The assembly line–inspired hierarchy rewards managers who squeeze more tasks/time out of their people. The fact is that people in the office have never been 100 percent productive 100 percent of the time. Humans are not wired that way—and also, eight hours for a workday is purely arbitrary. Focused time is likely half that, and that's being generous.

One study on productivity conducted in the United Kingdom revealed that "the average UK office worker is only productive for 2 hours and 53 minutes out of the working day; with social media and trawling news websites labeled as the main distractions affecting employee productivity each working day."[lx]

The future of work will undoubtedly be driven by measuring impact of work versus number of tasks completed, as discussed in the "Evidence" section in this chapter. Although the pandemic drove home the need to juggle the various aspects of one's life, it didn't change the items that were being juggled. In other words, when employees were commuting into work for that arbitrary eight hours a day, they still needed to find time for the other activities.

Happy people are more productive. Equilibrium also means allowing people to balance their various needs to achieve being content people, seeking to pursue happiness while driving impact for the business.

5. Ethics: Do the Right Thing

It's my belief that a vast majority of corporate managers and employees wish to live positive lives, use their intelligence and creativity to solve problems, and contribute to society. Yet the reality is that time and time again, corporations are busted for serious transgressions against the laws of society and common societal understanding of ethical behavior. While most human beings, including those who work in big corporations, believe they should adhere to the laws, they have a powerful ability to rationalize. They will allow circumstances—money, power, pressure, lack of understanding, inconsistent accountability— to sometimes override their better judgment.

Companies must do better. Scratch that. Companies don't make decisions, behave good or bad, rationalize or not—people do. Company management, including boards, needs to better define and model their mission, values, and expected behaviors. They must create a system that enforces rules and regulations, provides guardrails, and holds individuals accountable.

Society, through government, can improve, too. Laws must be clear and concise and as easy as possible to adhere to. They should also get boiled down to the level of expected behaviors in order to demonstrate their intent. Archaic laws should be removed. Laws should result in as little bureaucracy as possible.

The toughest part of this is the relationship between business and government. As mentioned briefly before, business is part of an economic system, the equilibrium of which is dependent upon the balance of several forces. The government is responsible for managing the balance based upon the desires of society. The system doesn't work if one of the forces controls how the government manages the balance. Balance is not possible in this circumstance.

Of course, a business must be allowed to manage the pursuit of its mission, within the laws of the land. But the deal is, then, that businesses *follow* the laws, and even stand down in their attempts to influence those laws through lobbying and funding candidates. Business managers, of course, are members of society and can fully participate in the democratic practice of choosing who represents their interests in government and the laws those representatives establish. But the *business entity* itself is not entitled to the same benefits of voting rights. This is the ethical take.

In managing its business, founders, and subsequently officers, define the reason the company exists. This is the company mission. It says whom you are serving and what you're hoping to help them accomplish, and how. The mission answers why customers choose to have a relationship with you. Hopefully, the mission inspires employees. It also forms the basis of the "contract" with investors. Part 1, Item 1 of an SEC 10-K filing: "'Business' requires a description of the company's business, including its main products and services, what subsidiaries it owns, and what markets it operates in."[lxi] This is what investors choose to fund, not an empty business entity whose purpose is subject to investor whims.

Company values represent what the company stands for in pursuit of its mission. They serve as guardrails for the organization's behavior in relationship with society. They are not aspirational; they should be grounded in reality. They must be defined at a level of specific behaviors that can be taught and evaluated. People must be held accountable to values, or those values are meaningless.

The twentieth-century focus on efficiency in the maximization of value for shareholders led to overlooking ethics, since abiding by ethics might have reduced value to shareholders. As mentioned before, if one looked instead at the actual relationship between businesses and shareholders, efficiency in the execution of their mission would perhaps have avoided some of the violations.

In many respects, the digital revolution makes managing ethics more difficult, since many workers spend a majority of their time behind computer screens and keyboards. Digital products collect vast amounts of data—not just the "private information" that Facebook gets dinged for mismanaging year after year, but personal behavioral data that exposes biases, fears, emotions, and even highly sensitive personal "secrets."

Businesses owe it to their customers to treat that information ethically. Values and behaviors need to reflect that. Protecting the information is consistent with their mission in creating value for customers through their products. Here's an example of where that fails:

Facebook's declared mission: "Give people the power to build community and bring the world closer together."[lxii] Facebook's stated principles:

- Give People a Voice
- Build Connection and Community
- Serve Everyone
- Keep People Safe and Protect Privacy
- Promote Economic Opportunity

Yet before a congressional antitrust subcommittee staff, a former Facebook employee testified on working to increase a specific user engagement metric: "Your only job is to get an extra minute. It's immoral. They don't ask where it's coming from. They can monetize a minute of activity at a certain rate. So the only metric is getting another minute."[lxiii]

Motivating and incentivizing metric optimization without managing employee behavior according to stated principles or values leads to unethical behavior. The result is selling diet pills to anorexia sufferers, gay aversion therapy to homosexuals, or political insurrections fueled by inflammatory conspiracy theories fed to anxious and fearful people vulnerable to such thinking. This runs directly counter to Facebook's declared values. None of this "gives people a voice" or "builds connections and community." At least not healthy ones. And the behavior clearly does not keep people safe.

As with the other elements, Ethics needs to be applied internally as well. This not only includes "human resource management," which seeks to improve how employees are treated in support of the organizational mission. But it includes diversity, inclusion, treating people with respect, open and transparent communication, and creating policies that allow humans to live balanced lives.

Ultimately, the test of real values is determining what company managers are willing to forgo in order to stay true to the values. In other words, choosing to stop a behavior that would lead to increased market share or profits because it would violate values. This seems reasonably easy to do, but as history informs us, it requires an iron-clad commitment from top to bottom, leadership to rank and file, and back.

Agile practices can help enforce values. Specific team-level mission statements should include behavior guardrails that reflect corporate values and empower employees to safely refuse to do tasks they deem unethical. "I did it because I was told to" should never fly.

The fact is that the best way to enforce this ethos is through the social nature of agile teams. Rather than the dystopian method of "spying" on colleagues, agile teams have a natural way of discussing ethics and including such practices in their sprints. In agile organizations that live up to the original principles, culture reinforces ethics and people hold each other accountable.

The Five Elements need to be applied by all people within the organization. They form the basis for the desired behavior. Leaders, middle management, and grassroots team members apply them in their own way, in service to their missions. In other words, this is not a top-down mandate to march down the right side of the hallway in single file, as some of us used to do in elementary school, but rather are applied in a decentralized way that achieves the desired behavior.

The behavior makes individuals more aware of the environment within and outside the walls of the organization. Awareness means people pick up on both subtle and significant changes in the environment that might affect the missions or the ability to do work. A more aware organization picks up on economic changes, acts of god, or ripples of chaos sown in various corners of Earth.

Having employees working in agile teams, self-organized and empowered to act in the best way they deem fit, means an organization is dynamic, able to respond quickly to changes, and able to take action to the benefit of the company's mission. Organizations whose people must wait for permission to act respond slowly to changes and breed inaction. The opposite is also true: Granting authority and responsibility to people makes them proactive problem solvers.

Ultimately, a resilient organization is one that is sensitive to changes in the environment and able to adapt. In addition, it must be both flexible and strong. It must be able to take a hit but continue to function. In my early IT days, we never had a proper disaster-recovery plan until after the disaster. We were more resilient after the event than before. I recommend not waiting for the disaster.

CASE STUDY
INNOVATORS STUDIO

Cargill is a 155-year-old company with 155,000 professionals in 70 countries. Cargill is a "global, privately held company that brings together the worlds of food, agriculture, nutrition and risk management with the purpose of feeding the world in a safe, responsible and sustainable way." It is a decentralized company, but its seventy-plus business units are consolidated under one Cargill roof. Innovation is one of the strategic drivers for the company and is encouraged at the grassroots level, keeping it as close to the customer as possible.

As part of this effort, Cargill's Marleen Dekker was asked to establish a global Center of Excellence (CoE) for Innovation, to offer programs that build internal innovation capabilities, help accelerate transformational innovation, set standards for processes and tools, and so on. One such program is the Innovators Studio, which is essentially the CoE face to the business units, connecting and empowering innovators across Cargill's businesses.

The Innovators Studio goes down to the level of those grassroots innovation efforts, offering services to groups trying to do innovation in the modern world. The food and agriculture industry is changing rapidly. To operate successfully, insights to the changing needs of consumers are a starting point. The Innovators Studio seeks to leverage these insights, with the independent groups understanding their local markets extremely well, and use them as input for longer-term, customer-driven innovation. The studio also seeks to improve the skills of the network, while not forcing frameworks top-down.

"When we took the approach of an Innovators Studio, we knew we couldn't have a one-size-fits-all innovation framework or a very defined set of capabilities," says Pete Richter, chief customer officer. "We need to mirror the needs of our customers and the new realities of changing consumer markets. We launched the Innovators Studio concept to take advantage of our expertise, while moving quickly to bring new value-driven solutions to market with our customers."[lxiv]

Chuck Gitkin, chief marketing officer at Cargill Protein, says, "Cargill has invested in R&D, sales, and business management. We realized that we needed a more integrated approach to win with customers and drive growth through innovation."

Richter describes fundamental changes to Cargill's business model: "Consumers historically didn't have the ability to customize their own buying experience. A large percent of our customers used to buy very similar products from us, standardizing the consumer experience. Consumers today want a personalized experience that fits their unique set of buying criteria. We see this across all of our key customer segments. Cargill's innovation process and corresponding value proposition integrates this level of supply chain agility and customization. We can't simply bet and scale singular solutions today."

Gitkin adds, "In the past, Cargill competed on economies of scale and as a low-cost player. As markets have become more commoditized, the company's focus now is moving up the value chain. We aim to be more strategic partners to our customers, bringing them innovative products and solutions."

Launched in early 2019, the Innovators Studio now is a thriving network across Cargill businesses, functions, and regions. The Innovators Studio teaches people how to think about customers and consumers: about market segmentation, developing new business models, testing them, how to differentiate based on need, and also how to apply those skills to the product development the groups already do well. It acts as the connective tissue between functions and roles. Innovators can participate in an Innovation Catalyst Certification program, follow Innovation Masterclasses, and more; the managers of the participants are involved as well and actively participate in learning programs, as well as active innovation projects. This way, Innovators Studio is scaling innovation skills across the company.

Sensitive to the perception of an internal CoE sweeping in to tell teams how to "fix" themselves, the Innovators Study took a grassroots approach, inviting innovators to help move the needle. This ran counter to the consultants' recommendations, who prefer to "drive efficiencies" using the CoE model. Richter shares, "The sustainability of a Cargill CoE and a program like the Innovators Studio is directly linked to establishing creditability, building trust, and serving the customer and business needs. Your ability to influence broad-scale change only comes after these areas are established."

Global CoE Lead Dekker says the idea is to find the champions in the businesses already applying some of these skills or eager to bring them in. "We want to create the appetite, the feeling of need in multiple places in the company. And that means not only skill building, but also that by people doing design thinking and more agile work, others begin realizing that the traditional way to organize themselves doesn't really work anymore."

Business leaders start to feel the pressure from the grass-roots work. "I think we created a lot of fire at their feet and we're now seeing a significant number of leaders coming to us and saying, 'We need some help because we see how this could work, but we need some different ingredients,'" says Dekker.

This is how momentum is created. Gitkin says, "You're seeing Cargill leaders sharing best practices, saying 'I've got to change my business model. I noticed that you've done some interesting things. Can you tell me about that?' We have seen this dynamic really pick up speed in the last twelve months, where people are willing to have the hard discussions."

Dekker adds that this creates new scaling issues: "I see the role of the CoE as helping to scale so people become self-sufficient and we keep the CoE team as small as possible. How can we equip other people to act and take the lead? We keep trying to find examples, stories, tool sets, skill sets, and connecting them so we can scale capability development. The core role of the CoE has become to connect the dots."

The first step in disruption-proofing your organization is through **Kickstarting** grassroots behaviors, which are defined well enough to result in quick impact, but with loose controls so that groups and teams can find what exactly works best for them. **Acceleration** happens by doubling down on the behavior that works, providing the coaching resources, tools, training, and other resources that make the new behavior easier to do in daily work. **Scaling** requires broader systems that expand and protect the behavior from resistance that emerges from legacy parts of the business, while also helping those parts of the business change. **Endure** happens with enough of the new behavior entrenched in all levels of the business, as well as a structure that in itself reinforces it.

And like Cargill, the new business your organization will become emerges from within. It retains the legacy of your DNA, the positive aspects of your culture and ethos, even your original entrepreneurial spirit. But it must change to become more **resilient, aware,** and **dynamic (RAD)**, and this happens in the four-phase process described previously, which we'll unpack in the chapters ahead: Kickstart, Accelerate, Scale, and Endure—that is, KASE.

The Five Elements—Empathy, Exploration, Evidence, Equilibrium, and Ethics—are now downloaded and embedded in your gray matter. But the real work of applying these 5Es remains and will require regular practice across your organization. Whether it's your wily senior leadership team, steady middle management, or hungry rookie front line, everyone can hone their work in this arena. As NBA legend Allen Iverson put it well, "We're talking about practice."[lxv]

Now it's time we turn the page and get to kickstarting, the first phase of building a disruption-proof organization. It's how we build momentum. Let's get moving.

Chapter 5

KICKSTART CHANGE FROM WITHIN

L ife is full of opportunity. Every moment we can choose to do something different. Obviously, and for good reasons, most of these moments pass us by. Change in our personal and professional lives is hard. Yet we have the ability and even the responsibility to make positive change. Often it's a matter of getting out of our own way. For myself, whenever I really want to make a change in my life, I put myself into a situation where change is the easiest, most inevitable course of action.

On a Christmas morning sometime in the 1980s, I paddled out into the ocean alongside my brothers; the swell was pumping. Back in those days, with luck and good timing, the break was a spot where you could stumble upon uncrowded peaks that were *going off*. This was one of those days.

Again, I am no great surfer, but since I was young and dumb, paddling out into large surf seemed like no big deal at the time. There was danger, sure, but I was extremely confident in my swimming ability if my surfing were to fail me. This was an opportunity I could not pass up. My memory of the experience remains clear; in first person, real time, it went something like this:

Getting out into the lineup requires digging deep. The lull between sets is just long enough to allow me to paddle furiously through the channel right to the point of clearing the break, only for a set of waves to crash in front of me and push me back inside. By the time I finally am out, my arms feel like spaghetti; I'm not sure I will have the strength to push myself up to actually ride a wave.

Seeing an opportunity, I paddle out beyond the break to sit and rest. I can feel the incredible energy below me as I roll up and down with each wave. It's a full-body pulse. The sound is tremendous: crashing thunder over and over again, deep and percussive. It's not until I'm out there, in awe, that I begin to consider, Am I in over my head? My brothers are fine. Me? Hmm. Not so much.

The thing is, I've already made my choice. I am in the system. There really isn't an exit ramp. There's not a lot of difference between paddling in, until a wave takes you the rest of the way, and surfing. In many ways you have less control trying to paddle in, because you don't get to choose which wave picks you up and carries you the rest of the way. Plus, I think, is it really *that* dangerous? I mean, what do I have to lose?

I decide to just do it. I turn and paddle. The trajectory I take is based on the subtle shadow and color variations that indicate where the wave will likely crest. This particular break has a very soft lip, but quickly hollows a bit, which means taking off is pretty easy, but the drop is steep. Eight feet at least.

You may think that a wave would seem the biggest when you're paddling toward it. But somehow, it's when you're moving in the same direction, paddling furiously, and the wave picks you up that you get a real sense of its size. You're no longer in control, being raised up. You have milliseconds to bail and even then might be sucked "over the falls," depending on the power and shape of the wave.

Remember, technically the water doesn't move that much—it's pitched forward as the wave crashes and then gets pulled back. We surf energy.

I rocket across the water, and as I'm lifted up, I leap to a crouching position, then am literally tossed forward with the lip. I feel as if the board is barely touching the water; the nose is facing sharply down. My stomach is in my throat as I shoot down the face of one of the biggest waves of the morning. I hear my brothers yelling "Woooot!"

I am blessed or perhaps cursed to live very mentally aware of the moment I'm in. I can pause and think about virtually anything—where are we going to get tacos?—even while being turned, tossed, and pummeled at the bottom of the ocean floor, like a lone sock in a sudsy, agitating washing machine. The wave rolled me forward, the rest I left up to choice and chance.

JUST DO IT

You may be wondering about the point of the tale. The startup world is filled with "Just do it" advice. People misconstrue this to mean "Don't write a business plan" or "You don't need to get your finances in order." These are just excuses, so the tech bro mythology goes, to keep you from achieving your grand vision. "Forget all that, take the leap!"

Like most things in life, both sides of the binary view are wrong: "don't plan" versus "plan until everything is clear." Big businesses have been planning and trying to drive lasting change for ages, but perhaps most fervently since the Great Recession. Most of these endeavors, despite some tactical wins, have not had the desired outcome.

Though, I should say, there are many promising stories of companies well into their transformational journeys.

No matter the story or the details of the change you desire for your particular business, I want to provide you with some ideas on how to either kickstart the transformation that's required or find the momentum that gets you over the proverbial tipping point. The Five Elements described in the previous chapter represent ideals that should eventually be diffused and instilled throughout the company, from leadership to the front line. Is there planning that needs to be done for this to succeed? Of course. But relentless planning can be and often is the enemy of progress. There are ways to get moving without dozens upon dozens of meetings, leadership alignment sessions, consultant PowerPoint presentations, or months of planning.

First, it's important to imagine the difference between what I will describe and the mythology the Innovation Industry would have you believe. Contrary to popular opinion, you will not disrupt yourself. You will not become a startup again. You will not cannibalize yourself. You will not be a snake that eats its own tail.

The new business you will become emerges from within. It retains the legacy of your DNA, the positive aspects of your culture and ethos, even your original entrepreneurial spirit. But it must change to become RAD—more resilient, aware, and dynamic. Like the wave that emerges from within the depths of the ocean, you need an event to get the change going. If all progress is motion, Kickstarting is the way to start to ride that wave, followed by Accelerate, Scale, and finally Endure.

In the Kickstart phase we want to define, iterate, and practice desired behavior. Launch an initiative so that the work can begin. Produce small wins and shine a light on them. Tear down one wall of the old way. The demolition is under way, the remodel begins, there is no going back.

The objectives for Kickstarting change:

- Define your company's "RAD mindset."
- Find your champions: those who will lead by example and prose-lytize the call.
- Practice the new mindset.
- Invite everyone—not just for the chosen few, the new way is for all.
- Drive some amount of organizational impact.

From the onset I want to demonstrate that the transformation work we're doing is in service to the company's mission. The transformation must not only prepare the company to survive in the twenty-first century, but to thrive perpetually. It's worth noting and actually exciting to consider that, to a large degree, I am confident you already have the abilities to do this in house.

We're nearly a quarter of the way into this century. We've already had three major economic and societal disruptions. The next disruption is on its way, if not arriving tomorrow. To catch the wave, you need to start paddling now. There is no maybe in this decision.

Define Your Company's "RAD Mindset"

What is the desired outcome for your team, your organization, for you as a leader or an emerging leader? From a behavioral perspective, what I might suggest is similar to what I have already preached. Some combination of increased understanding of customers and the environment, decentralized decision-making to be more agile, and speed across the organization.

There are numerous popular practices that teach and promote understanding customers deeply. The most pervasive in large corporations is some version of design thinking or human-centered design. It's important to understand that the label of the practice is less important than the fundamental principle of truly understanding the needs, desires, pains, and passions of customers.

To reemphasize, the customer interactions defined by these sorts of practices are not about imagining oneself as the customer and documenting what you think is true as you try on their hat. Corporate implementations often use the term "customer-centric" without ever leaving the building. Customer research is fine, but insufficient; focus groups and surveys are superficial, designed for quantity of responses versus quality of insights.

Understanding the customer requires going to the source, learning directly from people, while in listening mode, with an open mind, one on one. This applies to all business models, whether selling to consumers or businesses, whether heavily regulated or not.

Agile principles provide team structure and work organization, and emphasize collaboration and team-improvement behaviors. As I've already indicated, the "team" is the new unit of work (as opposed to the individual). If you give a group of smart people a problem to solve and the authority to solve it, they will succeed. If your organization is not already there yet, you need to kickstart this agile team ethos.

Good agile practices work in a "continuous improvement" mode such that as a team, they hold themselves accountable to working more efficiently in pursuit of their mission. They focus on producing the best output possible for their mission's stakeholders. They report progress to colleagues and leadership. They share their learning. They are able to adapt to changing conditions, including those that alter priorities.

Diverse, cross-functional teams, given the time and space to learn and respond accordingly to customer or stakeholder needs, move fast. The continued pursuit of their "products" is funded based upon demonstrated success. While failure ends bad ideas fast, the learning informs future efforts. This contributes to speed. Money and resources flow toward high-impact projects.

Agile teams do not run amok. They have missions. Think U.S. Army Special Forces teams. Assembled with the right skill set, provided specific desired outcomes, their behaviors regulated by rules of engagement and law, the members design, lead, and execute the mission autonomously. They are empowered to make decisions based on learning on the ground, in the moment. Leadership of the team's activities changes as needed based upon the phase of the mission. This is agile.

Find Your Champions

One of the most striking parts of creating an emerging new business is that you already have the people to do it. This isn't to say you shouldn't receive outside help or recruit talented people with the energy and mindset you need, but people exist in your organization today who stand ready to dedicate their creativity and intelligence to moving the company forward. You must rally these people, regardless of their hierarchical place in the organization. You want vertical and horizontal cross sections of early adopters, from bottom to middle to top.

So who are they? It's likely you have people who are experienced and even currently practicing many of the skills mentioned earlier in this chapter, such as design thinking or human-centered design practitioners. You may have customer-experience professionals or lean innovation experts. You may have people familiar with agile, people who are entrepreneurial, have worked for startups, or started businesses themselves.

It's time to rally your disruption mindset early adopters. If you have an innovation group, the members likely operate with this mindset baked in. These people should probably be your first stop, but I wish to emphasize that I'm not talking about creating an innovation program. This is not another program to be siloed. This is to become a company-wide endeavor to support the current business mission. Innovation is needed and it's great, but that's not where this change effort lives.

There are likely community groups within your company that leverage some of the keywords mentioned: #agile, #empathy, #innovation, #startup. Reach out to them. Other than using these ideas to figure out who and where these people are, you can also practice what I'm preaching. Run your first experiment.

Send out an email or post a message to whichever internal messaging platform you're using, inviting people to a "Disruption Mindset Happy Hour." (Call it whatever you'd like.) This event could be in person or online, but should definitely be available to all workers, including those who work remotely. Make the message short and sweet. That includes:

- The why: help us define what our twenty-first-century mindset should be
- The what: happy hour, refreshments served (or whatever)
- The call to action: completely voluntary, sign up here

Take a stab at the response you expect: one hundred signups, or one thousand, or zero. You now have a hypothesis: "If we announce a happy hour event to discuss company mindset, 10 percent, or one hundred people, will sign up."

Post the message and measure the response. How did you do? Run the event and invite people to be coaches of the new mindset. How many people actually show up to the event? How many sign up to be coaches? Your early adopters are those who make the time to see what the fuss is about. They already believe in the approach that you're kickstarting.

Congratulations, you're in exploration mode! I told you it was easy. Just kidding. But seriously, you just need to get started, and the fastest way to do this is to leverage the people you have, practicing a mindset that is already known to some extent. These meetings may become monthly or biweekly, and the core team to drive this forward will reveal themselves.

Practice the New Mindset

Many programs exist that you may run to get started, but I want to give you one detailed example to establish a benchmark. I recommend you kickstart your efforts with a series of what I call "impackathons," short for "impact hackathons." Kickstarting the change requires you get people together, give them problems to solve, provide direction and coaching, and let them go off and try to solve them. These days, it's very likely the solutions to problems *can* be built; the question is: Will they actually solve the problems? Will people use them? Will anyone care? The impackathon teams focus on developing evidence that ideas will work before the solutions are invested in. This is the crux of exploration mode.

You may have heard of hackathons. Startup Weekend, founded by Andrew Hyde in 2007 and now part of Techstars, is perhaps the most famous version, becoming popular during the Great Recession. The basic idea is to bring a bunch of people together—software developers, product designers, and businesspeople with startup ambitions—to launch a business within fifty-four hours. These are fun community events where teams of people hack together product ideas they hope to turn into real startups.

Recessions always bring a new wave of entrepreneurship. In the late aughts, we saw Startup Weekend, the emergence of Lean Startup, and a new wave of "super angel" investing, all announcing the beginning of an economic recovery fueled by grassroots entrepreneurship. The proliferation of open-source, low-cost software development, the cloud, and the ability for people to come together in a social setting to innovate really represents capitalism at its core. Due to the wider adoption of technology, including mobile devices, and the continued drop in the difficulty and costs to develop products, all this is even more true today. This rise in entrepreneurial thinking and democratization of the ability to create products is also what fuels the ability for companies to reinvent themselves for the digital age.

At the beginning of the hackathon, people pitch their ideas and then all the other attendees organize themselves around the teams they want to work with. Originally, it was just hacking a product together. Teams would sit down and write code and others might write aspects of the business plan, like how the product will be marketed and sold. The teams would try to finish as much of the product over the weekend as possible. At the end of the weekend, teams demonstrate the product to a panel of judges, who choose winners based on the quality of the demo and its market potential. Successful startups have actually come out of these hackathons.

Many companies now have innovation labs and idea competitions and pitch contests, and they hold "Shark Tank" events, and they do all of these cool, fun things to try to emulate the startup world. And yet they make decisions on what to fund like they always have: putting their finger in the air and seeing which way the wind blows, or investing in a pet project or one that they absolutely believe is a sure winner based upon their biases and assumptions. In other words, *a decision based upon zero evidence.*

The impackathon takes its inspiration from the hackathon, but instead of trying to hack together a product, it's focused on driving impact for the organization. The idea is to bring volunteer employees together to test and validate ways to solve business issues. The aim is to produce evidence for an idea rather than working on the solution itself. In two days, teams attempt to produce enough evidence that indicates that more time and money should be invested in pursuing the idea.

More companies are looking at this approach because it drives better results. In 2015, Cisco launched their "Innovate Everywhere Challenge." In five years, more than 50 percent of employees participated at some point, more than 3,100 ideas were tested at some level, and eleven ventures were productized.

Nestlé launched InGenius in 2014, engaging tens of thousands of employees in creating and testing ideas to improve the business. Over the years they've generated more than seven thousand ideas, eighty of which achieved the "minimum viable product" stage, and over twenty-five that have been officially productized.

Adobe created an "innovation in a box" program called Kickbox that provides any employee with the means of testing ideas, including a small amount of funding. Thousands of employees have tested their ideas. Swisscom adapted its own version of Kickbox and launched an internal program a bit more formalized than Adobe's in 2015. Eighty of the ideas generated achieved the funding level, and twenty were implemented.

Bayer created the Catalyst Fund in 2017, choosing seventy-five ideas to pursue among four hundred submitted from across business lines from around the world. Seventeen projects ended up permanently integrated into business units.

Changing company mindset requires changing behavior. Nobody changed their outlook on anything because someone told them to. It takes belief, practice, and positive reinforcement. Belief requires using what has been proven to work, which is why you leverage the exploration skills that already exist in the organization. The champions you recruit coach and mentor teams during the impackathons. They recruit and inspire; they model the 5Es.

The teams themselves are naturally "agile" in that they are

autonomous and self-organized. They get to decide how best to solve the problem they are trying to tackle. For many, this is perhaps collaborating in a new way. By itself, it can be empowering and inspirational to employees. Further, due to the nature of the event, it's likely— or, at a minimum, it is encouraged—that teams are represented by people from a variety of different roles in the company. A wide range of abilities, backgrounds, and experiences is likely to create a more impactful and ultimately more scalable solution than one developed among those with similar roles.

Invite Everyone

Each impackathon team works on a real issue, big or small. The issues come from anywhere and everywhere. Employees of all levels come up with ideas on how to improve products and the way they go to market. Middle management experiences internal issues daily they'd love to find solutions for. Support functions are under increased pressure to serve their internal customers better. Leaders have challenges they don't know how to resolve.

Invite Employees

Many individuals in your company already have ideas they can't wait to test or have others test. Teaching people how to test ideas empowers them to scratch that itch. The experience of getting to work on their ideas inspires them a lot more than a suggestion box. They also see things from a different perspective. The greater the diversity of your people, the greater the diversity of ideas. Employees are often closer to the source of insights: customer knowledge and broken processes. They also are likely full of incremental product or market improvements that otherwise never see the light of day.

Traditionally top-down, big-change ideas are expensive and time-consuming, and come with the hope of generating big returns. They are big bets. But all the incremental items add up. They improve products and go-to-market tactics, and solve internal inefficiencies. They're typically inexpensive, and their benefits are often realized near-term, if not immediately. Plus, *they demonstrate the ability to do the work*, to operate with the RAD mindset.

Team members use these new skills—the 5Es—to learn how to understand the needs of internal stakeholders, as if they were external customers. It requires developing empathy for colleagues and leaders, further developing collaboration and a feeling that different areas of the business are all growing in the same direction. Collaboration, horizontally across departments and vertically from the proverbial mailroom to the C-suite, is sure to uncover more challenges and opportunities to drive impact.

Invite Middle Management

Middle management often understands where the bigger holes exist—new market opportunities and bigger product changes that may generate more revenue or improve customer satisfaction. They see where groups or departments are redundant or not working efficiently together. They have neither the time, the resources, nor the incentive to fix these problems. But these types of problems prevent future growth and create fragile workarounds that crumble when disruption hits. Often managers are incentivized to patch problems rather than fix them, in order to hit their numbers. They find themselves in a reactive mode, looking for the break to become proactive, which never comes. This is anti-RAD.

A clothing manufacturer in Seattle invested hundreds of thousands of dollars in digital fabrication equipment. With an eight-figure contract for high-end outdoor gear on the line, the equipment was supposed to reduce the time it took to produce product samples from four months to four days, but they weren't seeing the results. The bottleneck lay in the process used in designing, creating, and iterating on new product samples between the design group and the manufacturing team.

Interestingly, the manufacturing team was very reluctant to have anyone look at the problem—they were defensive, accustomed to shouldering the blame for any and all product woes. Finger-pointing, of course, is not uncommon in hierarchical, siloed organizational structures. When I suggested the design team would act like the internal "startup" and the manufacturing team the "customer," the guards immediately fell. After all, the customer is never to blame.

In two days of empathy development, rapid experimentation, and process iteration, the agile startup team completely reinvented the way the two groups worked together. The return was immediate, reducing sample production to two weeks. And while they leveraged the new digital equipment, the improved process was very analog, using descriptive tags to exchange information.

People are still analog. "Innovation" and "digital transformation" focus so much on technology that organizations miss where the real inefficiencies reside, which is often in the way people are organized and the industrial-age processes they must follow.

If prompted correctly, the middle management of the company is a gold mine for uncovering opportunities to drive immediate results. They are not conditioned to think about uncertainty, but you can be sure that they don't know how they will deliver 100 percent of the results they're signed up for. As a matter of fact, if you believed they did know, you'd likely up their numbers! Performance is viewed as purely an execution exercise, but the real world doesn't work that way. Everyone faces uncertainty and thus needs to be equipped with the skill set to deal with it.

Invite Leaders

The best way to include leaders is to work to solve their problems. When I traveled to India in 2016, I spoke to several senior executives at different Indian business units of major U.S. tech companies and I heard a similar refrain: "India is a market that is about to explode; we could make small changes to products designed for the U.S. market that will prepare the company for the Indian market. U.S. HQ does not want to listen to us. 'Build what we specify' is their command."

Huge opportunities are lost because communication must run up and down hierarchies and across departmental silos. In one fell swoop, impackathons or like events eliminate the barriers to testing and producing evidence for ideas that might unlock huge growth opportunities.

It's quite possible that the most senior executives have the most pressing needs—the biggest uncertainties that span a broad time horizon. It doesn't mean, however, they have the best ideas for how to address the needs.

The best way to get leaders on board for adopting the new mindset—and allowing their employees to participate in the impackathon—is to tackle some of their challenges, such as strategic initiatives that are not achieving their expected outcomes, zombie products that cost as much as they earn, or entrenched organizational issues that don't seem to go away. These are big problems that won't be solved in two days, but the process is the same: applying exploration principles to understand issues deeply, dive into stakeholders' immediate needs, reduce the uncertainty, and generate evidence for a particular approach. This is a less costly and more efficient use of resources than making large investments in one unproven idea, or no investment and expecting people to execute their way through the unknown.

Organizations have run similar events that ended up revamping sales scripts, fixing backend financial system holes, raising customer Net Promoter Scores, and even launching new products. Some of this is low-hanging fruit that doesn't require much of anything other than the time and mindset to get it done. Working through even basic problems will allow your people to practice a new framework, and that practice is the key to changing behavior. Leaders tend to believe that the risk is greater to try something new because they fear it takes more time and effort to pause, think, and act than to simply cajole people to work harder. The former always works; the latter ends in failure.

Invite Support Functions

When attempting massive change, especially with respect to a new mindset, one often hears about the corporate "antibodies." This typically refers to the processes put into place by support functions— Human Resources (HR), Finance, IT, Legal, and so on that serve to protect the core business.

The people in these groups are typically the furthest away of anyone from actual customers or thinking about customer problems. Of course, they all have internal customers. But fundamentally, their job is perceived to protect the mother ship from anything that threatens it. As such, they tend to squelch initiatives that strive toward mindset change, or fall outside conventional wisdom, or might be considered as straying from the efficiency mantra. This is not out of a conscious maliciousness, but because "out of the ordinary" is perceived as a threat.

Of course, when massive disruption approaches externally, their practices are suddenly myopic, and their practices and processes suddenly create fragility. In order to create a resilient organization, these groups must be intimately involved in the change. They must be invited to the game. Ironically, these groups are often the most squeezed by the ever-enduring efficiency mindset, since they are considered an overhead cost—in other words, don't directly contribute to revenue. Imagine being part of a group who is forced to say no to requests that might lead to change yet are also being considered only as costs.

This is a dynamic that impackathons help address. Back-office support teams need to learn the RAD mindset skills like everyone else. The challenges they take on should include improving the services they offer to colleagues internally, as well as concerns held by their senior management. Even the uncertainty around transforming company mindset makes for a good challenge to explore. Ultimately, these teams help create the internal systems and processes that enable the rest of the organization to work in exploration mode. In other words, the fundamental changes necessary to be a resilient, aware, and dynamic company require specific changes to back-office rules, process, and behavior, which can be understood and tested.

Drive Some Amount of Organizational Impact

100 Startups in 100 Days (100s/100d)

There are many great resources available for teaching mindset at such events, including how to do customer interviews, run rapid experiments, build prototypes, create landing pages, and so on. As such, I will not cover them here. Additionally, it's likely your existing event resources know how to execute the operational aspects of events such as impackathons.

The bold move is to aim for 100 internal startups in 100 days. Set an audacious goal. You can schedule one a month so that each has thirty-three teams of two or three people (or more), or you can do smaller events every couple of weeks, and you will have 100 teams trying to solve real business issues, acting like startups, in 100 days.

Or aim for 100 startups in 200 days—the point is, don't do five teams in an innovation silo. Don't wait until all the growth or innovation planning is done; don't do another reorganization. You can take the first steps to create momentum for change by getting lots of inspired people working together to drive impact, tomorrow. Literally, tomorrow.

CASE STUDY
INTUIT AND THE FIVE ELEMENTS IN ACTION

Intuit, the long-standing Silicon Valley software company and makers of QuickBooks and TurboTax, is well known for its innovative culture, building empathy, exploration, and evidence-informed decision-making into its daily work. Unlike many multi-billion-dollar companies, Intuit benefits from the fact that its founder is still involved with the company. Several decades after founding it, Scott Cook remains an inspiring force, helping employees to align with the mission of being more customer-focused and entrepreneurial in all aspects of their work.

As current chairman and former CEO Brad Smith says, "True customer-centricity existed before I joined in the early 2000s. It started at Scott Cook's kitchen table when he and his wife reached the conclusion there was a better way to manage finances and they gave birth to Quicken, with cofounder Tom Proulx."[lxvi] In order to maintain the customer-focused mindset as the company grew, Cook created a technique he called Follow Me Home, inspired by Procter & Gamble's practices, which were not about market research but rather *direct observation* of customers' behavior. The practice was literally following a customer home (with permission, of course—no stalking!) to watch them install and use the product. Every employee, according to Smith, including himself when CEO, does Follow Me Homes every year. (Many other corporate empathy success stories have leveraged this approach over the years.)

When Brad talks about customers, he doesn't mean asking customers what they want and doing what they say. *He means developing deep customer empathy.* The name of Intuit's innovation methodology is Design for Delight. Brad tells a story that when he was running the TurboTax business as a general manager, he met with an elderly woman who was using the product in the Intuit lab (which she preferred versus her home). She clearly struggled to use the product.

"How did you feel about the product?" the Intuit team asked.

"I think it's an amazing product," she said. "I'm just not smart enough to use it."

Taken aback, they asked what she specifically meant.

"You have this one screen that said 'charitable donations,' and I do give to charity, and the options were cash and noncash, but I wrote a check. I don't know which one that is."

Brad says, "We ended up hiring an editor from *People* magazine to reread every screen we published and rewrite it in regular-person language. And that was a big step forward and why empathy and observation matters."

When Intuit's innovation and transformation leader Bennett Blank brought Lean Startup to Intuit, he did so with impackathon-like events he called Lean StartINs. He and his coconspirator, Aaron Eden, were able to leverage Intuit's 10 percent free-time policy, which allows employees to spend up to 10 percent of their time working on projects they think they'll get funded. Early on, Blank and Eden started their events on Friday and ended them on Monday, telling people that working over the weekend was their decision. Most people did work over the weekend because, just as with the hackathons, there was a social aspect to them, and oh, by the way, they were fun.

Most corporations, of course, do not have a 10 percent free-time policy; some have tried and stopped. I suspect there's a cultural ethos that is required prior to implementing such a policy, which Intuit had. Zappos' policy is that an employee can work on any project they'd like, but they must first find funding from a sponsor. 3M has such a policy as well.

Without such policies, the choice is to mandate that leaders allow their people to spend the two days needed in order to practice this new mindset, or to run an experiment to see if people will actually do it over the weekend purely voluntarily. Obviously, providing food and drink, a fun environment, and coaching, and having leaders or outside speakers make an appearance, will go a long way to inspire people to try it out.

Blank and Eden invited Brad Smith to their second event to spur interest, resulting in twelve teams showing up. From there they convinced leadership from Intuit's centralized Design and Innovation Group to fund hitting ten locations with ten teams each over the course of ten weeks, with help from Intuit's network of Innovation Catalysts.

The budget was modest but enough to cover travel and move the program forward.

Over the course of the next one hundred days they created eighty-two "startups," just short of their goal. Two weeks later and with one more push, they reached 120 total internal startups created through the Lean StartIN events. Within the following year, products, improvements, and insights that spun out from experiments run during the series of workshops accounted for more than $20 million in benefit to the company in the short term, and an estimated $90 million over the long haul, including new product revenue that continues to this day. That's a pretty good return on investment.

Dan, digital president of a large Midwestern insurance company, told me, "You've seen all organizations for ten to fifteen years now say, 'We need to be customer-centric,' which means, 'We have clever products and we'll use sales and marketing techniques to drive them out there.' And that evolved to 'I have a great idea, and in addition, I will tell you what the return on investment is going to be, because I have two customers who tell me they really liked it.' No customer input. It was just a checkbox. And that customer-centric facade lived for ten years at least."

The most fundamental work is to go talk to customers. It's a skill like any other, where the best practices need to be taught, tailored, and democratized. Yes, engineers can do it. Yes, you can talk to customers in highly regulated environments. Yes, your business customers are busy, but early adopters especially want to hear from you.

The entire key to changing your organization is changing behavior. This must be kickstarted. The desired behavior is pretty well known these days, but it must be tailored to fit the needs and mission of the organization. But in all instances, this means admitting what is unknown, understanding customers deeply, working through assumptions, and cutting through biases.

Kickstarting is accomplished through launching an internal program with the goal of achieving 100 startups in 100 days, and to always have at least 100 kicking at some stage. The biggest obstacle is getting going. You've achieved Kickstart when you have an ongoing program that identifies and tests ideas that improve the business. The program is open to employees across the organization working on ideas that originate from anywhere. You have also identified the individuals who are interested and capable of taking the program to the next level, early-adopter practitioners, coaches, and leaders.

Your next phase, Accelerating, requires adding a more informal investment arm, doubling down on the behavior that works, and beginning to implement support mechanisms to reinforce the new behavior.

Chapter 6

ACCELERATE THE CHANGE WITHIN

When I attended college, several times a year I used to make the drive between my parents' home in San Diego and my school, UC Davis, which is twenty miles east of the California state capital, Sacramento. In those days with the speed limit, the quality of the cars on the road, and the fuel stops, the drive totaled about nine hours. It was a ride of reflection and forward thinking, and I made the trip in a variety of hand-me-down vehicles, with my favorite being a 1974 blue Fiat 124 Spider.

Each trip was not without its challenges. Within the first couple of hours of getting on the road, I knew whether my car would endure the drive. And in my five years of making the trek up or down, several times a year for summer vacation and holidays, I broke down near virtually every single exit along the four-hour stretch through the San Joaquin Valley: in Buttonwillow, Coalinga, Los Banos, Modesto, and on and on. "Fix It Again, Tony!" was a meme I came to know all too well. But the Fiat was also a sports car with a quintessential Italian feel: sleek, sexy, and, on the days it did survive, a joy to drive.

But how did I know when it wouldn't make the trek? The intuition that the car would break down was based on subtle feelings about how the vehicle was running on any given day; I could sense the tiniest anomaly. If the engine hum sounded off, that was an easy giveaway. I wouldn't always be able to articulate it, but I could feel it. And I was right 98 percent of the time. I should've hosted my own version of *Car Talk*. Over the vast number of hours driving a car great distances, a car becomes an extension of yourself. It becomes familiar, like a well-worn baseball mitt. Like with Serena Williams, whose tennis racquet is an extension of her body. Or in the case of a startup investor, who develops a sense of the soundness of a business plan and the abilities of the founder.

In the case of leading large organizations, you feel a vibe for how the business or a division is doing. You can feel when things are not right, even when you don't understand why. You also develop a sense of ways you might take corrective action. This is not to say you are always right, especially when it comes to how to fix problems. Especially when things change. My sense for the car was different on other routes. The sense needed to be rebuilt for different vehicles.

Intuit (the company) uses what it calls "SUCCESSion metrics" to measure whether an internal startup is ready to move from its nascent idea-validation stage, "Horizon 3," to scaling stage, "Horizon 2." These are the only qualifications leaders should look for in the early-stage teams to evaluate readiness for Horizon 2:

1. One person loves it (quantitatively delivering value to the customer, demonstrated active use, and a Net Promoter Score that is favorable)
2. Can reliably create more customers who also love it (there's some evidence of a market)

One of the biggest obstacles to getting teams to successfully work in this RAD way is that leaders ask the wrong questions or hold teams to metrics that are not reasonable relative to the stage the team is in. Business leaders, understandably, want to see a large number of customers. I pressed both Brad Smith, executive chairman at Intuit, and Ben Blank, an innovation and transformation leader, on this point, and neither would budge: "There are no hard numbers for the number of customers needed to move to Horizon 2."[lxvii]

When Netscape cofounder and venture capitalist Marc Andreessen coined the term "product-market fit," he said, "There is no forward-looking way to define it, but you know it when you get there." Blank said the same thing about knowing when teams are ready to be moved from Horizon 3 to Horizon 2.

The point of all this is that unlike my old Fiat, this is a *new* car we're asking leaders to drive, with a set of entirely new features and bugs, and it will require time for familiarization. The intuition needed to know how to manage teams, projects, and endeavors in the twenty-first-century digital age is new. Leaders will get it wrong. They know it's more than one customer and less than 1 million. Depending on the business, it may be 2, or 10, or 10,000 customers. Or 42.

Blank pointed out that it's a skill like any other; it needs to be learned and experienced. You sometimes get it right and you some-times get it wrong, until you have enough experience to feel it, to intuit it. Pun intended. As to my broken-down car on the road? After eight or so breakdowns, I developed the feel for sensing pending breakdowns.

The same goes for all the 5Es and RAD mindset skills we've discussed. The twenty-first-century digital-revolution skills that must be taught include the ability to listen to customers, understand their needs, diagnose problems, and test ideas. Those who already consider themselves experts on these skills need to transform themselves by becoming coaches and leaders in making this the newly established way of doing business, of training teams and boosting the potential for success.

While I urged in Chapter 5 to "just do it," I suggest now that as you move into the Accelerate phase, you do some planning for how to move forward. The Accelerate phase requires you to create momentum with the new behavior. You want to double down on what works. To do so, you create your remodeling plans, formalize the Kickstart program, and add some mechanisms to spur more use of the new behaviors. Specifically:

- Create the RAD team and the road map.
- Brand your particular RAD.
- Determine how you will communicate RAD.
- Measure RAD.
- Build behavioral support mechanisms.
- Build new leadership skills.

If you go all in on a RAD program, the new company emerges from the Kickstart phase, your version of the 100-startups-in-100-days program. It's not that an internal startup will succeed and bring about a new billion-dollar market, but that the behavior *fixes* the business, creating a new normal that will result in continuous innovation and reinvention.

It's vital for leaders to watch, attend, and participate in those one hundred days. You can see the teams in action, see them inspired, entrepreneurial, agile, moving fast, understanding customers and internal stakeholders. You can see their ability to solve problems. You witness management participation, the coaching skills, and, yes, even the impact the projects have.

You will be able to imagine what your company might accomplish by making such behavior the standard way of operating. It turns out, working this way does not delay successful execution, but rather speeds it up. It makes the company more efficient in support of its mission. Rather than dreaming of a spinout that is supposed to eventually disrupt your business, as the Innovation Industry would have you believe, your company is re-formed from within your existing company.

You define what you think the business might look like in service to its mission. You practice and iterate the behavior, using the principles of the 5Es, in service to the mission. You reinforce the desired behavior and build the structure so it not only supports the behavior but induces it.

RAD ROAD MAP: PLAN TO LOOK BACKWARD BEFORE MOVING FORWARD

In the Acceleration phase, the goal is to create momentum for lasting change from within, across the company, from individual to team, top to bottom, and back. But to accomplish this effectively and efficiently, you need to take a step back. It may strike you as a counterintuitive chess move, but driving forward requires getting a few key organizational and operational north stars aligned. That means looking back on foundational elements of the company, creating a vision for change, and iterating on a plan that sets in motion transformational changes while achieving wins that generate momentum.

As a leader, you need to look with fresh eyes at your company's mission, values, and vision. Easy to think about, yes, and hard to do. Now, I'm not going to go all *Mad Men*–style branding on you, but you should take a look at why the business exists. What did it initially set out to achieve, what did you stand for back in the day, and where do you stand now relative to that ambition?

At the most basic level, your mission describes the business you're in. It should define who your customers are, it should describe the needs you're fulfilling, and it should include the products or product lines. Ideally, the mission also includes why you do what you do, an aspirational component to the reason you are in business. What are you seeking to improve, how are you trying to make your customers feel, and why is that important to you?

There may not be anything legally binding, per se, regarding your mission, but the foundation of capitalism here is that your company supplies something of value to a customer in exchange for something the customer has (typically, money). It is a mutually beneficial relationship, an agreement to an exchange of value.

The first order is a contract with your customers, but it also forms a basis for a contract with your employees, who are agreeing to help you create the value you agreed to provide the customers. It's a contract with your shareholders. Investors invest *in your mission.*

In the end, if you want to define your mission as just the products or business lines and the customers you sell to, that is okay, too, but not ideal. Adding a more aspirational component helps define which investors wish to join you on your journey and why customers should choose you and inspire employees to be part of that mission. But it's up to you.

The mission should be factual and succinct. "We help Spot run" is a better mission statement than "Our mission is to be the industry leader in facilitating the boundless energy of beloved, fluffy pups springing across the lush green meadows of life." Once you have found the right words to encapsulate your mission, that statement should appear on your website, and it should appear in your filings with the SEC if you're required to file those.

Company values are the ethical principles that define and regulate the behavior of all employees, including management, in pursuit of the mission. The values should drill down to the level of expected behaviors and include examples within illustrative scenarios. You must be willing to forgo benefits to the company—revenue, profits, growth—in favor of the values, or those values are meaningless.

In the digital revolution, the behavior of company executives is increasingly scrutinized relative to their values. With shareholder activism and boards that include people interested in sustainability, diversity, the environment, and how employees are treated, as well as social media callouts, websites dedicated to reviewing workplace culture, and media awards for popular companies, it's part of the digital-age new business order to couple mission and values with real behavior. Ignore at your peril.

The vision for your RAD program defines what is on the other side of the new emerging business, built to survive and thrive in the twenty-first century. What does the company look like then? How do managers and employees behave in support of discovering and creating value for human beings? What will the business be known for? Will that align with the story the company tells? The vision articulates the outcome the desired behaviors achieve. Is the desired disruption mindset, the behaviors associated with the Five Elements, captured in your current values? Do the values need to be updated?

Empathy goes to the heart of understanding customers deeply in order to create value for them. But also, understanding employees and the heterogeneity of shareholders allows their concerns to be properly considered.

Exploration behavior is perhaps captured in whatever innovation principles you may have. Essentially, a curious, value-creating mindset is important for businesses to succeed, as they pursue the discovery and development of new products and services that deliver on a promise of value to customers.

Evidence is perhaps a bit more difficult to capture as a value, though it may be incorporated in other areas regarding cutting through biases and the ethical treatment of data collected from customers. It also includes embracing science, if that's a relevant value for your organization.

The Equilibrium element respects that human beings—the employees and customers—need time and space to create balance in their lives. It also entails striking the balance between being efficient yet staying committed to exploring new opportunities. Finally, at some point, businesses may want to consider how much growth is actually necessary. In other words, is there a place for a company to be the right size? That within a community or within an ecosystem the company has found its own balance and doesn't need to continue to grow?

Ethics more obviously correlates to the values, but it also necessarily reflects social norms, as well as legal obligations. Social norms evolve over time. Ideally, corporate values reflect an awareness of the ecosystem within which it exists. Values should clearly state that the business commits to adhering to the laws of the land, and respect citizens' right to determine the social responsibilities of companies.

The vision for the RAD program acts as the clarion call for employees to join the journey. Once that is established, it's time to take a stab at how it might be expanded upon, beyond the 100-startups-in-100-days program.

Where inside the company might you attempt a permanent change to the way the people work? When? What are the milestones that mark progress toward desired outcomes?

To develop the RAD road map, you will likely need to establish a team. The RAD implementation team composition should reflect the principles that you're trying to establish, populated with people who are familiar with the behaviors you're trying to establish. It should be cross-functional and cross-hierarchical. It is a two-pizza team, as Jeff Bezos might call it. In other words, only big enough to consume two pizzas.

The road map is like a business plan—it's going to change. The team you put into place is an internal startup. They will apply the RAD principles in the development of a plan for broader implementation of the principles. They'll use an iterative learning process to figure out what works best inside your organization in order to achieve your company's vision in service to its mission.

Additionally, a governance body is needed, a steering committee; perhaps the senior leadership team will do. Their job is not so much approval or disapproval as much as providing the strategic priorities, adherence to the vision, and guardrails that govern where the company can and cannot go. They ensure that in a very flexible, adaptable way, the program stays on course.

It's not there to put the brakes on or be a bottleneck to progress. But there are barriers, impediments, the program will run into. The members of the RAD implementation team need to have a course of action for seeking help in overcoming these obstacles. This might be a business unit leader not being on board, inappropriately holding up progress, or not supplying resources. Or the team may need help overcoming human-resource allocation or legal issues.

To establish the road map, you need to figure out the criteria for establishing what groups in the organization may use the new mindset first. Where you will begin formally implementing change. Is it with a particular business unit because leaders have already bought into the mindset changes? Is it another part of the company that is struggling, so leaders will take any help they can get? Perhaps the business is behind in terms of digital transformation of a particular product line. Perhaps a program to revamp a product line will potentially provide a big impact. Perhaps it's a project around a new opportunity that cuts across multiple business units.

It's best to start with early adopters and monitor the laggards; one can think of the different stakeholders along that continuum. Early adopters may be motivated because they've already developed the RAD mindset. Or it might be because they have the biggest need.

RAD PROGRAM METRICS

Just as a startup or any part of an organization in Exploration mode, the RAD implementation team needs to adopt learning metrics to track the progress of change. In the "Evidence" section of Chapter 4, I introduced the Learning Impact Metrics framework, which helps determine how to track the progression of behavior change for stakeholders—for example, senior executives, middle management, coaches, and sole contributors.

The framework is used by startup teams to hypothesize, test, and measure what it takes to move customers from where they are today to where the startup wants them to be. The seven states include the marketing and sales customer creation states: Aware, Intrigued, Trusting, and Convinced; the realization of value proposition states: Hopeful and Satisfied; and the additional aspirational state, Passionate.

For each of the states, teams ask the question: What customer behavior indicates they are at that state, and how do we get them there? This same method applies to the RAD program. For example, a senior executive is "satisfied"—in other words, an engaged participant in the program—when they see or experience the value that was promised to them. So what might that look like? It starts with a hypothesis. What is the behavior exhibited by a senior leader that indicates they have shifted over to the new mindset?

Example behaviors might be that they submit new challenges for teams to work on once a month. Or it could be that some percent of their direct reports are working within an agile team structure. Perhaps they nominate individuals to be a RAD program coach; they attend investment board meetings and ask the right questions of the internal startup teams. They demonstrate how they provide time and space for teams to operate with the new mindset.

For the RAD program metrics, the implementation team asks these questions regarding each of the stakeholder groups, which are akin to market segments. What is the behavior that indicates that they are in a particular state? Measuring this behavior becomes the bellwether for the progress of stakeholders adopting the mindset. Metrics that don't move month over month become warning flags. Early on, it could be that you have only one leader engaging in the desired behaviors, and then you have two, and then you have five, and so on. Just like any new business.

At some point, hopefully, you see momentum where the growth in the number of individuals exhibiting the right behavior grows month over month, or quarter over quarter. The number of leaders that are in that behavior cohort is increasing. The team tracks that just as if you were in a startup tracking the growth of a SaaS application. The indications of satisfied stakeholders become the dashboard that the implementation group is sharing with the steering committee and management team.

The normal top-down method for implementing such change focuses primarily on measuring outcomes—in other words, the impact the change of behavior has on the organization rather than the behavior change itself. But what this means is that nobody sees the value or the benefit from the program for potentially years. People become impatient because the wrong thing is being measured. This often results in responses where people believe the program is merely this year's version of innovation. Or this year's version of culture change. People become skeptical and cynical.

Achieving RAD starts with ground-up behavior change focused on near-term impact that then meets top-down proselytizing. It's a pincer move that establishes the behavior and generates impact sooner rather than later by focusing on the core business rather than nebulous, poorly defined "innovation" or "digital transformation."

Additionally, top-down programs focus on making people aware of the program, without ever figuring out if the program drives the behavior change needed. The impact will never be realized if the behavior doesn't change. While typical milestones established in the program road map are necessary, they are check marks on a calendar that indicate time has passed, but not whether one is progressing toward the desired outcome.

It's important to start by measuring whether you're seeing the behavior change that indicates value is being delivered, not whether people understand that the program exists. This is perhaps a subtle change that makes all the difference. Execution-mode metrics measure outcomes by calendar, without ever evaluating and thereby iterating on the efficacy of tactics required to deliver the promised value of the program.

The other states prior to Satisfied outlined in the Learning Impact Metrics are important, too, in their proper turn. After the RAD implementation team establishes the right systems, tools, and processes that get the leaders to the level of being satisfied, then they can start marketing the program more widely internally. They start asking questions like "What tactics could make more people aware of the program?" "How can people be convinced that they should participate?" "What might make people passionate, so they become proselytizers?"

In tracking these metrics, it's important that you remain both responsive to sites of stagnation and flexible on the timeline for progress. The most important element of old-world companies is the calendar. The calendar determines when a product is done, marketing launches, execution metrics come due, and investors expect results. This model is layered on top of the reality that only the customer determines when a product is done. A customer-endorsed product with no marketing launch performs better and grows faster than the massive launch of an unfinished product. Results are dependent on what happens, not what was predicted.

If you manage by predictions and not reality, you most assuredly will fail. Periodic measurements of progress make sense, of course, but failure to achieve expected results likely has as much to do with the prediction as performance.

Like many companies, at the first startup I worked at, Tumbleweed Software, managing by calendar meant the management team had to report earnings results to Wall Street. Sales had aggressive numbers to hit by quarter's end. Engineering was focused on completing its core product that served a completely separate market segment, while also trying to demonstrate its platform bona fides by releasing a second application. All implementations sold required serious, complicated integrations by Professional Services, where I lived. The Professional Services Organization (PSO) was stuck: It helped Sales close deals through customization, but also required help from its overburdened big-brother Engineering team in order to complete the customization projects. The company could not recognize revenue until the product was live, putting the PSO team in the middle. We were a family of ducks trying to cross Highway 101 in the middle of the day in 1999 Silicon Valley.

The joke inside PSO was "Who owns the spreadsheet?" This referred to the spreadsheet that represented our reality, which eventually fell under my control. The reality was that the colored cells of the spreadsheet showed that no projects were resourced fully and that the percentage completion of the projects did not match the due date. I owned a digital file, but not the resources or the authority to change anything other than the color of the cells. I held reality in my hands, but had no way to change the outcomes that success was to be measured by.

In a sane environment, promises are not made to Wall Street. (This includes public companies today. Seriously, just stop.) Investors should measure progress, but the speculation surrounding earnings predictions is counterproductive for companies and misaligns interests in the company's mission. Adapting plans and resource allocations based on reality is a more efficient way of achieving ambitions than basing those on incorrect assumptions. The structure of work reinforces desired behavior. Purposeful, networked communications keep reality front and center, overcoming hierarchical incentives to "manage up" or achieve siloed victories over the company's overarching success.

Measuring progress on missions from the ground up is more effective than dictating outcomes and timing top-down, thereby incentivizing middle layers to manage up. In the Tumbleweed example, middle management swore upstream that everything was hunky-dory, based on, you guessed it, the spreadsheet. The fact that it didn't truly reflect reality was a dilemma to address another day.

RAD BRAND

You are welcome to use the RAD program, RAD implementation team, and so on, but I will hazard a guess that you will want your own name. Branding your disruption program is important to its success for several reasons:

- Employees want to know the program has been designed by and for the company.
- It strengthens the tie between company values, program, and desired behavior.
- It cuts through the dogma brought on by silos and particular frameworks.

Intuit calls its program Design for Delight. ING calls its program PACE. P&G's is GrowthWorks. Each of these has similar characteristics but is owned by the company, with each incorporating their history, culture, and specific desired outcomes.

One of the obstacles you're likely to encounter is that people become attached to their particular expertise. It's built into employees' desire to become irreplaceable and leaders' desire to command a fiefdom. Whole departments become attached to a specific implementation of a framework because they then are seen as the experts in that. Organizations often mistakenly brand their program based on a specific dominant framework and then suffer from the associated dogma.

A large European life sciences company, representative of many others, decided they were to be an "agile" organization. They developed an entire internal website dedicated to being "agile." The first problem is purely semantic. Just as with the diffusion of the meaning of "innovation," words like "agile" have meanings independent of the companies' use, which causes confusion. What does "be agile" mean to the human resources folk who put up the internal website, or launch the company's agile group chat channel on Microsoft Teams?

The second problem is with people who actually understand the word in its business context. Their R&D team, in fact, had recently gone through a formal Agile implementation. R&D looked at HR and said, "That's not *real* agile." I spoke to the CTO, who was very guarded with me until I said, "When I say 'agile,' I mean agile with a small 'a.' I'm referring to the principles, not specific implementations such as Scrum or Kanban." He was fine with the discussion after that.

I've seen this happen with other frameworks, too, like design thinking or Lean Startup. Marriage to the terminology creates unnecessary conflict in the company, where groups declare, "We're the only ones who can engage properly with customers." Or, "We already do that." Or, "We tried that and it doesn't work." Even, "You're doing it wrong." (Rolling-eyes emoji.)

This mentality is an artifact of the hierarchical, command-and-control company, where people measured their value based on knowledge and expertise, versus learning and impact. That is the ethos that we're trying to break down in order to create this new twenty-first-century organization. How you brand the program either helps or hurts that effort.

Branding couples desired behavior with desired outcomes. It connects the program to corporate values. It provides an aspirational component tied to the program vision and the company's mission, inspiring people to work in the new way to achieve common goals.

In the end, it's the behavior you want to see, not the framework. If there's a part of the organization that wants to do a specific flavor of agile, and that works for them, so be it. But another part of the organization needs to be able to do their own, as long as both result in the desired behaviors relative to their duties.

RAD COMMUNICATIONS

How one communicates the disruption program is also important. The top-down, big-consulting-firm method is like the *Mad Men*, old-school branding done internally. Pull out the big megaphone, stand on the high perch, and tell everybody how it's going to go. This method creates anxiety, disbelief, and cynicism inside the company that will impede whatever change was being imagined.

Communication needs to be two-way. It must be ground-up as well as top-down. The whole nature of the RAD mindset means that the grassroots layer, the agile teams, are empowered to make decisions. Data, information, and knowledge flow up from the source. The RAD program is just another example of the implementation of the mindset. Desired outcomes, priorities, and guardrails flow down; feedback, evidence, and actual outcomes flow up. The two-way communication of the program is part of breaking down the silos that slow the company and make it less nimble.

The communications strategy for the RAD program should include these components:

- Mission: a reinforcement of company mission
- The why: What is different in the world, the market, or the company itself that drives the need for a permanent change?
- Vision: What does the company look like on the other side; what's the outcome?
- Road map: light version on how it will be rolled out, subject to iteration
- Method of communication, including ideas, feedback, and dialogue

SUPPORT MECHANISMS

The Kickstart phase pushes the organization to act in an agile way, using the RAD mindset. A hundred or so teams have a mission, defined by the team founder or a stakeholder, the challenge itself, and an idea to address the challenge. The teams' missions align in some way with the organization's mission. While the term "startup" is anathema to many large businesses, we need to capture the mindset here. The agile, internal startup teams practice empathy, explore needs and solutions, use evidence to inform their work, balance execution and explore tactics, and maintain behavior within the values of the business in service to their mission: solve the given challenge.

The way these startup teams behave represents the future way of working. The RAD program is not an innovation silo that exists in a corner of the company, supposedly figuring out the future version of the business, the snake that eats its own tail. That is innovation fantasy. That is the exception, not the rule, a product of the Innovation Industry.

Startup teams use the RAD mindset to solve today's business issues, within the landscape of the current business. During the acceleration phase, along with developing your road map for RAD rollout and tracking new behavior implementation, you also want to insert mechanisms to support the behavior and construct scaffolding to protect the behavior. "Scaffolding" is a term I heard first in a series of YouTube videos about organizational design called *Dave Snowden & Friends,* though Ann Pendleton-Jullian is credited as the originator of the concept. These form the systems, processes, and structure that sculpt the emerging new business. You literally begin building the new business from within, without needing to tear down the existing one. The existing core continues to execute on existing products and markets, and over time begins to adopt the practices of the new mindset. The snake doesn't eat its tail; rather, it eventually sheds its old skin.

The support functions, often considered antibodies to change and innovation, begin creating the very systems and processes that make change possible, that ensure RAD mindset is repeatable, scalable, and efficient. In other words, they make the new mindset the new norm.

In most organizations, these groups aren't viewed as allies to change, but as obstacles. This is why these groups should be invited to be part of the programs in the Kickstart phase. How each internal support function can support the first wave of RAD teams is a challenge in itself that can be tackled using the Five Elements in impackathons. During Accelerate, this thinking is formalized by functional leaders forming teams to test how they might serve their internal customers better.

The human resources management group(s) responsible for training, company culture, performance management, organizational design, and recruiting are critical to the success of RAD. Early on, Human Resources may set policy or recommendations for how much time company employees can spend on projects not formally funded. They can offer guidelines for incentives and rewards. They should likely be involved in determining RAD program branding and the implementation of the communications plan. Human Resources or another learning-and-development group should also think about training in the RAD mindset.

Many regulated industries, such as banking, insurance, health care, must adhere to laws with respect to how they interact with the public. Internal legal or compliance teams can establish rules of engagement with respect to how employees interact with both existing customers and potential customers. Oftentimes, employees overcompensate about compliance, out of fear of violating regulations they're unsure about. Compliance teams often create overly stringent rules, hoping to avoid giving the impression that they're stretching the laws or skirting on the margins.

Legal should take another look at the actual laws to evaluate where the appropriate, ethical line actually is. They can then establish rules of engagement that enable agile teams to move quickly and confidently when interacting with people. They should practice the RAD mindset in coming up with the rules of engagement. They ask the question "As the legal team, how can we enable the RAD mindset?"

Marketing controls the use of company brand elements and the ways that teams are allowed to portray the company to the outside world. In the digital age, many of those rules are anachronistic and should be updated. Customers want relationships with the companies they engage with. They want innovation. They want their needs addressed. In fact, that's a key component of whom they decide to support. Marketing teams can benefit from updating their rules such that customers might learn that the business is trying to discover new value for them. Creating that understanding encourages them to willingly participate in experiments and empathy interviews. Marketing has a role to play in supplying new brand guidelines to RAD teams, access to customers, and freedom to experiment.

The marketing department can make or break RAD initiative

success. For example, in one global health care company, the marketing division controlled go-to-market messaging and positioning centrally. This created obstacles to learning what tactics would work in emerging countries around the world. During a ninety-day commercialization accelerator, agile teams worked with country managers to explore local needs and requirements, marketing and sales tactics, and compliance regulations in fifteen countries, with five emerging and existing products. Until the accelerator, local input was virtually ignored by the global organization, including R&D product development, the innovation group, compliance, and marketing.

It's tough to ask a functional group to delegate power to regional offices, but it's likely to be necessary, while still maintaining some centralized control. They should practice the RAD mindset in figuring that out.

Sales and account managers have a role to play as well. Especially in businesses that sell to other businesses or are in a highly regulated environment, the individuals in the company who own the relationships need to share. Again, most often, customers and regulators want more dialogue. It's up to the sales teams to provide access to other parts of the organization.

RAD teams may need small amounts of money to run experiments. The finance team can make that easy by providing reimbursements up to a certain amount for specific uses, such as landing pages or digital advertisements. Adobe's Kickbox program, for example, includes a small amount of money in each of its innovation tool kits, available to any internal startup team testing a new idea.

IT may help RAD teams with access to digital tools that are useful in running experiments or prototyping ideas. If you create digital products or products that have digital components, ideally this is done through an internal (including cloud) IT service. In other words, business groups (composed of agile teams)—including product engineering, user experience design, marketing, and customer service—develop, experiment, research, and support customers through IT interfaces that deploy to the customer-facing environment. Depending on compliance requirements, IT may also approve guidelines for using infrastructure to run experiments, leveraging a sliver of web traffic, for example. Or they may need to approve applications like Slack for team collaboration or apps for split testing, landing page design, or sending emails. The goal is to allow agile teams to move fast, so providing guidelines that offer the freedom to act without seeking permission within specific guardrails is critical. IT can provide those guidelines for best security practices and other guardrails for the use of such tools.

Again, each of these groups acts as an internal startup asking the specific question "How can we support the RAD mindset?" But also, generally, "How can we better serve our internal customers?" Internal support functions can act as an agile team, just like any other, by balancing the work they have to get done with exploring how they can better serve their customers.

NEW LEADERSHIP SKILLS

The purpose of the impackathon was for teams to spend a couple of days generating evidence for an idea and what its impact might be on the company. At the end of the two days, they pitched to leaders their results—not just their ideas—to see whether they had generated enough evidence to continue with the project. Leadership decides whether they want to go forward with it or not. Very similar to startup investors. But also not that dissimilar to the numerous idea competitions and internal corporate shark tanks that occur regularly around the globe.

"Accelerate" means formalizing this process. In other words, leaders need to pony up. Those with budgets choose to sponsor projects that demonstrate they are worthy of a tranche of funding to get them to the next milestone. Pressure may need to come down from leadership to force a percentage of the budget to go to these endeavors. But they get to fund the ideas that have demonstrated success. It's an internal "market"-based approach to innovation.

Investment decisions should be based upon the generation of evidence that a viable business model exists. The job of these impackathon internal "startups" is to pitch evidence. Those in the company with budget responsibility, or those leaders responsible for implementing the idea, decide whether or not they would like to fund that project, based on the evidence. The return could be something as simple as scratching that itch a leader couldn't get rid of. It could be productivity related, or efficiency improvement, or cost savings. Or it could be pure revenue.

If a team pitches an idea, there's an infinite number of reasons why that idea might fail. And if you pitch an idea to smart people, they will poke holes in the idea. Critically thinking, analytical people do that. The fact that smart people can think of some of the potential pitfalls and point them out is actually not very insightful, nor is it very helpful. If the team pitches evidence—data and insights from customers or stakeholders—smart people will still poke holes, but now it's about the evidence—and that's fair game. The leaders at that point are saying, "I will invest in this idea if you generate x amount of evidence."

A key part of accelerating 100 startups in 100 days, or whatever your RAD program includes, is teaching leadership new investment skills. Sounds simple, of course. It's complicated because leaders want crystal clear evidence. They want statistically significant evidence, even though we're not really targeting a random audience when we're doing this sort of early startup or innovation work. So we're not going for "nine out of ten is better than three out of a thousand with a standard deviation of whatever." What we're trying to find is a pattern among stakeholders, among customers, that indicates that we should receive the next level of investment. It isn't "Here's $10 million, go build it." It means "Here's enough money and time and space to go produce the next level of evidence."

But with the right help, leaders can learn how to use learning metrics, mentor rather than simply manage execution, clear the path for teams to find solutions to real problems. This increases the trust between the teams and leadership. It not only empowers teams to tackle wicked problems with bold ideas, it empowers leaders to trust in delegating authority to agile teams.

DEALING WITH SUCCESS

Once you have your vision, your road map, and your support and protection mechanisms scaffolding the new behaviors into place, you'll see how progress on your RAD journey is accelerating. It's not unusual for the Accelerate phase to produce one or more internal startup endeavors that show real market promise. I mean, you hope so, right? Not surprisingly, success breeds new issues to overcome. Success has lots of company. Whether the startup effort is kept inside the core organization or moved away is a management decision based on a number of factors you might consider:

- Is the aim of the startup to cannibalize or compete against the current business?
- Will the startup behavior disrupt or inspire the core business?
- Will the startup benefit from core business assets?
- Will the core business attempt to squelch or dominate the internal startup?

The Innovation Industry, with their academic-inspired ambidextrous, bimodal, dual-operating-system organization, will have you believe that you must spin these entities out. But it's just not that simple. The very same Innovation Industry thinks your people should hang out with startups in order to be inspired by their agile, fast-moving, inspired activity. Which is it?

Suffice to say at this point, it's a good problem to have.

CASE STUDY
ACCELERATING AN INTERNAL STARTUP

A Midwestern financial services company decided to house their promising insurance startup—we'll call it FinCo—outside the main organization, but it also wanted core business representation on the team. The startup "founder"—we'll call him Dan—is a longtime lean innovation believer who from the beginning was sensitive about how the startup would be perceived by the core business. He didn't want the startup to appear to be a purely academic endeavor on the one hand, nor a bunch of Nerf gun–toting, scooter-riding hipsters on the other. "We wanted to bring some people over to the startup who were open-minded to where we were going, but also possessed deep business capabilities that were understood by the executives like actuarial, underwriting, and legal."

Core business representation in the startup not only ensures executives are more comfortable, but it also has the potential to bring elements of the new mindset back to the most conservative parts of the business. "We grabbed a thirty-five-year veteran from Legal who was in line for general counsel, as well as one of the business's top actuaries. I told their superiors: 'Feel free to talk to them directly about the work we're doing.'" This is a good example of using empathy to build trust inside the organization.

Primary customer research pointed to a large opportunity within FinCo's customer base. They had an idea on how to tackle it, but existing financial services regulations that protect consumers from fraud were in the way. They were written in such a way that you must find where something is *explicitly allowed*, rather than simply being able to demonstrate it's not illegal. The thirty-five-year legal veteran helped FinCo navigate the regulators, another circumstance where empathy was key.

"Meeting with regulators, we talked for the first twenty-five, thirty minutes about our mission and about what we had heard from consumers, who were struggling. We talked about the data and the fact that 47 percent of Americans can't come up with $400 in an emergency. We gave them real stories of families in this situation that we had learned about firsthand. There was a lot of nodding going on, but finally they said blandly, 'Why are you here?'

"We shifted our tack to convincing them that we were a mission-driven team committed to solving the problem, whether it was through this product idea or some other method. The head regulator's deputy, sitting at the end of the table like he was the Godfather, slowly looked through the slide deck for several minutes. Finally, he looked up. 'Okay, how do we do this?'"

Ironically, the original product idea that showed so much promise failed. "We built a base of customers and successfully serviced them and treated every customer fairly. But we did not get to a point where we had a sustainable business model.

We completed our commitments, but decided to not renew the contracts."

Pivoting is hard, but the market need persisted. "We knew from the start that we had to build a business that would be modestly profitable. For a year and a half we tested the assumptions that would lead us to a profitable business. We almost got there. It's really tough to get that close and then have to say, okay, we're going to shut this down. But we were still doing research with consumers. We were still talking to these people to understand their needs."

While pet insurance has traditionally been thought of as a scam, the fact of the matter is pets are considered an integral part of the family for most households. The fact that 47 percent of families can't come up with $400 for an emergency makes it difficult for them to put any money toward the health of their pets.

"Like everything else, we tested our pet insurance idea and it tested better than anything we had ever tested by a magnitude of five. Seventeen percent of people 'out in the wild' said they'd buy it. We put it in the market and had very modest goals around it, understanding saying is different than doing. When we hit our annual goal in the first three weeks of the year, we realized we were on to something."

As they thought about new features, multiple assumptions were cut down. "We actually had an active hypothesis that consumers don't want to pay for specific additional product features. We thought that was an added bell and whistle they don't want. But they're telling us, 'Hey, this thing doesn't cover the annual physical for Fluffy. It doesn't cover immunizations. It doesn't cover heartworm medications, the stuff that I have to deal with every year.'"

Product-market fit is when the market pulls the product out of the company. The business continues to grow 40 percent month over month. The new dilemma facing the startup is the natural tension with the core business.

"When do I get to offer this through our core channels?"

"You're launching a brand. How does it fit with the corporate brand?"

"We need this capability in the core business."

"I have a great product idea for you to test."

Make no mistake, throwing the startup over the transom to the existing core business will kill the startup. This type of internal startup win, even if it doesn't end up producing a unicorn—a billion-dollar new business—demonstrates the ability of the organization to do this kind of work. Phases of the business are financed in tranches based upon achieving both learning and growth metrics.

The more of these internal startups that are launched, the greater the chance of one big success. Ideas worthy of investment must prove their worthiness. The more ideas tested, the more ideas worthy of investment will be found. The required scale of ideas to be tested can come only from the core business, not the innovation silo.

You can't overcome an obstacle until you run into it. The next obstacle is: How do you get from Accelerate to Scale?

Chapter 7

SCALING THE CHANGE

I f violent images and disturbing screams of a passenger being forc-
ibly dragged off an overbooked plane come to mind when you hear
"United Airlines," you know all you need to know about its brand;
Rhapsody in Blue, "Fly the Friendly Skies," and logo be damned. In
the face of the viral uproar, it took CEO Oscar Munoz several attempts
to respond in a way that evoked empathy in any real way.

The first missive included a bizarre euphemism: "I apologize for
having to re-accommodate these customers," while the second, an
internal memo sent later that day, praised employees' actions and
described the passenger's behavior as disruptive and belligerent. But
the third attempt was actually pretty darn good. He apologized to
employees for putting them in such a situation. He apologized to the
passenger, stating, "No one should ever be mistreated this way." He
took responsibility, declaring, "It's never too late to do the right thing.
I have committed to our customers and our employees that we are
going to fix what's broken so this never happens again."[lxviii]

This is not a PR problem. I mean, it's a PR disaster, but the root
cause of the incident is the real issue here, not the response to the

event. Despite the first two hiccups, I believed Munoz to be truthful in the third. The backstory to the event is decades of deregulation and the government turning a blind eye to corporate consolidation. But it's also a complexity problem. The airline essentially bought out the government, which, in return, effectively raised barriers to market entry, allowing consolidation that reduced competition, and fought against "customer rights" regulation. The government stood by while the airlines destroyed the customers' product experience, all for the sake of "efficiency."

It's bizarre that so many believe these developments represent a "free market." The airline industry is actually like the pre-Uber taxi industry.

The great irony is that allowing corporations to run rampant over the government ultimately hurts business. Airline deregulation and efforts to undermine antitrust were, if you can believe it, done in the name of "customer welfare." Such efforts also hurt employees, who are pitted against customer wrath. It hurts pensions and wages, and, in turn, happiness and productivity. It hurts the general economy when the traveling employees of other businesses suffer the ever-shrinking seat, the ever-diminishing customer service, the ever-expanding nickel-and-diming of basic flight amenities. What is the lost productivity in the economy due to airlines' quest for increased efficiency? It's difficult to understand who benefits other than stock day traders and the CEOs with their eight-figure compensation. Certainly not the majority of shareholders.

Recall the Facebook employee, pressured to expand seconds of engagement time, regardless of the ethics of the tactics employed. This, too, is for financial efficiency. It destroys customer, employee, and long-term shareholder value in order to squeeze out short-term profits.

David Dayen points out in *Monopolized*, "Before deregulation, seats were on average 18 inches wide, with 35 inches between rows. By 2016 the width had dropped to 16½ inches and the seat pitch to 31 inches....Every inch removed between rows equals more rows of seats that can be added to the back of the plane, and six or more potential fares."[lxix] On average, planes were 83 percent full in 2018, up from targets of 55 percent prederegulation.[lxx]

Fast-forward to the pandemic, and you once again see federal bailouts of this same "efficient" airline industry, while CEOs maintain more than 90 percent of their compensation and lay off thousands of employees.[lxxi] What exactly is the capitalism contract here between company and society?

Of course, unlike the taxi industry, there is no app-in-waiting to disrupt the airline industry. Not yet anyway.

FROM ASSEMBLY LINE TO DIGITAL FAB

Reaching into the past, imagine the business structure required to produce Henry Ford's Model T "in whatever color you want as long as it's black," and compare that to looking forward a bit, to a business that uses digital fabrication technology to completely customize a product to the demands of the customer ordering it. Two ends of a continuum—from core, heavy infrastructure-based companies, to edge-dwelling, nimble companies—upon which all businesses exist somewhere.

If your business is more akin to Henry Ford's assembly line, then command-and-control and efficiency of execution works fine to deliver your mission, except for two caveats. First, from a product perspective, the old model is subject to technological innovation; significant changes in technology very quickly crush old business structures, allowing emerging competitors to dramatically reduce the cost of production, improve quality efficiency, or significantly reduce time to market. Second, from a market perspective, these heavy infrastructure-based businesses are vulnerable to the whims of the edge. In other words, the power consumers have gained through the digital revolution can rock the world of old-school industrial companies overnight, like what happened to United Airlines.

The big industrial companies attempt to ward off the former through owning the levers of government. And because these silverback gorillas have been focused on optimizing efficiency for fifty years, they don't know how to create new customer value anymore. Meanwhile the production process remains consistent, but is under constant pressure to lower costs and increase productivity, as with robotics. (In other words, digital transformation.) Stuck in a flywheel of optimizing efficiency purely from a financial perspective, they are still vulnerable to market disruption.

From the ten-thousand-foot perspective, the organization of any business must reflect the complexity of interactions within its business ecosystem—in other words, all the entities in society the business interacts with in pursuit of its mission. In the early automobile industry days, for instance, the ecosystem included customers, parts suppliers, dealerships, gas companies, financial services companies, and the government entities responsible for developing highways.

The relationship between the business and its ecosystem entities, and the dependencies among groups inside the business, determine how employees are organized. In a simple relationship, both parties know what information they need to exchange, the mechanism for the exchange, and the frequency. The relationship is relatively static.

The employees are therefore organized in a static way, where each department is responsible for some portion of the various value exchanges among the ecosystem entities. Department members interact, establish dependencies, prioritize the work, and lay it all out on the calendar. Milestones are established and appropriate KPIs assigned to groups, subgroups, and individuals.

The basic unit of work is the individual, a cog within the department gear within the business machine, executing its mission. Optimizing the efficiency of this machine makes sense, since the mechanisms are well understood and relatively unchanging. Execution efficiency ensures that all the cogs are properly aligned, the gears in sync, working together as a unit in order to create specific products for specific markets.

Imagine now a business tending toward the opposite end of the continuum, say a medical device company that provides an internet-based platform for a global network of devices that monitor patient health. The ecosystem includes patients, health care providers, labs, hospitals, insurance companies, government regulators, government payers, hardware manufacturers, cloud service providers, application developers, competitors, standards bodies, and who am I missing?

This is today's world and the complexity is immense. For example, the interaction between the cloud provider and the medical device company's IT team affects the devices R&D team, the software applications team, third-party-application developers, and all customers using applications or IoT devices, as well as doctors and patients. It *may* make sense that the relationship between the cloud provider and the medical company is wholly owned by a team of IT professionals grouped within the IT department, residing together on the third floor of building 14 on their San Antonio campus, who have never interacted with labs, doctors, patients, application engineers, or hardware API developers, but it's not *obviously true*. Intuitively, it doesn't strike me as particularly *efficient*.

Not that I delight in kicking any one company when it's down.

Nor do I need to make mention of the role of our tax dollars creating a lifeline during the COVID-19 pandemic slowdown, but let's be honest: United Airlines, like many airline companies, remains united in an old-guard, command-and-control, assembly-line mix of products and services scaled with limited competition to deliver a not-so-great product and so-so customer experience. An experience that's grown infinitely more expensive and less satisfying over time for end users. One might say they've scaled at the expense of the customer to deliver the opposite of what Zappos' Tony Hsieh referred to as "happiness."

The old-school business management has devolved into efficiency for efficiency's sake. Rather than work to create more or better value for customers, companies trim muscle in the name of trimming fat. Business managers break down the business components and reduce costs regardless of the adverse effect on accomplishing the business's mission, the very reason the company is in business.

There's a better way for United and for any organization willing to do the work. And in this chapter, we'll tackle the immense work of scaling the right way by introducing alternative organizational structures.

Scale phase: As discussed, the desired outcome of this RAD journey is that a new business eventually emerges from the old, based on everyone in the organization adopting some version of the 5Es behavior. In Chapter 5 we kickstarted the behavior to define and practice it, as well as demonstrate its effectiveness in solving problems. In Chapter 6 we formalized it, while also implementing operational mechanisms to support teams working this way and adding a way for leadership to become integrated into the program.

Scaling requires continuing this work. Successful projects from the 100-startups-in-100-days program, or your equivalent of it, are either integrated into the business or must continue to be nurtured and protected as they grow. New organizational structural components are added to the mix and are applied to specific parts of your existing business.

The new components are described in:

- Team as the New Unit of Work
- Scaffolding Scale
- Managing Communications Flow

There are two parts to scale: push and pull. The first is pushing the new behavior, mechanisms, and structure into the core business. You choose parts of the organization to change. You repeat that, touching as much of the business as possible. The second part occurs after businesses become aware of the RAD benefits and begin pulling it into their daily work.

TEAM AS THE NEW UNIT OF WORK

In a scaled agile organization, the team is the new unit of work rather than the individual. While individuals are still important—you want them happy, engaged, and productive—everyone is part of an agile team. The team is provided a mission, which is a subset of a group's mission, which is a subset of the division's mission, and so on, cascading up to company mission and strategic priorities.

A team of individuals is more capable of handling complexity than a collection of individuals. One can imagine organizing a company using a network of Jeff Bezos's two-pizza teams, where teams are organized and resources allocated based on a mission's requirements. The teams are given the authority and responsibility for accomplishing their missions the best way they deem possible. The teams are grouped not necessarily by function, but by how they can collectively best serve the group's mission. Team composition depends on the skills required for the mission, as well as by the level of uncertainty they face.

Where there is little uncertainty, the team looks more similar to an industrial-age team. The mission is tightly constrained. The skills required are known and often similar, less interdisciplinary, less cross-functional. They use best practices in the execution of their mission. The metrics measuring progress and success are well understood. The dependencies of relationships with other teams and with external entities (if any), the inflow and outflow of their communications, and the resources they need are also well understood. Like an army squad, the agile team is responsible for looking out for each member's well-being, as well as the team's productivity, continuous improvement, and progress toward accomplishing its mission.

Where there is a lot of uncertainty, the teams must be more dynamic. They are like a special forces unit. The skill set is more specialized, cross-functional, and interdisciplinary, dependent not only on the skills known to be required, but also on contingencies. The team must be able to learn, to respond to changing conditions, and adapt to the unexpected. In Snowden's Cynefin model, teams use best practices when dealing with well-understood challenges, leverage team expertise when facing the complicated, but also have the ability to explore when faced with complex situations. In other words, they're able to learn and adapt quickly to conditions on the ground. A combination of execution KPIs and Learning Impact Metrics (LIMs) track their progress toward accomplishing the teams' missions.

All teams, whether facing uncertainty or not, should use the "agile with a small *a*" in the application of the 5Es of Empathy, Exploration, Evidence, Equilibrium, and Ethics. In their missions, teams should be provided objectives, execution and learning metrics, and "values" statements that provide guardrails around acceptable behavior in pursuit of the missions from an ethics point of view.

As the teams go, so goes the group or the divisions they belong to. Tracking the team's pursuit of its mission keeps the team moving in concert with the rest of the group, as opposed to managers trying to track the KPIs of each individual. The aggregation of the team's progress marks the success of the division in achieving its mission. Again, "agile" doesn't mean no hierarchy, it means less hierarchy.

What does that hierarchy look like? Ultimately, this was what General McChrystal wrestled with in Iraq. After forming autonomous tactical teams to take on specific missions, how could he organize the teams? "It was not possible to make the Task Force one big team," McChrystal writes, "but we also could not stick with our command of teams compromise; stacking our small teams in silos had made us unwieldy."[lxxii]

How might he construct the necessary structure that brings together the special tactical combat teams with other operational components within their service, as well as with other military services and civilian agencies?

There's a Buddhist parable called "The Blind Men and the Elephant." To make a point, a king in the ancient city of Sāvatthī instructs a man to round up all the people who have been blind since birth, and show them an elephant. The man does as he is told. He shows one group the tusk and says, "This, blind people, is what an elephant is like." He shows another group the ear and another the trunk, and another the tail, and so on. The king asked the people if they had seen the elephant:

"Yes, Your Majesty. We have seen the elephant."

"Now tell me, blind people, what the elephant is like."

The blind people who had been shown the elephant's head said, "The elephant, Your Majesty, is just like a jar."

Those who had been shown the elephant's ear said, "The elephant, Your Majesty, is just like a winnowing basket."

Those who had been shown the elephant's tusk said, "The elephant, Your Majesty, is just like a plowshare."

Those who had been shown the elephant's trunk said, "The elephant, Your Majesty, is just like the pole of a plow."

Those who had been shown the elephant's body said, "The elephant, Your Majesty, is just like a granary."

Those who had been shown the elephant's foot said, "The elephant, Your Majesty, is just like a post."

Those who had been shown the elephant's hindquarters said, "The elephant, Your Majesty, is just like a mortar."

Those who had been shown the elephant's tail said, "The elephant, Your Majesty, is just like a pestle."

Those who had been shown the tuft at the end of the elephant's tail said, "The elephant, Your Majesty, is just like a broom."

Saying, "The elephant is like this, it's not like that. The elephant's not like that, it's like this," they struck one another with their fists. That gratified the king.[lxxiii]

Not sure, exactly, why the king enjoyed that so much, though I suppose it's like our reality TV. It actually reminds me of the management team of the software startup I discussed earlier, where company strategy was determined by whoever won the argument week after week.

The hierarchical structures we need in place are those that are responsible for the bigger picture. As team missions roll up the various levels to the company mission, so, too, does context. This is what McChrystal means by "Team of Teams" in his book of the same name.

Thinking about the parable again, the agile version is a team composed of representatives of each of the groups shown one part of the elephant. They work together to aggregate the information they've collected in order to accurately describe the whole animal. The nonagile version is what we see above—multiple silos of like-minded people each insisting their perspective paints the one true picture. Division wide, a team-of-teams-of-teams layer can describe the ecosystem of a herd of elephants. Company-wide, perhaps the entire zoo is understood.

The Swedish audio-streaming company Spotify, for example, is a popular example of an organizational model that scales agile. (Even major consulting groups now offer it as a reorganization service, so you know it has come of age.) Forewarned is forearmed. You cannot copy a model: You can study it, learn from it, but then you must model your own version of it.

Spotify named their agile teams "squads."[lxxiv] Squads are autonomous, while belonging to a larger entity called Tribes. Spotify lives in a more complex ecosystem than one might imagine, but they produce one primary product, so most Tribes are assigned missions relating to that. The Squads' missions include the metric they're accountable to, as well as a value, such as "customer safety," that they are supposed to adhere to when trying to improve the component they're responsible for. Contrast this to Facebook allowing teams to do *anything*, regardless of customer safety, in order to improve engagement. "Customer safety" is still a bit nebulous, admittedly, but clearly better than nothing.

At one point in Spotify's history, it was noticed that their users were suffering from a lack of consistency among the different components. The overall user experience suffered because there was not a layer responsible for the overall product experience. They lacked a layer that would adequately aggregate the layers beneath it to provide a seamless experience. (What was supposed to be an elephant was actually Snuffleupagus.[lxxv]) Adding a Tribe responsible for the "core experience" was implemented to resolve that. Squads determine how best to accomplish their ambition, while Tribe leaders ensure alignment with other Squads.

The Tribe is a "matrix organization" within which individuals belong to both squads and chapters. Squads focus on product delivery, whereas chapters focus on domain competency. Guilds are a third dimension which, according to senior agile coach Jason Yip, are either "communities of practice," which serve to improve strategic capabilities, or "communities of interest," which serve people's hobbies.[lxxvi] Think of them like networking "meetups" around particular topics, where anyone can join, discuss, learn, and so forth. Individuals' managers might be intra chapter or intra tribe.

Finally, Spotify culture is experiment friendly, with an infrastructure to support the ability to constantly test new ideas with a low risk of disrupting customers' experience. They openly discuss and share failures and subsequent learning. They heavily rely on evidence to inform decision-making. They even provide 10 percent free time to work on new ideas and run a "hack week" once per year to test new ideas.

Spotify's organizational structure is a mature example of organizing people around aligned missions, rather than basing it necessarily on function. Scaling RAD requires that in addition to ramping up successful 100-startups-in-100-days teams, company leadership and the RAD implementation team find initiatives that serve as program launch points. Remember Cargill, which implemented its Center of Excellence to promote new behavior through defined "innovation practices," did just that with their alternative proteins project. The key to such endeavors is that they touch multiple parts of the organization horizontally and earn leadership backing.

CASE STUDY
ALTERNATIVE BUSINESS STRUCTURE FOR
ALTERNATIVE PROTEIN

Cargill, the global food, agriculture, and nutrition company, was a bit of a laggard of the traditional protein players to enter the alternative protein space, but for good reason. Elizabeth Gutschenritter, managing director of Cargill's Global Alternative Protein business, says that they were interested in the market as it was initially developing, but looked for ways Cargill might provide unique value. In other words, rather than pretending that innovation requires disrupting the current business, or greenfield invention, Cargill was willing to take a wait-and-see approach to how the market developed. "What we saw," Gutschenritter says, "concerned raw material access, operational and supply-chain efficiency, and customer intimacy, all areas where Cargill has a strong history of performance."[lxxvii]

Based on market evidence, they could see that their expertise might improve the efficiency of the industry as a whole. Interestingly, the expertise touched various parts of Cargill, rather than, say, one specific business unit. So rather than launch a product in the old way, they spun up an interdisciplinary team to tackle the go-to-market strategy.

Florian Schattenmann, Cargill chief technology officer, explains: "One thing that we had not taken advantage of as well as we could have in the past is leveraging our cross-business capabilities. For example, understanding the transfer functions between ingredient chemistry, formulation, and processing, and taking the breadth of expertise across various businesses and central R&D and seeing them through all the way to the final application. For alternative protein, we chose to put one dedicated team reporting into the R&D function, but aligned with the global business under Elizabeth. But that dedicated R&D team engages a much larger network of these relevant capabilities and technical expertise across the company."

"One of the first hurdles," Gutschenritter shares, "was to challenge the normal process of starting in a new category with six to nine months of strategy work. Traditionally, the commercial effort would follow the strategy work. Given the dynamic nature of the developing alternative protein business, our approach was to lead with a go-to-market plan—learning from customers, from consumers, from the marketplace, and then doing the strategy work as a pressure test of our hypotheses."

The process of developing the product becomes iterative, reaching from the core chemistry in Cargill R&D to the edge where consumers live. Schattenmann states: "There's a feedback loop that goes back and forth between the consumer, the customer, our product, the meat alternative, the processing, the formulation, and the ingredients. From consumer insights all the way through the ingredient, it's a sustained, agile way of working. This is an iterative and continuously improving system."

The team is visible to leadership throughout Cargill. When the team gives a progress update, it goes not only vertically to the executive team, but also out to business leaders in other parts of the company who feel shared ownership of the results. To keep them on board, however, requires storytelling. Since financial results are not impressive during the initial launch phases, different metrics must be shared. Learning metrics demonstrate progress, whereas mature business metrics focus on financial efficiency.

Gutschenritter observes: "Cargill's mature businesses are very much profitability driven. In our startup business, we shift the focus to top-line growth, sales revenue, and distribution—how many stores or food service operators are we in? How robust is our sales pipeline?"

"The result is you see other people all over the organization move mountains in order for this to be successful," Director of Strategy Bruce McGoogan says.

"Leadership support is such a critical aspect," Gutschenritter says. "We have very robust processes for our mature businesses, some that we felt could be detrimental if we followed in the same way. We want to make sure we have alignment across the business, but understand the need to be agile and flexible when it comes to the application of these processes—and the support from leadership has made all the difference. Our meetings run differently. They go pretty quickly and provide more of an awareness and direction than the details."

The key to this type of innovation is that it isn't invention led. It's market led. It requires an awareness of market needs and trends. A business must understand its core strengths and capabilities and that it is okay to not be first. Waiting, watching, then being able to move quickly to leverage strengths to compete can create more value more efficiently. This is not bimodal or ambidextrous innovation. It's learning to balance execution and exploration throughout the core business to capitalize on opportunities.

Schattenmann summarizes the approach: "That's where the sweet spot is for Cargill to win: bringing together the different expertise, different capabilities across organizational borders. That's why Cargill has a strong, functional identity for R&D. We come around to areas like health, alternative protein, pet food, and other markets where we bring a unique, broad set of expertise and capabilities."

As with the Cargill team that launched a whole new subcategory of products, the agile team is the new unit of work.

SCAFFOLDING SCALE

Ultimately, you hope the RAD implementation team morphs into a "Center of Excellence," like in the Cargill case study described in Chapter 4. Business units pull the new behavior out of the CoE, which provides the support necessary to teach, coach, and mentor using the RAD mindset to drive impact on the current business.

Alas, to truly scale, this isn't enough. We often see that the type of programs we introduced in the Kickstart phase lose their luster. Change requires momentum. Momentum requires numbers. If an insufficient number of employees experience a change in the way they work, the programs will gradually fade away and die. Within the honeymoon period of the RAD program, the leadership team and RAD implementation team need to go bold and push out to the business units, one by one.

Scaling requires continuing to bring the mindset to more people, to train more leaders, to shine a light on success, to push until you feel the pull. I tell entrepreneurs great marketing isn't meant to create buzz, it's to amplify the buzz your product is already creating. Same goes for RAD. Think back on the RAD metrics. If you have a stable, ongoing version of 100 startups in 100 days, then you should feel buzz around it. You should see behavior change that indicates your different stakeholders—support-function people, leaders, middle management, and team members—are behaving in ways that indicate they are realizing value from the program.

It may very well be that the insurance startup described in Chapter 5 remains as a startup, independent of the core business. But typically, pressure from the core business to get a piece of the startup's action is difficult to avoid. Business units want to absorb the successful internal startup. (Or, perhaps, an acquired startup.) If it's integrated incorrectly—and it's done wrong more often than not—the value of the startup will be crushed.

Successful internal startups and RAD initiatives require "scaffolding" to protect them from the core business. A large local communications company saw one of its promising internal startups run through a bizarre maze of startup clichés in only a couple of years:

- Closes a series of six-figure business deals in a brand-new market
- Company reorganizes so new business unit could take over the startup and build
- CEO lauded for "innovation"
- Company's revenues flatten
- New CEO onboarded to the company
- Startup kicked to the curb

Guess what? To a multi-billion-dollar business that dominates a particular global market, a new, successful startup earning less than $1 million a year in a new market is meaningless. In the Silicon Valley tech-style startup, lore has it that the two primary reasons startups fail are (1) there's no market for the product, and (2) premature scaling. Business units absorbing internal startups too soon is the corporate version of number (2).

But all this is true of *any* business initiative subject to the old-school efficiency-for-efficiency's-sake mentality. It doesn't matter whether or not it's called a startup. New initiatives are killed when they don't produce enough money quick enough. It's the mindset that must change, not believing in an ambidextrous, dual-operating, bimodal system. Whatever that means.

Recall the original Horizon planning model I talked about earlier with respect to how Intuit advances its internal projects: Horizon 3 is an early-stage idea, Horizon 2 is testing scale, and Horizon 1 is ready to be integrated into the core business.

The model applies to any idea attempting to traverse the life cycle adoption curve of disrupting conventional wisdom. It doesn't matter whether you call it a startup. It matters whether it will benefit the company in pursuit of its mission.

The trickiest are those in Horizon 2. Even poorly executed idea competitions might get you a handful of Horizon 1 projects. And if you don't know how to manage a Horizon 3, well, I guess that's a good problem to have because it's potentially making you a lot of money while you figure it out. The only way to get to a Horizon is to make a lot of Horizon 1 bets. But following the 5Es means you don't have to spend a lot of money.

Horizon 2s, however, do not yet guarantee a positive return on investment and yet require a significant allocation of time, money, and human resources. This is why, quite rationally, if core business KPIs are applied they will be killed, since they haven't yet proven they can scale. Horizon 2 initiatives need to be close to the business, but not integrated. They exist in what I call a "docking station."

They have an agile structure, with a base layer of agile teams, and a team-of-teams layer, and then a management-team layer that reports into the business unit management. In this sense, the startup team's management team acts as an additional team-of-team layer in the hierarchy. Business unit leadership manages them, but perhaps more like a startup board of directors.

They do not dictate the business of the startup, but they fund based on their achieving agreed milestones. The business units are smart money, which in the startup world means they provide value to the startup that goes beyond dollars. They make introductions to stakeholders, they provide resource assistance from the core business, they help overcome obstacles. They mentor, advise, and invest. Because these leaders have participated in the Kickstart and Accelerate phases, they've already practiced these new ways of "managing" teams working in uncertainty.

MANAGING COMMUNICATIONS FLOW

In order to be resilient, an organization must be able to bend and not break. It must be able to withstand storms and bounce back from disruption. To do so, it must be aware of things that are going on internally, as well as externally, with respect to customers, economy, other members of the ecosystem, and the world at large. Awareness, plus built-in agility, allows the organization to be dynamic, to both prepare for change and quickly adapt to it.

Obviously, communications inside an organization have always been important. There are communications advantages to the assembly-line style of corporate organization, including the hierarchy. In that style of organization, through sheer power, the top sends communications down a well-worn path. Information is shared on a need-to-know basis. You could make a case for your need to know, but the default was that you don't. If you think otherwise, you know where the suggestion box is. A mere acknowledgment that the communication was received was all that was required. If you received no updates, you executed the last known command, theoretically no matter what you saw on the horizon.

In a RAD organization, however, this isn't the case. Those closest to the problem make decisions on how to resolve them. They are also likely the first to see the outcomes. So each agile team might produce:

- Tasks they are working on
- Insights on the problem to be solved—for example, a previously unknown customer need
- Solutions they tried that didn't work
- Solutions they tried that did work
- Stakeholder response to solutions, both positive and negative
- Progress on metrics
- Obstacles both internal or external they need help overcoming
- Wins or praise for others who have helped
- Resource needs or salient information regarding individuals

I'm sure you can think of more. All this information doesn't need to go to all people. And yet, for non-privacy-related items, limiting who receives information based on an arbitrary evaluation of "need to know" is severely limiting and likely very wrong. Transparency can be an overused concept because autonomous teams might lose autonomy by sharing too much. On the other hand, borrowing from retired U.S. Navy captain David Marquet, "thinking out loud" helps stakeholders understand the reasoning behind decisions.

In *Turn the Ship Around!* Marquet shares an extraordinary story of overcoming the obstacles of empowering sailors on a nuclear submarine in the extremely hierarchical, command-and-control, execution-minded U.S. Navy. Much of the empowerment came down to intentional communication, and in this case, promoting informal sharing of reasoning, rather than just the "statement of doing" that is favored by Navy protocol. In other words, stating what is being done, but not why:

We worked hard on this issue of communication. It was for everyone. I would think out loud when I'd say, in general, here's where we need to be, and here's why. They would think out loud with worries, concerns, and thoughts....[We] encouraged a constant buzz of discussions among the watch officers and crew. By monitoring that level of buzz, more than the actual content, I got a good gauge of how well the ship was running and whether everyone was sharing information.[lxxviii]

Similarly, McChrystal didn't think predicting what needed to be shared was possible. He erred on the side of transparency. "The daily O&I [Operations and Intelligence] briefing lay at the core of our transformation: this pumped information about the entire scope of our operations out to all members of the Task Force and partner agencies, and also offered everyone the chance to contribute."[lxxix]

Increased information sharing generates trust. Leaders working in a new way, no longer dictating work to be done, will feel more comfortable with more information. Agile teams that share the context of a dilemma and reasoning for a decision—in other words, sharing their work—allow leadership to understand the decision. It also may demonstrate to other teams how to leverage evidence for making decisions.

As mentioned in Chapter 4, human beings store information best in story form. People literally fill in gaps with imaginary facts in order to more efficiently recall a memory. Only they don't realize that's what they're doing. In other words, if you don't supply the why regarding a decision, a leader will fill in their own version of the why. I think this is usually referred to as "jumping to conclusions." The more completely teams share the reason behind the decision-making, the more likely the leader will go along, because it doesn't feel like there are gaps.

Some of the information shared by individual agile teams needs to go to the other teams in their group. In Agile implementations, this is often managed by "standups," which are often daily and include tactical-level items people are working on; "retrospectives," which come at the end of a set period of work ("sprints") and are used to share outcomes both good and bad, as well as thoughts on improving performance; and "demo days," which are held periodically to allow teams or groups to share major accomplishments, or significant progress on work. In reality, how teams share information is up to the teams and groups.

Similar to McChrystal's O&I briefings, other layers at the group, division, and company levels should regularly share updates, progress, changes, priorities, strategy, and so on so that teams and team members can better understand the broader context for what they're working on. I'm a big believer in increased transparency top-down, but I also recognize that not all information should be shared with everyone and that some information is better shared using more personal methods. Information and knowledge flowing *to* groups and teams is as important as that coming from teams. Mandates from division and company leadership, such as changes to priorities, missions, and policies, and how they affect teams' missions and behavior, require direct sharing with teams.

Still, the larger-scale briefings need some element of two-way, such as Q&A or postmeeting feedback mechanisms. Additionally, even though these briefings seem very top-down, it's important to include a mechanism for the participation of specific groups or teams, based on the subject. Remember, they are often the direct source of on-the-ground information. As noted above, McChrystal's O&I briefings "offered everyone the chance to contribute."

Finally, a big gap currently exists in most businesses with respect to horizontal communication. Again, it's the very siloed structure of the present assembly line–based organization that causes this. The world is already in an interconnected, networked communication mode, yet silos hoard information that may benefit others. It's not uncommon for half a dozen or more independent communications platforms to be running within one company with no knowledge of the others or interplay among them.

A multitude of tools exist to help with this, of course, and the work-from-home mandate caused by the pandemic has resulted in more corporations using them. But it's also an ethos that needs to be developed and practiced. Sometimes the old-school methods still work.

I'm a huge fan of Techstars-style emails, named after the well-known startup accelerator founded by David Cohen, David Brown, Jared Polis, and Brad Feld. The startups are supplied a basic email template with which they share progress on a consistent basis in a consistent format with all stakeholders and anyone who opts in to receiving them. In this way, teams regularly share their progress through top-line metrics, lessons learned, insights, needs, and other context that might directly impact or benefit other parts of the organization. Other ideas for horizontal information sharing could include: run biweekly happy hour with team share-outs, form communities like Spotify's Guilds, schedule regular conference calls with R&D inventors, formalize how conference attendees share learnings. The RAD implementation team can help different parts of the organization implement, market, and scale these knowledge-sharing activities.

CASE STUDY
DIVING INTO A TEAM OF TEAMS

Imagine a global medical device company (MedCo) seeking to transform into a twenty-first-century medical diagnostics platform. The company already exists in a large, complex ecosystem that includes labs, hospitals, doctors, and patients. They deal with different government agencies in each country they operate in. They must manage relationships with supply-chain vendors, manufacturers, and other technical and strategic partners.

The company has a broad portfolio of devices for different medical diagnostics, suitable for a variety of environments and customer needs. The products, which span the life cycle from new to legacy, live in several different divisions. The company sells direct, as well as through independent agents; they have both medical science and technology R&D groups. The professional services organization is required for some implementations.

The new platform will monitor and maintain devices on customer premises, and collect and aggregate data where authorized. New applications will use the aggregated device plus third-party data to improve and expand diagnostic ability. Applications will be developed by internal engineering teams and customers, as well as independent and even competitive companies. Applications will be available through a platform marketplace.

The company employs approximately thirty thousand people in fifteen departments, distributed across one hundred countries. Much of their R&D has implemented some agile principles, some groups more formally than others. They have user experience design and customer-experience professionals, entrepreneurial people from startups acquired in the recent past, as well as their share of "change agents"—in other words, people seeking to bring a more agile, innovative, or entrepreneurial mindset to the company. This includes people up and down the existing hierarchy.

Approximately 10 percent of MedCo's employees contribute a portion of their time to this new platform endeavor. MedCo's senior leadership team creates a digital leadership transformation team (DLT) pulled from leaders across the departments. The DLT sets the vision, mission, and road map. To kickstart this massive effort, the company does not do 100s/100d, but rather takes a focused approach on building a temporary structure to frame the work to be done in the early phases.

The DLT forms seven agile teams composed of seventy interdisciplinary, cross-functional, cross-hierarchy employees from the fifteen departments. Each team is assigned its ambition, which is frankly the right word, since at the beginning of such a project, so much uncertainty exists that hard outcomes are impossible to predict. Each team's ambition is to generate enough customer and internal stakeholder evidence within their domain to create a solid road map for how to proceed. The work to be done is focused on learning, as well as planning execution on what's known or learned.

The teams are organized around these streams: data management and flow; application ecosystem; commercialization, including brand; platform architecture; communication among MedCo products, customer locations, the cloud, and so on; operating model, including governance; and deployment. The leaders of each team comprise the team of teams at the layer above. A second group of three to five leaders, pulled from the DLT, as well as others not officially part of the project, form an innovation board or a growth board.

The first phase is ninety days, the time rather arbitrarily

chosen like a typical startup accelerator cohort. Each month is an agile sprint, with a repeated structure:

- Week 1—learning sprint, where team members learn and apply empathy and exploration skills
- Week 2—team members consolidate data and insights, including coordinating with other streams
- Week 3—team members continue to explore, perhaps tend to "normal" job duties, while the team-of-teams team meets to integrate learning; develop a unified road map aligned to DLT mission; share out results to growth board
- Week 4—team members plan their next sprints, incorporating new information based on the team-of-teams work, growth board input, and updates from DLT

Each of the teams is provided coaching in different innovation practices, such as design thinking, Lean Startup, jobs to be done, or customer-experience journey mapping. They are expected to use these when interacting with customers and external stakeholders to understand needs, environment, decision-making process, constraints, and aspirations for their specific ambitions. They interact with internal stakeholders to understand their needs as well, and domain experts to learn what is already *known* inside MedCo.

The teams use Agile to structure their work, planning sprints, determining what experiments to run, figuring out access to customers, and documenting what MedCo already knows to be true versus the myriad of untested assumptions. They run daily standups (short, organized meetings) to coordinate work internally and with other teams, to align customer interactions, compare notes, and determine interdependencies. They run weekly retrospectives to improve their performance as a team. This follows Alistair Cockburn's Collaborate, Deliver, Reflect, and Improve description of work.

Based upon their ambitions, teams must interact with a variety of other entities in MedCo's ecosystem. Part of their learning is to define the two-way dependencies in their relationship with the entities required to accomplish their ambition. For example:

- Money in exchange for value with a customer
- Access to an application programming interface (API) in exchange for shared revenue with a technology partner
- Endorsement in exchange for superior diagnostics with a doctor
- Customer premises data in exchange for better applications

The information gathered by one team might be pertinent only to that stream, or also to other project streams or different parts of the company. The information is shared through collaboration with other teams, but also as part of the team's communication responsibilities. The stream-of-streams team is composed of the leaders of the agile teams (organizational hierarchy doesn't matter). They're responsible for aligning the layers vertically from teams through the DLT, as well as, to some degree, horizontally across MedCo departments, ensuring communications are working and the teams are progressing well.

I like to use computer APIs, that is, application program

interfaces, as an analogy. An API defines an interaction between two components. It describes how they connect, the syntax of the conversation, what information can be exchanged, and how they can interact with each other. These must be defined prior to any communication occurring. If you wanted to make a piece of software independent of the hardware it ran on, for example, you would define an API to provide "hooks" into the software to access specific functions. The hardware engineer that wants to communicate with the software uses the defined API.

The team of teams, if not actually defining the interaction between entities, defines what APIs are needed and establishes the minimum requirements for the communication between teams, between teams and other ecosystem entities, to and from the growth board, as well as the DLT. The APIs define the minimum interaction required to accomplish the mission.

The team of teams presents to the growth board each team's output, as well as the aggregated view. They provide an update on metrics, obstacles, needs, team issues, and anything else relevant to the project. The growth board acts similarly to a startup's board of directors. They hold the team of teams accountable to performance metrics, which are composed mostly of learning metrics, since the project is in an early, highly uncertain stage. The board asks questions, challenges assumptions, offers assistance in overcoming obstacles, makes exploration suggestions, and shares its own evidence when it has it. These are often new skills for leaders, and so they go through their own training to learn new skills and are coached before and after share-out sessions.

* * *

In the end, the new business endures because the new behavior is standard everywhere. Why keep the virus of old-school management around? A business set up to endure doesn't require explicit mechanisms to change behavior, until at least the next revolution is identified. But even in that case, the organization is designed to spin up the right mechanisms and scaffolding to adapt.

Scaled change has resilience, awareness, and dynamism built in.

Chapter 8

THE ENDURE PHASE

Like the waves tossing and turning me in the salty surf, it's likely that the greatest lessons in life have completely whooshed over my head. But two stand out that I was able to latch on to. The first occurred a couple of years out of college, while I was sitting on the stoop of the house I lived in, just across the Rosslyn bridge in Northern Virginia. I was working nearby at a small consulting firm, a "regular job" I didn't want. On that day, I decided to quit my job. And I did, with no other prospects in sight. And after a drama worthy of a 1950s noir film that literally included a crying damsel on a train platform, I ended up in Fredericksburg, Virginia, where I wrote a book I was convinced was destined to be the next Sophomoric American Novel.

Not much winning there, but understanding that I could take care of my own economy was freedom to me. In other words, my confidence that I could depend on myself to find work and build savings allowed me to leave work. I recognize the inherent privilege in that statement, in that this isn't a possibility for many people. To make that privilege a reality for as many people as possible is an ongoing mission of mine.

I am fortunate to have realized that power at a young age, without any obvious reason.

The second lesson occurred decades later and was perhaps the flipside of the same coin. After holding numerous "regular jobs" again, I eventually started my own business. I like to tell people I eventually struck out on my own (again) because I was a bad employee. Most jobs I held saw me tossed from manager to manager like a hot potato. I was always a square peg in a round hole. Was that because my managers were all bad or because I was an obstinate square? I'm going to save a bit of my fragile ego by voting for a bit of both.

To perhaps excise any remaining bits of ego, I must admit that no company suffered any enduring loss due to my exit. I've said it many times, and it bears repeating: *No company should ever suffer ill through the loss of any one individual.* I would go so far as to say that it's a failure of the individual if an organization can't survive without that individual. It's worth looking at the founder if a company does not survive the founder's departure. The legacy of a founder should be a culture that endures on its own strength. But that doesn't mean it's an easy pill to swallow: No matter what our role, even as founders, we're not as indispensable as we think we are.

I speak to you, here, dear reader. You likely have the power to walk away from any work you don't find meaningful. If not, you may want to develop an entrepreneurial spirit and financial savings that can help you realize that power. The business or role you leave will suffer little long-term damage. This last point is also imbued with power. *It means that you can make your current job meaningful.*

At any time, a CEO can announce to Wall Street a new mission for the business, recommitting to the specific ways it seeks to create long-term value for customers, employees, and shareholders. This bold action will, quite obviously, not adversely affect the business. The business leader can announce a RAD restructuring of the division, knowing that while it's a difficult undertaking, the business will not cease doing its business. It may (or may not) temporarily affect the public valuation of the business, but not to an extent that it adversely affects the economics of business. In fact, if the RAD work is accomplished, it is very likely the long-term value of the company will increase.

Similarly, senior leaders can, at any time, decide to delegate many decisions to employees and teams who work for them, without hurting the business. It may ding their egos to learn that the business won't subsequently collapse, but it does provide an opportunity to become a leader for a new age. (Perhaps a leader worth promoting.)

The twenty-first-century RAD organization endures with the structure, systems, and processes in place to produce, encourage, and support the RAD behavior. Employees and leaders act in ways that demonstrate their Empathy for customers and colleagues, and they Explore ideas in the face of uncertainty. They leverage and share Evidence, even when it runs counter to their wishes or beliefs. They establish balance in their life, while also seeking balance in their work and supporting Equilibrium in economic society. They act Ethically, with a foundation based in principled behavior and doing no harm.

The enduring organization acts in the interests of the business in the short term (in other words, executing and hitting its numbers), while also exploring and investing in the future. Both of these are in service to its mission, which is based upon creating value for customers. So what does Endure, the final of the four KASE phases, look like, and, more important, what does it mean for you?

Endure phase: Endure exists when the RAD mechanisms are no longer overt systems to support new behavior, but are locked in as established practices and processes. Protective scaffolding disappears, and the emergent business we once had to protect is now the primary business. New scaffolding and mechanisms appear as needed in order to continually adapt to changing conditions.

In this stage, the implementation team goes away. The work they pursued and the principles they proselytized over the course of the previous phases have evolved into permanent systems and processes. They are reflected in the normal course of business. Ensuring the new business endures requires leadership to finish up the organizational design. This includes:

- Governance Practices Based on a Needs Portfolio
- Restructuring to the Rest of the Company
- The Enduring Power of Conscious Culture
- Practicing Disruptive Leadership

GOVERNANCE PRACTICES BASED ON A NEEDS PORTFOLIO

All successful products have a life cycle. New products are built and released, and combined with marketing, sales, and so on, they find a niche market segment, generate some amount of buzz, establish momentum, and grow. Eventually the growth peaks, endures for a while; then either the market slowly tails off or perhaps precipitously collapses. The lifetimes of products vary widely, subject to competition, changing technology, economic conditions, demographic changes, and in some cases disruption—something new and incredibly popular that turns the market upside down.

Many businesses rely on the practice of "portfolio management" to manage a pipeline of products, such that declining revenue is continuously replaced. Indeed, the product plans are laid across the time horizons I mentioned earlier, stretched out from today into the distant future. Portfolio management tracks incremental product improvements to grow and extend the life of existing products. It plans how to start now to create incremental innovation to find new growth a few years out. And then, the holy grail: By iterating through various experiments in your business model canvas, you unleash your inner unicorn; the plan is for the innovation lab to achieve disruptive innovation, putting Kodak, Blockbuster, and Nokia to shame.

As I've discussed, while the idea of product portfolio management is good and needed, the innovation model above is wrong and not helpful. It leads to lots of investments into projects and initiatives that will never see the light of day. For all the innovation professionals who complain that "leadership is not bought in," this is why. It's highly likely you *don't* need disruptive innovation. Not if you're managing a RAD business.

A different approach to portfolio management is to consider that while product demand changes, foundational needs don't. Products address the particular needs of a specific market segment over some finite period of time. A need can be described at various levels, but at its most fundamental, the need itself doesn't change regardless of new market dynamics. *Who* has the need changes, as does its priority relative to other needs. *How* needs are addressed also changes. Customers' expectations change, as do other market conditions, but not the need itself.

Peter Drucker points out in *Innovation and Entrepreneurship*, "By 1970, it had become crystal clear that the number of children in America's schools was going to be 25 to 30 percent lower than it had been in the 1960s.... Yet the schools of education in American universities flatly refused to accept this. They considered it a law of nature, it seems, that the number of children of school age must go up year after year."[lxxx] The need for education didn't change, but its market conditions did. The product portfolio management approach would be to add an annual growth target rate to each product, since they are analyzed separately from the market needs.

An innovation strategy or product portfolio strategy in isolation doesn't take into consideration demographic changes or technology trends that might affect market conditions. They both also focus only on new technology or new products solutions, when there are all sorts of other ways a change in the need market might be addressed. Sales and marketing come to mind. Or a different business model. Or acquisition. Those are addressed in their appropriate silos, if addressed at all.

In 2006, the question "How do we incorporate mobile technology into our product line?" was a purely technological one, the answer to which would be obsolete in less than two years once the iPhone blew up. "How will mobile technology change our customers' expectations?" is a bigger, albeit more complex, question, but is still relevant decades later.

The difference comes about from focusing on need versus product or technology. While most businesses focus on the technology of innovation or "digital transformation," focusing on need instead provides different opportunities to assess how to address the underlying reason for transformation. Teams can test where the market is headed, seeking to understand trends that affect the market and how to overcome market risk. The legacy of twentieth-century technology invention is that organizations tend to worry about overcoming technical risk, which in the digital age is often a low hurdle.

The Jobs-to-be-Done model, popularized by Clayton Christensen, is a good example of assessing needs, though the internet cliché example is amusing. "People don't want a drill bit," so it goes. "They want a hole." The funny thing is that people don't want a hole. I mean, most holes are undesired: holes in socks, gopher holes, college dorm room walls riddled with nail holes.

People want to hang a picture. Or a doctor drills a hole in a femur to repair an ACL. It's important not to stay at a superficial level, but to look upstream of that hole to what the *real need is*. The needs portfolio helps create strategic guardrails for future product development, and for technical companies, future invention.

Managing a needs portfolio versus a product portfolio or an innovation pipeline is a more effective way to address future revenue goals than a siloed approach, where the responsibility for each potential growth source is distributed across the organization without coordination. Product portfolio management, innovation strategy, corporate venturing, mergers and acquisitions (M&A), and new market development are often each off on their own, lacking coordination, information sharing, and alignment to company priorities.

A needs portfolio analyzes demographic trends, emerging economies, technology movements, and competition (including startups), all of which provide information on how needs can be better addressed today, as well as how they might be addressed in the future. A needs analysis expands your visibility into potential adjacent markets other companies dominate today, as well as new markets that appear too disparate at first glance, but actually may be closer than you think. Being product or technology agnostic in the analysis of needs allows you to see how your existing technology might be used elsewhere.

The work done up to this point has largely been ground-up behavior change, with overarching steering, managing, and cheerleading from the top. Needs portfolio management is a way to align organizational design from the perspective at the top with the work done below. Managing the needs portfolio of markets you are currently in and might go into is a broader approach that creates a better understanding of how you might leverage existing abilities and helps focus invention or innovation efforts.

Currently, it's likely that R&D, marketing, sales, corporate venturing, and M&A each think about products and markets relative to their own view of the world, loosely aligned with corporate strategy. The time horizons they work with are those that drive immediate results, and so longer-term opportunities are missed. Instead, a needs portfolio can be used to determine corporate strategy, where each part of the organization works toward fulfilling its portion of the needs the company wishes to address. Only in this way do you truly have a portfolio approach.

If M&A is focused on their own priorities and objectives, for example, they look for opportunities for acquisitions independent of what's happening in their own R&D or with sales in emerging markets or research trends uncovered in marketing. Again, this is the siloed approach. But similar to a cross-functional agile team or team-of-teams layer, representatives of M&A, sales, marketing, R&D, and so on can create a diversified approach to creating growth strategies in the needs areas mapped across time horizons.

CASE STUDY
3M REINVENTS AGILITY

As mentioned earlier, 3M was born of invention, but succeeds by discovering market applications. 3M looks for applications for their inventions and has added specific capability to do so more efficiently. Recognizing the need to coordinate efforts across the organization to find and capitalize on growth opportunities, 3M created a growth team responsible for, to a certain extent, herding cats.

In 2014, Laura Nereng, new business development leader at 3M, was working a booth at the U.S. Department of Energy's Innovation Summit. Next door was Stanford University–spawned startup SkyCool demonstrating an innovative, electricity-free cooling idea. Nereng, a natural technology and startup scout, planted a seed with one of the founders regarding 3M technology, and several years later she invited the founder, Aaswath Raman, to speak at a 3M tech forum.

There the SkyCool founder met 3M scientist Tim Hebrink, with whom he discussed his technology needs. Hebrink provided Aaswath with samples of commercially available visible-light reflective film for their prototype, but knew of a new solar reflective technology he had developed that would be better suited. The startup entrepreneur was able to use the sample to prove the technology could work. For Hebrink to show him the better-suited film, however, would require a confidentiality agreement, *which took two years to complete.*

Funding was not immediately available to formalize the new solar reflective technology at 3M. "The business units thought the technology was way too far out for commercialization," Hebrink says. (This is similar to challenges Spencer Silver and Art Fry had with finding an application for the adhesive eventually used in the Post-it notes product.) Hebrink says: "After demonstrating the technology worked outside in a parking lot under the sun, the business people still questioned its business value, since our idea hadn't been validated with customers yet."[lxxxi]

Hebrink applied for and received a $15,000 3M Discover Grant in order to show market feasibility.

"We showed feasibility, but still more proof was needed. We applied for, and won, a $100K 3M internal funding opportunity called a Genesis Grant. The grant was awarded to make the new solar reflective film at a scale large enough to demonstrate the technology in a real-world situation." With that money they were able to make enough of the right type of film that could be applied to the SkyCool project.

In partnership with the SkyCool team, the collaborators successfully demonstrated the technology, the idea, and the value of a real commercial convenience store with a walk-in freezer and an HVAC system in hot, sunny Sacramento, California. In a couple of months the store saved 20 percent on its electricity bill.

That was good enough to get the business managers interested, though not enough to provide funding. 3M turned to the U.S. Department of Energy, which ended up granting millions of dollars to enable 3M to develop an improved film specifically designed for the application.

Nereng commented on the serendipity of discovering Sky-Cool, but also that the opportunity for that has to be created: "It's fun to be able to take disparate parts of the organization, connecting dots from over here and over there and then bringing ideas to the scientists and saying, 'Intuitively it seems like there might be something here. What do you think?' It's very much a team sport."

Based on her experience she sought to formalize it. "After years of advocating for changing how we develop new business at 3M, we formed this growth group, and part of what we do is scout externally. It's my responsibility to look for connection points that might make for new business opportunities. 3M has long been a technology push company, because it has a bunch of great inventors and tinkerers that come up with new inventions and ask themselves, 'What might this be good for?'

"It's worked pretty well, but as things change in the world, we felt like we needed to get out in front of this a bit, and the mantra in our group is, 'What's an unmet need that we could find a solution for?'" The idea is to keep the inventors inventing, but also to help direct the smart people to where the money is, and let them invent with needs in mind.

"Seeing is believing, of course," says Hebrink, "and more than understanding that the technology works, I encouraged people to touch these prototypes and feel that they were colder than the air."

Similar to Intuit, 3M has a 15 percent free-time policy, where employees can work on any project they'd like up to 15 percent of their time. The concept at 3M goes back to their early days, when company leaders saw the value in letting employees work on passion projects, or "bootlegging" as they called it.

As it turns out, "bootlegging" is well adopted within the technical community, but not so much on the business side. "One of the issues," says John Morrow, who is the insights lead on Nereng's growth team, "is that the business isn't involved at the beginning of one of these projects. The technical side is really good at inventing things, and a lot of it is done on their 15 percent time, but when they bring it to the business, it's been harder to make that connection. With the kind of inter-disciplinary team we have in place now, we can take a more holistic view of markets, needs, and solutions." In the SkyCool example, the technical team did the early heavy lifting on the business side, but now Nereng's growth team can build the business case in terms that 3M executives and customers will understand.

"We learned through customer interviews," Morrow says.

"Initially we were thinking, 'Is 10 or 15 percent energy savings exciting for a potential customer?' The supermarkets said 1 percent savings excites them."

"We de-risked the project in other ways to get more support," says Ryan Rogers, also part of the new business growth team. "We went through the process in a robust way, taking out some of their perceived risks. We filed additional IP, executed the partnership agreement, found the key market applications, all of which had been flagged when we first started engaging on the project."

RESTRUCTURING TO THE REST OF THE COMPANY

I've covered at length agile teams and their missions, as well as the organization of layers that exist above them. This is perhaps easily imagined within the context of a growing startup or how one might design the organization of a business unit from scratch. But what does this mean to the existing businesses?

It may make sense to structure divisions or business units based on the needs portfolio being addressed. These groups will naturally be aligned around optimizing the efficiency in accomplishing their mission, rather than merely the financial efficiency of producing output. As discussed before, missions cascade down to the team level out on the edge. Customers don't view their experience with a company by departments. Well, at least until something goes wrong.

The Learning Impact Metrics framework discussed in Chapter 4 tracks the seven states a customer goes through from becoming aware to being passionate. That journey, being Aware, Intrigued, to Satisfied and Passionate, is how a customer experiences the company, responding to its marketing activities, sales methods, and product experience.

People don't think about the structure; they think about their experience across the company. Yet companies are structured based on how they produce output.

Does that still make sense? I venture not. Let's return briefly to the "assembly line to digital fabrication continuum."

The old-school manufacturing company was optimized to produce a Model T in any color, as long as it was black. "Scientific management" means that you understood every task that needed to be done by every employee in order to produce, sell, and distribute the one automobile. In such a scenario, you rationally organize people by function and measure the number of tasks over time. The purpose of the layers of management hierarchy was to maximize this number.

The desired behavior was doing, not thinking; executing, not learning. The organizational structure purposefully reinforced the behavior. Any options, any deviations, would result in an ever-so-slight decrease in efficiency. It would make drawing a line from employee tasks over time to company revenues ever-so-slightly more difficult. The complexity of today's world is reflected in a multitude of options and deviations from the Model T example. You cannot, in fact, draw a line from managing employee tasks to business unit profits.

The goal in the twenty-first-century organization is to organize the work such that teams are aware of when they face uncertainty, collaboratively explore when they need to learn, and execute upon what they've learned. Accomplishing missions directly impacts group missions, which directly impacts company missions. Further, middle managers can more easily reallocate resources on the fly based on changing needs, instead of the current phenomenon of endless reorganizations, which are highly destructive to desired behavior. In the end, you want to be able to draw a straight line from team performance to company performance.

CASE STUDY
DISRUPTING STRUCTURE AS A COMPETITIVE ADVANTAGE

The bank ING created its own version of the Spotify model and deployed it company-wide. This restructuring plus a massive wide-scale behavior change initiative were two distinct efforts that came together in an unforeseen way. In the end, the structure change reinforced the behavior change. Like with many organizations, ING leadership, including the board and C-suite, had determined that banking was going through massive change and would soon look quite different than it did coming out of the Great Recession. Again, like many organizations, they realized they needed to be more customer-centric in order to learn what the bank needed to become.

"We needed," says the former chief innovation officer and current CEO of ING Spain, Ignacio Juliá Vilar, "to reinvent how we are solving customer problems and how to help them on their journey."[lxxxii] To do so, they needed to change the culture, specifically how to get their people to start thinking in a different, more customer-centric way. They also decided to open up a bit; in other words, to connect to the outside world where they could learn what others were doing. "The world is just going too fast to do everything yourself."

In 2015, ING launched their PACE lean innovation program, combining design thinking, Lean Startup, and Agile principles. They created three layers: one called PACE Everyday, which applied the practices to core business functions; a layer for new products and markets where the return was a few years out; and an innovation group, which spun up internal startups expected to scale in five years or more.

This laid the foundational layer of the desired behavior. The top-down portion was "we are doing this," and funding for the training, coaching, and implementation. But the approach was very grassroots. Led by Ria Escher, former global head of innovation transformation, ING's internal innovation champions built up the capabilities and supplied the coaching and support for every country they rolled this out to.

"Several factors were important to scaling this," Escher says. "Leadership is always important, but people on the ground do the work. The first reaction will be, 'Oh, the head office, again, has invented something new we have to do.' But in the end, the people fell in love with the way of working."[lxxxiii]

Meanwhile, at the ING Netherlands retail bank, leadership decided to restructure the organization after visiting Spotify, Zappos, and other high-tech companies. Fresh off a big acquisition, and because they were rapidly digitizing their products, the time was right to look at how to redesign their organization. The goals were to:

- Decrease time to market to respond faster to changing customer needs
- Break down organizational silos to empower individuals and teams
- Create more motivated, passionate, and self-starting employees

Payam Djavdan, ING program director at the time, led the effort: "We put about 1,000 people from the business and 2,500 people from IT together in 350 squads; multidisciplinary teams of about 9 people each. In six months we were already working in these agile teams."[lxxxiv] Each squad is given end-to-end responsibility for a mission, part of a larger tribe with its own mission. The tribes and squads adapt what they work on based on need. People often imagine that it's difficult to organize everyday work in this fashion, but in reality it doesn't have to be. Here's an example Djavdan shares:

"In the old way of doing simple things—for example, sending a communication to customers—the marketing group would think of a message they want to send. They'd ask the data management department to come up with a query for each customer segment. The data scientists would eventually create a model for that. Then they would ask the IT people to write a tool to make that happen. Then the product management team has to adapt the product and process and the operational risk management team has to check the related risks of the particular campaign. Somebody in Finance must sign off because the business case should be correct. Then after a couple of months, they would send the marketing campaign.

"In the new way, a squad is composed of a data analyst, a marketer, a product manager, an IT person, and a designer. They had the skills on the team they needed. But in one case, they made a mistake and sent a message to the wrong data query. Students got the message instead of a group of older people, whom the message was designed for. In the old world, they would analyze what happened and point fingers. It would take four or five weeks before they could send another mailing to the customers telling them that they had made a mistake.

"But in this case, because they had everybody they needed, they immediately sent a picture of the team apologizing. 'We made a mistake in the last email. Please accept our apologies. As a way of saying sorry, we have a special offer.' They did this within two days. A normal marketing campaign had a click-through rate of 0.3 percent. More than 30 percent of the recipients clicked the link and a total of 6 percent accepted the offer."

It's a simple example of the speed at which agile teams can work, in this case responding quickly to a simple mistake of little consequence.

While initially the PACE program and Agile implementation were separate efforts, leadership noticed that those banks that had been restructured did better with the PACE program than those that hadn't yet been. This isn't surprising, since the skills taught in PACE, including developing empathy and rapid experimentation, become tools in a squad's arsenal, as opposed to needing leadership to dictate or urge their use in the old structure.

This organizational design was subsequently replicated across all ING banking units in all countries.

THE ENDURING POWER OF CONSCIOUS CULTURE

A McKinsey survey says more than 80 percent of reorganizations fail to deliver the desired impact and 10 percent cause real damage to the company. I suppose at some level I'm offering up another reorg. But the key difference is that I propose you *allow the new company to emerge*, not merely shuffle the deck chairs.[lxxxv]

The difference is significant. The new organization is built around desired behaviors that drive impact, while the rest of the old organization continues to operate unchanged. There's no strict time frame for the shift. The process of change leverages the desired behavior of the 5Es we want to see in the emergent company. This results in a change that is itself resilient, aware, and dynamic. The need for constant reorganizations, assuming they're not done for political purposes, significantly diminishes.

Most traditional reorganizations I've witnessed seem almost random. I'm sure there's more planning than I understood, but they are reactive to disappointing results in some measure or perceived to be for improving efficiency. I suspect they often have to do with executive leadership not truly understanding what to do in the face of disruption.

Management consultants, of course, have all sorts of prescriptions. Focus on profits and losses. Communicate more often, and better. Design the organization top-down, bottom-up, inside out, right side in, middle-up and over; take two steps back and one step forward. Plan the structure, the processes, every element that will need to change, in the correct order. Dot all the *i*'s and cross all the *t*'s. Write a business plan, including the financial spreadsheet with requisite hockey stick revenue growth. Our work here is done.

I jest, but it's not very funny: The typical five-year CEO tenure includes 1 mea culpa, 2 reorganizations, and 1 major acquisition. The next CEO gets 1 mea culpa, 2 reorganizations, and 1 major *divestiture*.

According to the 2016 McKinsey survey, four of the top seven reasons for failed or disappointing reorganizations include issues of people's behavior:

- Employees actively resist the changes.
- Leaders actively resist the changes.
- The org chart changes, but the way people work stays the same.
- Employees leave because of the reorganization.

The hierarchical command-and-control method of reorganization is deeply imbued with the consultant ethos captured in the movie *Office Space*:

Bob Slydell: Milton Waddams.

Dom Portwood: Who's he?

Bob Porter: You know, squirrely-looking guy, mumbles a lot.

Portwood: Oh, yeah.

Slydell: Yeah, we can't actually find a record of him being a current employee here.

Porter: I looked into it more deeply and I found that apparently what happened is that he was laid off five years ago and no one ever told him, but through some kind of glitch in the payroll department, he still gets a paycheck.

Slydell: So we just went ahead and fixed the glitch.

Bill Lumbergh: Great.

Portwood: So um, Milton has been let go?

Slydell: Well just a second there, Professor. We uh, we fixed the *glitch*. So he won't be receiving a paycheck anymore, so it will just work itself out naturally.

Porter: We always like to avoid confrontation, whenever possible. Problem solved from your end.[lxxxvi]

Scaling RAD requires conscious culture decisions. Beyond the behaviors represented by the 5Es, specific measures must be put into place that continuously reinforce and reinvigorate RAD. These include training, leadership development, and a commitment to diversity.

Not long after publishing *The Lean Entrepreneur*, I had the good fortune of doing some work at General Electric's famed leadership campus in Crotonville, New York. It truly lived up to its hype. Beyond the extraordinary resources available to employees invited there, I was duly impressed with GE's commitment to developing its people and, in particular, its future leaders.

While there, I was fortunate to hear Raghu Krishnamoorthy speak; he was chief learning officer at the time. He shared his perspective about building an environment where it was "safe to be bold." He also talked about the influence company structure had on culture. He remarked, "Culture comes out of structure."

As I said before, it should not surprise anyone that the assembly-line structure used to organize business produces slow, not agile, not customer-centric culture. But I also think the structure originated to reinforce the desire for noncreative, optimized execution behavior. When it comes to culture change, you cannot simply restructure. Instead, it will morph itself to reinforce the existing culture. This is what has happened to many formal Agile implementations. Hoping to get behavior or culture change, they instead got a changed structure that acts as scaffolding to the old behavior.

You must start with desired behavior first and build structure around that, hence the KASE stages. The Endure phase requires leaders responsible for culture to implement permanent programs that create an environment that is safe to be RAD.

Training

All new employees, whether gotten through hiring or acquiring, should be taught your version of the 5Es. I would recommend that this not merely be a classroom discussion or a classic corporate instructional video, but rather it should instill the behavior, which requires action. For example, form teams composed of new hires (cross-functional, cross-hierarchical, and interdisciplinary), then provide them a coach and a challenge.

The challenge assigned to the new teams might concern the

onboarding process itself. Stakeholders are each other or other teams, hiring managers, and human resources people responsible for the onboarding process. Actual challenges could be fun, like "increase healthy activity at work" or whatever your creative people come up with. Again, the idea is to practice the behavior on day one.

Stewardship

Like Cargill's Center of Excellence (CoE), companies must maintain their RAD point of view. Initially, perhaps based on the 5Es, it should itself be dynamic, able to evolve based on changes to the business and its ecosystem. The CoE is responsible for the evolution, based on its own awareness, as well as feedback from the front lines.

The CoE should provide support, coaching, and consulting to business units and functional support organizations. It is important that the CoE not dictate the exact process and behavior. It operates as a supporting function, not RAD police. It might maintain an internal coaching program or provide referrals to outside help. It provides input to ongoing communications, including continuing to shine a light on the work of RAD teams and positive outcomes.

Incentivizing

Work based on the 5Es and accomplishing missions with an organizational structure based on scaling agile teams will require different performance management than that used in the task-optimizing hierarchical model. Performance measuring should be ongoing based on metrics tracking team progress. Course corrections and management feedback should also be ongoing. Compensation should include team and group outcomes, not merely tasks per day.

Creating other incentives to apply RAD not only reinforces behavior, it's the right thing to do. Team members who by accomplishing missions, going above and beyond duty to drive impact, or by launching internal startups that win big, should get upside. This doesn't need to mirror the startup world, but this type of rewarding has always happened inside hierarchical organizations. Just in the past, the rewards trickled down from the top. Ideally, this is flipped, since the bulk of discovery and creation of value is happening at the ground level.

Managers and leaders need incentives, too, in order to keep them willing to delegate authority down the line. This is, of course, especially true early on in the implementation of RAD, but should be formalized such that it becomes the normal behavior. Even something as simple as demonstrating spending 15 percent of budget on early-stage (Horizon 3) ideas to get a full bonus, for example, will ensure behavior change becomes permanent.

Embracing the Value of Diversity

There are many purely ethical reasons to embrace diversity. But so are there purely rational, value-creating reasons. Women, people of color, those from economically disadvantaged backgrounds, and other marginalized people often demonstrate alternative skills as a result of their life experiences, skills that barely show up on the radar of those accustomed to being in power, if at all. Changes in the world—say, like disruption—suddenly and without warning bring these skills to the fore. Suddenly, they are required to succeed in business. Complexity, uncertainty, and decision-making moving to the edge are all such changes.

Increased diversity makes teams more discerning, able to understand context from different angles, and therefore better able to recognize and describe the "entire elephant," for example, than the nondiverse team. Increased diversity *understands* a broader market, brings more varied solution ideas, lends itself to an increased understanding of diverse cultures, including those that represent new opportunities. They can help you avoid product problems like handless soap dispensers that don't recognize dark skin(!).[lxxxvii]

Diversity, cross-functional roles, and interdisciplinary skills enable teams to solve complex problems better. An artist can help visualize a financial or mathematical quandary. A chemist can help solve a physicist's problems, as described in this article:

> Nathalie de Leon, an assistant professor of electrical engineering, needed to control the carbon atoms on the surface of a diamond, but the sheer hardness of the diamond was defeating all attempts—not just hers, but those of every physicist who had tried over the previous half century....
>
> "Rob [Knowles, a chemistry professor] came up to me and said, 'The surface chemistry can't be that hard,'" de Leon recalled. "I told him, 'Well, this is a 50-year-old problem, and nobody has made any progress at all.' And then he said, 'Well, I think we can do it in a year.'"...
>
> Working together, the chemist and the quantum physicist had discovered completely new types of chemistry that work at the diamond surface.[lxxxviii]

As with much of conventional wisdom, meritocracy sounds reasonable when you say it fast, but is actually rife with bad assumptions. "Luck intervenes by granting people merit, and again by furnishing circumstances in which merit can translate into success. This is not to deny the industry and talent of successful people. However, it does demonstrate that the link between merit and outcome is tenuous and indirect at best," says economist Robert Frank.[lxxxix]

It also is heavily biased, since the qualifications of success are determined by the successful. It's those who create the ladder of success who say (and enforce), "This is the only way up." This is, of course, particularly dangerous during massive change. Human diversity, just as with maintaining a diverse financial portfolio, protects against uncertainty and unforeseen change, while limiting downside risk. In other words, from a purely maximizing-value standpoint, diversity makes sense. It's characteristic of a RAD organization.

PRACTICING DISRUPTIVE LEADERSHIP

The leadership required to pull this off benefits from the diversity. If you believe you must change management styles from the twentieth-century command-and-control style, then hiring and developing leaders the same way as in the past will clearly not work. It's unlikely that you'll find them on the twentieth-century-defined corporate leadership ladder. You may need to look outside your normal view.

Can the twentieth-century leader evolve into a twenty-first-century leader? Of course. But for most, it's a difficult journey, as are all personal journeys of such magnitude. It is perhaps sort of clichéd, but one imagines the twentieth-century leader is like a stereotypical football coach: loud, forceful, induces fear, and demands respect. Also smart, capable, often charismatic, and inspiring.

Elements of this are still needed in the twenty-first century. But only at the appropriate times. I know firsthand that in crisis, a lot of people wait for a few to lead. We need people who can take up the mantle without hesitation. There are situations where near-term decisions must be made, and when made by committee they result in bland, uninspiring results.

As noted before, complex is different from complicated. Complicated issues are difficult, but knowable. Further, it's likely someone somewhere knows how to address them; often they are even already in your organization. Complex issues, however, don't have one solution. The multiple variables involved mean multiple solutions are likely. Complex issues require more than expertise; they require exploration.

In Dave Snowden's Cynefin decision-making framework, when faced with decisions that need to be made in simple, known circumstances, the twentieth-century execution-minded leadership style can lead to outperforming expectations. (Though other means may do even better.) In a complicated situation, extensive knowledge is required, so the leader may be better off bringing in experts to help. However, faced with a complex issue, a hierarchical, command-and-control leadership style is ineffective, since executing a "known" solution will likely be wrong. Perhaps counterintuitively, in a chaotic environment the domineering twentieth-century leadership mode might be the best way to bring elements of stability and safety to the moment, but then leaders must be flexible enough to pass the reins to others more able to assess the complexity of what's going on.

In the twentieth century, businesses certainly faced *complicated* challenges, but generally the market was less *complex*. When faced with the complexity of the digital age, these same businesses struggle to deal with the new reality.

This may explain the Kodak situation better than their supposed failure to recognize the changing market. Rather than failing to see the digital revolution and the future of the digital camera, as the Innovation Industry story goes, they recognized the coming role of digital cameras but failed to adequately explore various business models. In other words, they used a best-practices approach to complexity. Instead of experimenting, they successfully invented digital cameras, but they chose a familiar business model and executed that into failure.

Perhaps the most important leadership characteristic is self-awareness. Leaders must understand whether a pending decision falls within the realm of the known or the unknown. They must be aware if they have the required expertise to plot the course forward. They must allow others to step in where appropriate. There is a conscious relinquishing of ego required.

This isn't easy, but if you believe that the way people work must change to deal with the complexities of the twenty-first century, well, then you have to walk the talk. The way change begins is through a personal commitment followed through in day-to-day behavior. This is where much of modern leadership training, which teaches vital skills like empathy, vulnerability, and empowerment, has not achieved the desired results. Workshops are helpful, but how are the new skills applied to daily work, which is primarily executing, putting out fires, and attending meetings?

The Kickstart and Accelerate phases are for practicing and re-inforcing these new leadership skills so they are second nature by the Endure phase. Leaders will balance managing empowered agile teams working in uncertainty, while attempting to drive real impact for the business. Leaders practice *how to mentor teams*, not just manage people; how to create time, space, and a sense of safety for exploring, failing small, and discovering new ways of creating value. Leaders learn *how to empower teams*, through understanding fears, capability gaps, and resource needs, but also by giving them responsibility through learning metrics and behavior guardrails. And there's the internal empathy layer, a give-and-take between teams and leadership.

When my daughters were younger, I yelled at them once in a while. Not often, but anger is a valid human emotion that stress and anxiety can unleash in unproductive ways. Later, I apologized. Not to pat myself on the back, but what is the better life lesson? To bottle up anger, perhaps leading to other unhealthy relationship characteristics, or making a mistake that shows I'm human, owning up to it, and apologizing? Maybe I'm crazy, but I think it's the latter.

Walking the talk means being vulnerable. Admitting when you are wrong, admitting when you've failed, admitting when you don't know. Admitting you can and must try to do better. Ultimately, this is what you want to see in others, what should be communicated in the stream-of-streams communications.

HOW DOES THE NEW STRUCTURE REACT TO DISRUPTION?

Melanie Evans, CEO of ING Australia, came to ING with a strong, human-centered design background and saw immediate potential for its application. As opposed to such practices being exiled into far-out market research or innovation silos, "there was a huge opportunity," Evans says, "to take the concept of what we'd used in digital banking very well and apply it across the organization."[xc]

The existence of the PACE program helped create the expectation that everyone could work this way, not just those with a human-centered design background, or "innovation" in their job title. Evans understood that good leadership included communicating what was expected of people, but also ensuring they developed the skills to do the work. But also, the leaders themselves had to experience the way of working for themselves or they wouldn't understand the output.

"Getting leaders out on the street as part of training, asking random strangers about solving problems, that was probably the highlight of getting our leadership cohort trained on the method itself," Evans says.

Her three PACE leadership keys:

1. Championing the people who do the work. "Storytelling is a very good way of sharing with the organization the behavior, the insights, the approaches to leadership that work."

2. Get engaged. "People are sitting on some of the best insights in the organization. I want one-on-one time with them; I don't want a slide deck that's been handed around and changed four times. I want to know the richness of the insight, so I ask—'Tell me what you observed.'"

3. Be willing to change your views. "If senior leaders decide how to distribute the organization's resources, it's necessary to understand exactly what problems the organization is solving, what's going out into the market. I've had my definition of what opportunity or customer problem I think we're solving completely reframed by PACE."

"The minute that COVID hit," Evans said, "it was very obvious that a large number of our customers were going to be under financial hardship. The calls started in mid-March 2020, as businesses were forced to close with lockdowns, and so we put together a PACE team immediately. We didn't really have a defined scope. I didn't ask the team to solve the mortgage problem or talk about savings accounts. It was wide-open and we had a sense of the problem, but we had not defined exactly what needed to be solved."

She said, "The first response was getting the insights correct. While some responses, for example, focused immediately on solving problems for those most obviously impacted, our PACE work suggested there was a reassurance all Australians needed. At that stage, no one really knew where the pandemic was headed."

They also looked to leverage the trust ING had already established in the market. "We have a unique position in the market where people know the value exchange; that we're fair, we can be trusted.

We had an opportunity to move very quickly to reassure our customers about what actions we were going to take to make sure that they were okay."

Evans says there's a sense of resilience and optimism among Australians. "She'll be right," they like to say. In very short order, the PACE team was communicating with customers. While everyone else was zigging to get their digital products out since the branches were closed, launching ads to explain how to sign up for internet banking, ING was zagging:

"We recorded a TV ad that was reaching out to people to call us if they wanted someone to speak to. The ad was a playful vignette of our team members working from home at their kitchen table, with their kid in the bouncer in the corner. It was quite playful and fun, a dog farting and all the imperfection that came with working from your home. We wanted to say that we're human, too, we had to send everyone home, this is a horrible time for everyone, but if you're worried, give us a ring, we'll have a chat. She'll be right."

ING recognized the diversity of their customer base, so their response wasn't one-size-fits-all. They launched free, one-hour coaching sessions with qualified, independent financial coaches. They allowed people to pause all of their payments on their loans if they had income worries. They even partnered with Uber Eats and announced, "We know you're locked in the house, you probably don't feel like cooking every night; have a Netflix binge and we'll pay the delivery charge for your favorite takeout."

Changes were made internally, too, to their missions. According to Evans, "The PACE work sharpened our focus and three principles emerged: Care for the ING team, look after existing customers to navigate the pandemic first before chasing new ones, and protect the financial system from fraud and other risks that it might be exposed to in a pandemic. The strategy came second to these principles in terms of communication. Giving context, purpose, and principles is essential in a time of change when we needed everyone agile across the organization. When the purpose and principles are clear, a leader's role is to support and empower—which brings us back to some of the most fundamental principles of the ING agile model.

"It's probably one of the most devastating, horrible things that we've all had to face as humans, but we can still take PACE and apply it to this situation in order to maintain our high standards, being focused on customers, understanding what problems we're solving, reframing things slightly, so everyone benefits."

PUTTING THE PHASES IN LONG-TERM PERSPECTIVE

The purpose of the four KASE phases is to allow a new business to emerge from the old that is then built up to withstand the disruptions of the twenty-first century, one that operates with eyes wide-open to what's happening in the world, and that can respond as an active participant in society while accomplishing its mission.

The change required is behavioral from top to bottom and across the organization, from factory workers in developing countries to executives gathering around boardroom tables. Kickstarting change requires ground-up work. The thread that connects all companies highlighted in the preceding chapters is understanding customers.

The real work starts now.

To accelerate, you grow the kickstart, but also plan the placement of firestarters—places in the organization where you can implement RAD strategically in order to create momentum. Proof comes from small impact. Improving internal processes. Shine a light on them. Double down on the behavior that works; make it your own. "Language is so incredibly important," as Ria Escher says. "Everybody has a different word for this and the same word for different things."

The good story about Scale is that if you get that far it means you're succeeding. The biggest mistake is pushing successful efforts prematurely into the core business. In other words, if you move immature projects or startups into parts of the business without mechanisms to support and protect them, the old business will swallow them up. The grassroots autonomous teams are on the ground floor with the customers, understanding their needs; they are close to the technology, able to understand the possible solutions.

The key to the agile teams' structure is getting the communications right to align with priorities and ensure the different nodes know what the larger context is and what's happening in other parts of the organization. "All the different people," says 3M's Laura Nereng, "doing these seemingly disparate things around the company, and it's really not coordinated, but we have this chance to connect them all together around customer needs, and thereby drive a bigger role for 3M in the world."

The test of Endure is threefold: First, when you remove the scaffolding that has been supporting your sculpture, does it stay standing up? Second, does it weather the first storm? Sure, it may need some fixing, some tweaks, some new mechanisms, some new temporary scaffolding even. But if it's still there and functional, that's success. Third and final, if leadership moves on, those instrumental to the emergence of the new business leave, and yet the new business remains; it passes the third test of endurance.

In the end, as you've worked through the four phases, the final look of the desired emergent organization remains up to your vision. In my words, it will look, behave, communicate, and perform like a RAD organization:

- Resilient—able to survive disruption
- Aware—open to new information arising internally or externally
- Dynamic—able to adapt and move quickly

Perhaps the COVID-19 pandemic of 2020 offers an opportunity for a thought experiment. How would a RAD company have responded?

In early 2020, the World Health Organization (WHO) formally declared the outbreak of COVID-19, calling it "a public health concern." An aware organization perhaps takes note of that announcement, particularly if they have operations in or dependencies on China. A resilient organization has a redundant supply chain. A dynamic organization perhaps spins up a cross-functional RAD team to monitor the situation, notify people internally during the standing monthly briefings of division-level team of teams, and formulate high-level contingency plans, just in case the virus spreads. The purpose of the communications isn't to strike fear, but simply to alert those who have dependencies on China, as well as any other groups that might be affected by a spread of the disease.

In March 2020, WHO declared a pandemic. The COVID-19 RAD team already has a plan for their first steps. It understands what the typical government reactions will be, based on history. They predict transportation shutdowns, for instance. The team leverages internal and external experts to produce an analysis on the potential ramifications of the pandemic on the business, the U.S. economy, and the global economy, given mild, moderate, or severe spreads of the disease. The team creates lists of key contacts to other participants in their business ecosystem, including customers, partners, government agencies, and local communities. They organize and begin reaching out to them.

The report is shared to all stream-of-streams layers, where division leaders assess the portions most relevant to their teams, taking a swag at altering their division's mission and reprioritizing their actions. All agile teams respond to specific scenarios, which, depending on the business, might include:

- Repurposing technology to benefit the battle against the disease or consequences of the disease
- Communicating with customers to understand their situations
- Assessing the challenges of working from home, including IT challenges, and the difficulties of managing family dynamics
- Ensuring employee safety
- Alternative revenue-creating ideas
- Optional cost-cutting ideas

Even in the worst-case scenario, where portions of the business are completely shut down, a RAD company persists. One portion does not bring down the rest. A bottom-up idea-generation mentality, especially one with a history of learning and iterating until succeeding, means the likelihood of finding solutions to stay viable is exponentially higher than with the traditional, top-down, cost-cutting approach.

The RAD organization is capable of responding to classic Christensen "disruptive innovation" as well. The Innovation Industry peddles the myth that companies must stave off disruption by disrupting themselves. But what's the actual evidence that companies need to do this? What's the evidence they *can* do it? Disruptive innovation is unpredictable. Therefore, no matter how smart you are, a team can't sit down and *do* disruptive innovation. It. Doesn't. Work. That. Way.

Nokia, Blockbuster, and RIM (maker of the ol' BlackBerry) didn't fail or suffer tremendously because they failed to disruptively innovate. Their failure was their inability to respond to changing conditions. It was a failure of leadership. The former chairman of Nokia, Risto Siilasmaa, says, "I think one way of looking at that is the way we look at CEOs. They are on a pedestal. They are demigods. And, we assume that they know everything, and we force them to pretend that they know everything."[xci]

The RAD organization is built to be aware of the world, including technology, demographic, and environmental changes, to explore in the market, testing new ideas, different business models, different ways to leverage technology. This happens only by empowering the bottom of the pyramid to act boldly, explore, experiment, fail small, and learn. And that change happens only if leadership is vulnerable, admits what it doesn't know, and acts boldly in the face of uncertainty, telling Wall Street, "We will balance executing and exploring. If you agree, invest in us. If not, invest elsewhere."

Those who concentrate on creating wealth operate in a zero-sum world. They wish to get theirs by denying it to others. The idea that some bit of that wealth trickles down to the less worthy creates a world of huge economic disparity, anger, and turmoil. Evidence tells an unequivocal story that trickle-down economics doesn't work. Proponents evoke social-Darwin-type arguments, that such disparity is a natural human inevitability and so should be left alone.

These same people are at the front of the line, however, to prevent other natural human behaviors that threaten their personal well-being. So it might be worth considering that "value flowing out" is a powerful alternative to trickle-down. Capitalism is not zero-sum. By succeeding to create value for customers, wealth still flows to senior management and shareholders. Yes, profits are likely less, but not in a meaningful sense, and the increased benefits of a stable economic system that creates value for all flows also to senior management and shareholders.

The other consideration is that the digital revolution means the people have pitchforks in their pockets.

This is the new world. Adapt or die—maybe quickly, but more likely through a long decline into mediocrity. Who is the Jack Welch of the twenty-first century, who leads the way in redefining the way corporations are managed such that they are resilient, aware, and dynamic? Such that they create value for customers and treat employees with the respect they deserve? Whoever understands that this is the way shareholders also benefit over the long term understands what is meant by a RAD company that has the attributes to endure.

PART III

THE BITTER PILL
OPPORTUNITY AND TRANSFORMATION AHEAD

"What about business—which branch is that?"

Illustration courtesy of CartoonStock.com

Chapter 9

TOWARD A MORE RESILIENT ECONOMIC SYSTEM

D r. Seuss's Sylvester McMonkey McBean was the ultimate capitalist. The "fix-it-up chappie" sold star tattoos to Sneetches who felt they needed one because they were ostracized by the elitist, star-bellied Sneetches. More expensive was the star *removal* service, which he sold to the elitist Sneetches. They no longer wished to have stars like those ungrateful, peasant, noob, star-adorned Sneetches. Pure genius.

From what I hear, McBean was about to launch a star-on/star-off monthly subscription service, when the business collapsed after the Sneetches could no longer tell who was who. Though some say McBean is behind Twitter's blue check-mark scheme.

Regardless of whether you're a zero-sum-gain type of person (dog eat dog, art of war, greed is good) or a kumbaya sort (capitalism is evil, but please buy my T-shirt; the greater good comes first), these are immutable facts:

1. We all live on the same planet.
2. In Western-style democracies, capitalism is the chosen economic system.

3. In these democracies, most citizens can vote for congressional representation in government, and each vote carries an equal weight in the election.
4. Those representatives establish the laws capitalist entities must abide by.

Now, to be straight, the forces imperiling facts 1, 3, and 4 are many times more extreme than the forces against 2. Despite all the "socialism" rhetoric on TV, fact 2 is not under any significant threat at all. Even in "socialist" Europe, the trend is toward de-nationalizing businesses, not nationalizing them. There's little to no serious effort at all to nationalize businesses in the United States.

We—of all political stripes in the U.S.—tend to rush to the Constitution to validate our biases. The various interpretations of which justices are activists, originalists, founder channelers, and so on resemble the McBean circus. I mean, good luck knowing what's upside right. The Constitution is law, and like all law, it is a *model*, in this case overlaying ideals. The ideals are articulated in the Declaration of Independence.

The Declaration is not endlessly interpreted because (1) the ideals are clearly stated generally, and (2) it's not law. The Constitution is based upon philosophies of the Enlightenment, ideals reflected in the Declaration, common law of the era, and the clear recognition that society would continue to evolve. It's nonsensical to believe that those who were actively participating in a real, shooting-war revolution would somehow view a model of law as being sacrosanct to one particular moment in time. The Constitution was ratified in 1789. It remained unchanged for only two and a half years.

If you would like to argue the law, I recommend Reddit—I hear they have lively debates. If you would like to consider the ideals, I suggest you read it: "We hold these truths to be self-evident, that all men are created equal, that they are endowed by their Creator with certain unalienable Rights, that among these are Life, Liberty and the pursuit of Happiness." In a very real sense, the Constitution is a model meant to capture the spirit of the Declaration.

Fundamentally, we are all responsible for defining and pursuing our own happiness. I have a problem with the word "happiness," to be honest, but that's just my take. Happiness exists only as the other side of a coin. My hope is that I am content; that happiness and sadness, good and bad, are balanced in a way that represents the ups and downs, joys and sorrows, of life. Ideally, I don't seek happiness; hopefully, it is a normal part of the contented life I do seek.

But we also are equally responsible for not stopping others from seeking theirs. Why? Two reasons: First, that's what the Declaration says—all people have the unalienable *right* to the pursuit of happiness; second, allowing others to pursue their happiness does not adversely affect my own pursuit. Unless, I suppose, they're happy when I suffer, and that schadenfreude is a freedom they seek to enjoy. No offense taken.

The system I have laid out in the preceding pages suggests these ten laws of a capitalist economic system:

1. Companies belong to an ecosystem, other entities of which may have interests that run counter to their own.
2. Society benefits from capitalism based on free and open competition, and it is the obligation of government to increase free market qualities such as open information, competition, and free movement.
3. Companies have the right to pursue their own interests within the system.
4. Companies should focus on increasing value to all stakeholders as defined by their legally established missions.

5. Companies must adhere to law and social norms, including labor and consumer rights laws.

6. Companies must disengage from interfering with the legal rights bestowed upon *citizens* (not "persons") to establish law through legislative representation.

7. Companies must disengage from lobbying against regulatory changes established by law through citizens' elected representatives.

8. Companies shall benefit from government acting as customer, innovation funding, and other grants as established by citizens' representatives.

9. Companies shall be subject to limitations on intellectual property rights where they are funded by government.

10. Companies shall not be responsible for benefits to workers, other than those established by law, such as minimum wage.

It may, of course, be necessary to establish a similar set of rules for consumers and workers. In the agricultural society dominant in Adam Smith's time, the sheer quantity of suppliers of particular agricultural commodities drove farmers' effective profits to zero. In such a situation a government might (and did) provide subsidies to the producers due to the inequities of the given power dynamics. Such relationships become more complicated, given international exchange, where other governments might tip the scale due to the particular situations in their own countries. But suffice to say, governments should freely manage the power balances in economic systems.

In the previous chapters we worked to reimagine how companies could operate in resilient, aware, and dynamic ways to become capable of weathering the disruptive storms of an uncertain world. But we can also reimagine what societal institutions might look like.

Undeniably, we lead lives *outside* of work, and we can make this arena of life more disruption proof, too. We can change, protect, and enhance our world outside of business by making our economic, political, and social institutions RAD in the manner we did with business. Rethinking how we enact laws and balance economic powers to benefit a broader populace matters greatly in battling daunting inequality. As we know, disruption happens whether we like it or not, and therefore requires deliberate action on all fronts.

With this in mind, the heavy lifting required to build RAD companies and scale the Five Elements through implementation of the KASE phases is behind us. Let us turn to thinking more broadly about the disruption-proofing of other entities and systems across society, as disruptive waves come at us unabated. Think of the tragic winter storms of 2021, which left dozens of people dead and millions without power or heat for days on end in Texas and other states.[xcii] The lack of infrastructure to make the Texas grid more resilient was a purposeful financial decision. In other words, it is another example of what happens when leadership focuses on system efficiency only with financial metrics, rather than centering the *purpose* of the system.[xciii] We need RAD here, too.

Up to this point, my ambition has been to convince you that refocusing on creating value for customers is a more efficient way to conduct business than focusing on creating value for Wall Street. The former does the latter, while, ironically, the latter decreases the long-term value of the company. I say "ironically," because those who adopted the Milton Friedman Doctrine that company managers should focus on value for shareholders created a system that does the opposite.

My second ambition has been to convince you that you must do this work, that the digital revolution means that what you thought was optimizing efficiency was actually cutting into muscle you need to operate in a new disruptive, complex world. Indeed, the very structure of twentieth-century companies, organized as large, extended assembly lines, optimized systems in the Frederick Taylor mode of "scientific management," leaves companies vulnerable to disruption. They are unresponsive to market needs, unable to adapt to changes, and too slow to compete in an increasingly disruptive era.

Finally, my third ambition has been to provide you with ideas on how to manage the reemergence of value creation, beyond "innovation" or "digital transformation" sloganeering. Namely, that you have the people and skills within your company to reinvent your business from the inside out, and that you must start from the ground up. The top-down-only approach assures a slow, disheartening grind toward dinosaur-worthy obsolescence, at best.

I have also attempted to make the case that a business is not an empty shell of possibilities, the officers of which steer in any direction they wish in order to find profits. All businesses have a mission. The officers are responsible for creating profits in service to the mission, which is typically defined by the products or services offered to specific customers in specific markets. Customers, employees, and shareholders have real, trusted relationships with the mission through the business.

The distinction is important, since, for example, if one doesn't create a redundant supply chain because that is an overhead cost that reduces returns to shareholders, you have perhaps become more efficient in a pure financial sense in the short term. If in service to your mission, however, a redundant supply chain means you are no more or no less efficient as long as there are no disruptions. But you are massively more efficient when there is a disruption to the primary supply chain. Therefore, spending now on the redundant supply chain is the only way to be efficient to all stakeholders, including shareholders in the long term. It makes the company more resilient.

In the end, these are all microlevel decisions in that they have to do with individual companies and how their leaders choose to act within their ecosystems. But there's a macro view as well, and that is what I turn to now.

FROM MICRO TO MACRO DISRUPTION

Most entrepreneurs and business leaders I know believe in capitalism for more than just their "micro" concerns. In other words, the promise of capitalism resides in its potential benefits to society, in addition to its potential to make one wealthy. The United States serves as a beacon of hope for many, not only for the promise of being rewarded for hard work or for the right to openly criticize the government, but also, for many, to exercise their entrepreneurial spirit. The desire to launch a business is as prevalent as the desire to enjoy the proverbial white picket fence.

We've already discussed how we are presently doing as a country: declining number of small businesses, declining real wages, declining life expectancy, increased economic disparity, infant mortality rate significantly worse in the United States than in other developed countries. The literature is pretty clear why: less power for workers, increased corporate consolidation, less enforcement of regulations, less antitrust, less government investment in the future, and so on.

Reversing this trend cannot start without fixing corporations themselves. For half a century, many large companies have focused on growth through acquisition, anticompetitive behavior, thwarting laws and regulations, while lowering product quality, outsourcing their ability to build, and squashing the spirit of their employees.

Now in the face of the digital revolution, confronting extreme uncertainty, these companies don't know how to perform. Company officers can only do the same things they've always done. That's where we are. The natural tendency in the face of crisis, or chaos, or extreme uncertainty is to grasp for more control. Surely, if we try harder, what worked yesterday will work again tomorrow. Until it doesn't.

I have laid out a path to fixing the companies. It's just a path, however. Digesting the principles, making them your own, and getting the long, difficult work done still lies ahead. But here's the deal: It will work *only* if the economic system maintains some degree of equilibrium. This is the macro perspective.

The classic way to measure the balance in an economic system is capital versus labor. But this is an academic approach that obfuscates what's really going on in the world it's supposed to represent. Economic models based solely on math do not reflect the real world. Math is, of course, foundational to most economic models and that's fine. But using complex math to prove economic theories that in the end don't reflect reality merely creates a language for elites. It purposefully moves discourse from its human impact to whether the math equations and their myriad assumptions are correct.

Instead, we should look at the economic system as opposing forces with its human actors defined by business owners, workers, and consumers. All the human beings in this equation have a voice in government, which ultimately is the body that determines what an economic system in equilibrium looks like. Is full employment really the goal? Or is it maintaining the present value of capital owned by 0.1 percent of the population? Is it keeping interest rates low? Is it keeping inflation low?

As opposed to the stagflation of the 1970s that showed high inflation and sky-high interest rates, the second decade of the twenty-first century shows very little inflation, some deflation, and historically low interest rates. The U.S. government, in practice not particularly representative of the people, generally seems satisfied with that result, despite the painful number of people who can't find work and those who give up looking.

In 2020, at the height of the COVID-19 pandemic, NYU professor of marketing and best-selling author Scott Galloway captured this reality impeccably by stating, in the Dickensian sense, "We are barreling towards a nation with 3 million lords being served by 350 million serfs.... This is the best of times and the worst of times. We've decided to protect corporations, not people. Capitalism is literally collapsing on itself unless it rebuilds that pillar of empathy."[xciv]

While many things systemically improve through companies refocusing on creating value for customers and treating employees well in support of that objective, the economic system stays in equilibrium only when the opposing forces are balanced. To get there, we must increase the power of workers and consumers, and thereby decrease relative corporate power in the system. Let me explain.

A decrease in power does not diminish the ability of corporations to create value for their stakeholders, but rather *increases* it. This is the tough part to swallow, perhaps, but corporations owning the government hurts businesses, in the macro perspective. A balanced system forces businesses to compete on value rather than on "efficiency."

Acquiring companies for the sake of demonstrating revenue to Wall Street, finding new ways to cut costs, and squeezing productivity out of workers do nothing by themselves to ensure the business is operating optimally for accomplishing its mission. These are tactics used by those who don't know how to find new revenue streams. They are last resorts. Ultimately, they will not stave off failure in the digital age.

The remedy is to unhinge corporations from the government.

On Money in Government

According to an estimate from the Center for Responsive Politics, the amount of money spent on the 2020 elections in the United

States reached an astonishing level: $14 billion.[xcv] While reasonable arguments can be made in favor of groups of citizens—for example, businesses, nonprofits, or unions—having a First Amendment right to freedom of speech, the amount of money in politics continues to grow out of control and is destructive to the principles of representative democracy.

In the little beach town of Encinitas, California, recent city council and mayoral elections were heavily influenced by negative, often deceptive advertisements created by political action committees (PACs). The ads came from both sides, while both candidates insisted they had no connections to the PACs. They were literally outside agitators that drowned out the voices of the candidates themselves. Much like the worthlessness of economic models that never reflect reality, third parties that effectively silence the communications between actual candidates and confused voters are so obviously far from the intention of the country's founders that legal remedies must exist. Greater accountability, capping of spending, and better transparency are good places to start.

Let's look at the facts:

Society provides the right and the conditions within which individuals may start a business. Society also provides the right and the conditions within which businesses can seek investment from shareholders—in other words, go public. (These are still private companies versus public entities owned "by the people" through government.)

Laws—including the laws mentioned above, but also those that regulate business behavior—are created by congressional representatives.

Corporations and other entities composed of people, like nonprofits, churches, and unions, have specific rights recognized through court interpretations of the U.S. Constitution. It was only in 1978 that the Supreme Court first recognized that corporations have First Amendment rights.[xcvi]

It appears to me rather obvious that an incorporation of persons has some but not all constitutional rights. The Constitution, unfortunately, does not distinguish which rights of formal assemblies of real human beings versus those of individuals ought not be infringed. Thus far, companies as persons can neither run for office nor vote. Therefore, in my view, it's reasonable to conclude that corporations do not have a voice in the creation or enforcement of law, but citizens do.

This is the other side of the "social responsibility" coin. If, because corporations have heterogeneous shareholders, a heterogeneous customer base, and a heterogenous base of employees, such that they cannot be viewed as an assembly of people *organized around a specific set of social responsibilities*, then they should stay out of the structure that is responsible.

Household-brand-name companies contribute money, of course, across the political spectrum. But the radical ways the money is spent can cause deleterious effects to democracy.[xcvii]

Is, for example, the attempted disruption of the business of Congress an acceptable use of corporate-contributed money? In the wake of the early 2021 insurrection, many companies answered no, suspending their contributions to politicians and political party entities, only to resume them later. The issue, however, is larger than specific actions in response to specific events.

The startup Coinbase made a lot of noise on Twitter congratulating themselves on their "mission"-oriented culture. To the cheering of the venture capital class, they explained that didn't mean backing specific social concerns, such as Black Lives Matter. They would only act politically if it benefited the company's mission. This is an impossible and inauthentic distinction. If they were to give money to a politician who favored cryptocurrency deregulation, but also happened to be a flaming racist, they couldn't then declare they were funding only the deregulation portion of that politician.

Allowing parts of a company to act outside its values demonstrates poor accountability measures and a lack of leadership, and it's also quite reasonable for society to determine that such behavior violates the tenets of its contract with the business. For fifty years, the business world has openly declared they do not have responsibilities to fix social issues. It's a reasonable declaration. But it is equally reasonable for society to demand that business does not openly contribute to causing or bolstering social problems.

Significant legislative or court amelioration can and should reduce the impact corporations have on elections and legislation. We must ACT in new ways: Accountability, Checks, and Transparency.

First, let's build in some transparency. The digital revolution means that information on congressional and corporate behavior is— or could be—at our fingertips. In 2020, the stock exchange Nasdaq proposed to the U.S. Securities and Exchange Commission (SEC) that all companies listed on Nasdaq's U.S. exchange be required to disclose diversity statistics regarding their board of directors.[xcviii] Similarly, organizations like the Sustainability Accounting Standards Board (SASB) and B Lab create corporate reporting standards in order to enable investors to make informed investing decisions that include companies' sustainability efforts and performance. A system such as this should be mandated by the SEC. The certification processes are already in place, and many businesses already use them.

Requiring public transparency, including how companies are contributing to political campaigns and lobbying efforts, is a reasonable condition of incorporation or exchange listing. Such measures arguably have more potential for long-term value creation than sending money to the Republican or Democratic state leadership committees, no matter what favors that might curry. Investors have the right to know and society has the right to demand the disclosures.

The unchecked power of money in politics is actually a fairly recent phenomenon, overcoming two hundred years of precedent in the last forty years or so. The Brennan Center for Justice has several legislative recommendations to reinvigorate the checks on political money. These include:

- Disclosure of tax returns for members of Congress and the president
- Pass the DISCLOSE Act to increase contribution transparency
- Increase public funding of elections
- Bolster Federal Election Commission enforcement
- Work to limit corporations' contributions to elections

With or without help from the government and the business community (though obviously better with the help), citizens can hold businesses more accountable. The best way is to engage with organizations that represent your beliefs. Citizen boycotts of brands that do not adhere to social norms have become a powerful tool for raising awareness and ultimately effecting change, as have efforts by environmental nonprofits and shareholder groups. Examples of successful boycotts include those against giant organizations like Amazon (tax avoidance and treatment of workers), BP (Deepwater Horizon oil spill), and the NRA (Stoneman Douglas High School shooting). And when civil rights organizations NAACP and ADL banded together for the "Stop Hate for Profit" campaign in 2020, one thousand businesses joined them, including the likes of Unilever, Patagonia, Verizon, and Ben & Jerry's, to boycott Facebook for its "repeated failure to meaningfully address the vast proliferation of hate on its platforms."[xcix, c]

The proliferation of internet-based political action tools and mobile apps has provided access to information, as well as a means of taking action. None seem to have cracked the code for consistent results from their advocacy. But with better data from companies and government, and perhaps more startup gusto, they will be able to drive great impact. The bottom line is that the first step is greater transparency. The second is empowering people to make better purchasing, investment, and funding easier, based on the new information. The third is getting people to actually take those actions.

It's a market-based approach to holding companies accountable.

Enforce Antitrust

In my university comparative economics class taught by my thick-accented professor, the assigned textbook, *Comparative Economic Systems* (1980), by Paul R. Gregory and Robert C. Stuart, had this to say about antitrust in the United States: "In various rulings, the courts have decided that mergers involving combined market shares of 20 percent and even lower constitute an undue lessening of competition.... In the United States, the burden of proof lies with the merging firms, and if significant market shares are involved, the merger will be declared illegal *per se*."[ci]

I mean, this is almost quaint. An entire generation has since graduated college and entered the business world with the assumption that all mergers are fine, and that the burden is on the government to show why rolling up an entire industry into one giant monopoly so Warren Buffett might be interested in investing is not the most ingenious idea since paper bitcoin.

Gregory and Stuart add, "It is difficult to establish the effect of anti-merger legislation on the market structure of the American economy."[cii] With a good twenty-plus years of pro-merger legislation, I think we have our answer.

It is so ludicrously one-sided now that private equity firms buy up local dentist offices in order to create a monopoly and they don't even appear on the FTC or DOJ radars. Free market capitalism has devolved from the Adam Smith–ian version recognizing the significance of competition, where mathematical models demonstrated "perfect markets" as having perfectly free information and unlimited competition, to a magical belief in "economies of scale" for all things and no government regulation.

Incredibly, the three major federal antitrust laws—the Sherman Antitrust Act (1890), the Clayton Act (1914), and the Federal Trade Commission Act (1914)—have remained wholly intact for more than one hundred years. It is, instead, the courts, the Federal Trade Commission, and the Department of Justice, the bodies responsible for interpreting and enforcing the laws, that have changed their interpretations and enforcement guidelines.

Their guiding principle, which was historically defined by market share distribution, has been dumbed down to "consumer welfare" as represented by consumer prices. Effects on small businesses are not important. Quality of customer service doesn't matter. Innovation and the quality, value, durability, and efficacy of products are all immaterial. Is it cheaper? Good to go. It's a race to the bottom and we're winning.

The 2020s will perhaps be seen as the period the tides turned with several blockbuster antitrust cases announced, including those against Google and Facebook. The "big is better" mentality, however, is deeply ingrained in corporations, government, academia, and the punditocracy. "Economies of scale" is a conventional-wisdom mantra that will not die. Yet it is so glaringly untrue in much of business, especially in the digital age, if one cares to look beyond the slogan.

Or have fun with this koan: Big business is best and big government is awful, so be like big business.

The primary goal of government regulation should be to increase competition. This is a system-level action that allows the market to produce a variety of desirable outcomes. It is fundamentally arbitrary to say, "The current regulatory environment has allowed the market to determine that a functional market is not truly required. Therefore, we shall no longer enjoy the benefits of a functioning market." It is more reasonable to say, "The current regulatory environment should be modified such that we maximize the benefits of a functioning market, while allowing for profits and fair wages."

While many wonder what Big Tech looks like broken up, it's actually not hard to imagine. They would likely be separated into naturally occurring business units that would have to compete with other market players based on creating value. They would be very well poised to compete and succeed—in other words, they would not be crippled, but rather have their anticompetitive advantages structurally removed. They likely would be good investments.

As a matter of fact, neolibertarians don't argue against breakups because of the outcome—they couldn't care less. They argue that the monopolies deserve their status. In other words, the means justify the ends, no matter the anti–free market result.

The FTC and DOJ have been so absent that businesses themselves have become productized. Completely untethered to the value they create or the communities they serve, small and medium-sized businesses are being rolled up into monopoly portfolios by private equity profiteers. It's really hard to call this anything other than anticapitalist, since the sole nature is to create local monopolies and flip equity shares of the holding company. This should be flat-out illegal.

Power to the Workers

The path to a stable economic system relies heavily upon the concept of "freedom of contract." This is a doctrine that reaches back to the Fourteenth Amendment of the U.S. Constitution, which says individuals can freely enter into contracts if they so desire, including employment contracts. What's interesting about this fairly obvious idea is whether or not it's necessary for the balance of power between parties to be equal for the parties to actually be "free" to enter the contract.

In the early 1900s, courts ruled that labor laws violated "freedom of contract." Amusingly, the justification for striking down laws that protected workers is that workers should be free to choose to not be protected. The presumption was that the employer and employee were equally free to accept or deny the contract. In reality, of course, since there are more workers than jobs, especially at different levels of skill, the employer has the power to choose which employee to hire. The employee is choosing whether or not to eat. The New Deal era largely rejected the notion, which gave rise to major pro-labor legislation, including the right to organize.

Fast-forward to the late twentieth century and early twenty-first century: The laws have not significantly changed, but as with anti-trust enforcement, the courts and agencies responsible for holding employers accountable to the law have eroded to pre–New Deal status. University of Michigan Law School professor Samuel Bagen-stos writes:

> The judicial trend toward ignoring imbalances of bargaining power has accelerated in recent years, with the Supreme Court under Chief Justice John Roberts issuing a series of anti-worker decisions. The timing is ironic, because these judicial develop-ments have occurred while evidence of weak worker bargaining power is accumulating. Working people's wages have stagnated, labor's share of national income has dropped, and inequality has risen.[ciii]

It's easy to fall into the trap of taking a principle out of context; I mean welcome to Economics 101. In perfect competition, it perhaps makes sense that the employer and employee have equal power in entering a contract together. Like the Adam Smith–era agricultural example mentioned earlier in this chapter, in a perfect competition mathematical model where number of jobs equals number of workers, the power is equal. But this is obviously not true in the real world. Within the law and social norms, a principle that doesn't reflect reality should not trump the real world. People move very quickly between ends justifying means and means justifying ends depending on the personal biases brought into the equation.

From a policy perspective, there are a number of positions that directly impact the power dynamic of workers. Minimum wage is the most obvious. Not including the economic turmoil of 2020 caused by the pandemic, in 2018 the "real average wage (that is, the wage after accounting for inflation) has about the same purchasing power it did 40 years ago. And what wage gains there have been have mostly flowed to the highest-paid tier of workers."[civ]

Incredibly, the U.S. federal minimum wage has not changed since 2009.

That large corporations pay full-time employees below the poverty line makes no sense and, to be frank, is clearly unethical. Forcing people into multiple jobs or receiving government aid in order to survive is not beneficial to either businesses or society. Again, returning to the Friedman Doctrine, relying on the government to fill the gap between wages and living is participating in the social-responsibility sphere, only to the business's financial benefit.

It is worth saying, given the corporate positions I am advocating for, I do not believe that businesses should be responsible for health care or retirement benefits for employees, either. The exchange is that the government should be responsible for those and businesses should not stand in the way of the government implementing them, if that's what citizens demand.

A job guarantee is another idea whose time has come. It's difficult to argue that the right to earn a living isn't a foundation for the right to life, liberty, and the pursuit of happiness. How it's implemented matters, of course. There's no shortage of work to be done, but the government should generally not compete against private industry. The potentially catastrophic needs for infrastructure work, for example, might be conducted by private companies hired by the government as opposed to expanding the federal payroll.

Modern Monetary Theory, popularized by Stony Brook economics professor Stephanie Kelton, describes one way the system might work. The program would act as an automatic stabilizer to the economy, as opposed to suffering the lags from government-led policy changes, assuming those policies ever get passed by Congress and actually work:

"Instead of leaving millions jobless, the government would establish an open-ended commitment to provide job seekers with access to the currency in exchange for performing public service work."[cv]

Critics immediately point to the theoretical—that is, non-evidence-based—inflation fears. But they also ignore the high costs of real unemployment and underemployment, which include the direct costs of welfare, food stamps, and unemployment insurance, but also costs incurred due to crime, health problems, substance abuse, homelessness, and domestic turmoil, and even "soft costs" like quality of life, missed human creativity and ingenuity, and political unrest.

Other examples of power imbalances that should be addressed include forced arbitration clauses for workers, as well as overly expansive nondisclosure agreements. The terms in such contracts come about only due to the imbalance of power. It should not be legal for businesses to force employees to give up fundamental human rights.

At-will employment law hurts worker power. "The reason why [eliminating at-will employment] is so important," says senior economist Dean Baker, "is it gives employees much more security. But also, if a worker knows that the boss can't just fire them because they don't like them or they criticize them, then it means they're more willing to speak up in the workplace."[cvi] Unlike most of the developed world, the United States allows companies to lay off workers without cause and without severance. (Wisconsin is a notable exception.)

Better yet, rather than focusing only on the outcome of an unbalanced power equation, we should change the power dynamics so that terms can be negotiated from more equal positions. Increasing the ability of people to be more responsible for their personal economy is freedom inducing, increases their negotiating power, and is fundamental to free market capitalism.

Instead of debating whether a worker is legitimately classified as an employee or a contractor, for example, we should simply pass many rights to all workers and be done with it. Increasing minimum wage and a job guarantee also increases systemic power to workers. The output of the economic system after rebalancing from this power shift will better achieve the desired outcome most people strive for: more employment, a stronger middle class, a raised standard of living, and safer communities.

Increase Power of Consumers

The fluctuation of consumer power follows much of the discussion in the "Power to the Workers" section, though its heyday perhaps started a bit sooner, pre–New Deal, and lasted a bit longer, until the late 1970s. In a growing industrial economy where businesses reach massive scale, sucking up resources, spitting out waste, and interacting with millions of customers, negative consequences also act on a massive scale. Food and medical product safety is life and death. Pollution of resources "owned" by the people affects quality of life, and also can be a matter of life and death. Clearly, regulation concerning these is not only vital but is a fundamental right of the citizens of democracies.

As efficiency for efficiency's sake reigned supreme in the latter stages of the twentieth century, society-protecting regulations came under increasing attack. The argument that U.S. businesses could not be globally competitive because of regulation is hard to believe, but even if true, so what? The United States became the wealthiest country in the world because of successful innovation and commercialization, often funded by the government and despite the laws of capitalism that were in place. The same rules apply today. Regulations spur innovation. This is a simple, factual statement. Forcing businesses to innovate and compete on value, based on the rules society creates to protect fundamental rights, is the game. The winners of capitalism should not be those that succeed by overcoming or ignoring society's rules, but those that succeed notwithstanding them. If you are not able to succeed in a fair and balanced system, you are not really a success.

The digital revolution brings increased power to consumers through social media, access to company information, ability to invest, and increased access to congressional representatives. Groups of consumers are loud and have had success changing company policies through protest and active campaigning. But fundamentally, again, a wall needs to be constructed between business and government, such that businesses cannot bypass or change regulations that the people have implemented through their government.

The most concerning practices in the digital age are the inadequate protection of privacy, the monitoring and manipulation of behavior, unethical practices that exploit human vulnerabilities, and click-through agreements where opting in to give up rights is the default behavior.

Where the small print and legalese obfuscate disclosures, and where opting out means inability to use a product, the balance of power is out of whack. In many cases, similar to the employer-employee relationship, the power is out of balance such that consumers don't really have a choice to opt out. Consumers are forced into accepting arbitration clauses, which waives their right to go to court if they have grievances. If you don't like it, no internet. Or no phone service. Or no health care.

Neolibertarians have long argued that government shouldn't regulate business because if they err, the market will correct. But what happens when those businesses eliminate the ability for the market to correct? Again, that's not capitalism, that's organized crime.

A STEWARD OF THE PLANET

Extraordinarily, in 2004, the Pentagon made bold predictions on the nature of climate change. The gist was that political structure or religious beliefs would be less contentious than the very struggle for survival due to the need for fundamental resources.[cvii] The predictions have not come true. Yet. They warned:

- By 2007, violent storms smash coastal barriers, rendering large parts of the Netherlands uninhabitable.
- Climate in Britain becomes colder and drier as weather patterns begin to resemble Siberia.
- Access to water becomes a major battleground. The Nile, Danube, and Amazon are all mentioned as being high-risk.
- By 2010, the United States and Europe experience one-third more days with peak temperatures above 90°F. Climate becomes an "economic nuisance" as storms, droughts, and hot spells create havoc for farmers.

While none of these have materialized within the dates foretold, the trends are certainly apparent. Just one example among hundreds:

Shifting temperature patterns across the globe fueled several dangerous summer heat waves that broke records in Europe and the US. Another heat wave rolled all the way up from the Sahara to Greenland, where the high temperatures threatened the world's second-largest ice sheet.[cviii]

Exxon and other oil companies apparently knew long ago about the very real nature of climate change[cix]—I mean, duh, they are a science company. It's interesting that two very old-school, command-and-control organizations, the military and a substantial global fossil fuels company, allow antiscience to proliferate among the citizens, while knowing it to be false. Is it participating in social responsibility to purposefully make citizens less informed?

Like telcos squeezing the last dime out of miserably slow DSL modems in the 2000s despite the proliferation of overpriced high-speed communications technology sold to businesses, many corporations seek to extend the life of old products explicitly in lieu of "innovation." Corporate power consolidation causes this.

The true test of whether corporations are maximizing value for stakeholders over the long haul or the short haul can be seen in their response to climate change. By definition the future circumstances of humans on Earth—their ability to work, buy, *pursue happiness*—are directly linked to the climate. While solving climate change is clearly outside the scope of most businesses' mission, minimizing damage is the very least they can do, which links directly to the long-term value of the company.

The economic system can help companies do this by incentivizing desired behavior. The U.S. Department of Energy doles out $100 million per year, which often is tied to innovation to help reverse climate change. (See the 3M case study in Chapter 8.) Further, the SEC could mandate public companies share sustainability metrics, along with their financial metrics. That isn't a requirement that corporations change their behavior, but rather provides incentive to do so, since investors may make choices based upon those disclosures. This is a free market–based solution, since it simply increases information flow, allowing consumers and investors to make more informed decisions.

TAKE BETTER CARE OF PEOPLE

Society and the economy are complex because humans are complex. Humans are complex because all of nature is complex and humans are nothing if not part of nature. Human beings need a balance—an equilibrium—within their own system. How the system looks when opposing forces are in balance represents the state of their *pursuing happiness*. The basic forces might be summarized as:

- Wellness, including health, food security, shelter, and safety
- Social relationships, such as family and friends
- Contributions—in other words, the daily work performed regardless of whether it's for a business or for pay

Is there any reason we don't attempt to create a balanced economic system that creates an opportunity for a balanced human system?

Raj Raghunathan, professor of marketing at the McCombs School of Business, studies the pursuit of happiness. While many companies focus on measuring employee engagement, they really only measure whether employees show up. Employees' reaction to engagement questions, says Raghunathan, "makes them feel like a cog in the wheel, reasoning: 'They want me to be more engaged so then I can be more profitable to them.' But if you are truly interested in their happiness at a personal level, then they feel that you're treating them as human beings."[cx]

Raghunathan talks about the importance of "reflective" happiness, which has to do with "meaning and fulfillment" versus feeling happy in the moment. "I'm doing something that's contributing to the universe" versus "having fun or laughing in the cafeteria." Both of those are important, but organizations tend to measure the latter meaning in their employee surveys. "What we find is that reflective happiness is what contributes to employee productivity and also to long-term profits."

A RAD organization, with agile teams practicing the Five Elements of disruption, contributes to reflective happiness. For all the clichéd talk about millennials wanting to live a more experiential life versus a transactional one, welcome to the human race. I think people have it backward. Human beings are natural problem solvers and naturally wish to live meaningful lives that contribute to things larger than themselves. Millennials didn't invent this, though they are the first, perhaps, to have lived in a world where they exist in such numbers as to be so visible.

A RAD organization is the primary work corporations can do in contribution to a balanced human system. As discussed, government by the people has its role to play as well. Putting aside for a moment "how we pay for it" in support of this idea of a balanced economic system and a balanced human system, imagine:

- Employment guarantee
- Livable wage
- Health care and retirement funding

As Stephanie Kelton points out, a federal job guarantee instantly makes the economic system more stable, since employment and thereby economic spending are kept stable. Additionally, the system includes "on-the-job training and skill development; poverty alleviation; community building and social networking; social, political, and economic stability; and social multipliers (positive feedback loops and reinforcing dynamics that create a virtuous cycle of socioeconomic benefits)."[cxi] The latter includes more preventative health care, less crime and associated incarceration, less substance abuse, and arguably all the ills associated with loneliness and being disconnected from society.

Internationally, such a system propagated to other areas of the world hastens the growth of emerging countries, increases the well-being of trade partners, and ultimately, to be frank, reduces war.

Believe me, I am fully cognizant of the Pollyannaish nature of such arguments. It sounds too good to be true. But consider, American households held more than $98 trillion of wealth in 2018.[cxii] Real GDP (considering inflation) was more than $19 trillion in 2019. This is not a case of charity or redistribution or philanthropy; this is designing a market-based system that balances the power of the entities within the system, such that a more equitable distribution of the output is the result. It benefits all. It requires less "redistribution," fewer debates about the safety net, less tinkering with outcomes after the fact, since the changes occur on the front end, and the system does its thing.

The counterforce to this rebalancing is corporate consolidation and nonenforcement of regulations. Freedom of movement of workers and freedom of market knowledge choice among consumers raise significantly the power of those entities. These are the natural tendencies of the digital revolution. The argument about how to classify the so-called gig economy workers is the wrong frame. The future in a perfectly free market economy is one in which workers sell portions of their time to the highest bidder for whatever duration agreed upon for a specific outcome.

For free market enthusiasts, I'm not sure what the objection to such a system might be. The government currently creates markets, aligning forces to desired outcomes. The result has been massive wealth redistribution to the very wealthy. The lack of stability in the system means when disruption hits, the redistribution is accelerated.

Shifting this dynamic is by no means a losing proposition, however, for companies. It merely requires they compete on creating value for customers—in other words, on the very reason for their existence in the first place. Speaking of creating value for customers and rethinking the competitive arena entirely, one more unique area of disruption remains ahead in the next chapter.

Chapter 10

DISRUPTING CONFORMITY

I dig the concept of flow, popularized in academic and business circles by Hungarian-American psychologist Mihaly Csikszentmihalyi. To me, flow means high-performance action uninhibited by conscious thought. In music, it's being in a "groove." (Or at least it was called that during one decade.) It's the artistic part of craft. You have likely heard musicians or writers talk about their muse "flowing through them." In such circumstances, it's difficult for the individual to take credit for the work.

I've experienced it both in writing and music, although in neither would I consider my abilities to approach "art." When in the flow, time passes quickly, you accomplish a great deal, the work is of high quality, and later you can't really recall the details. It's like hitting boost mode on a video game. You can go for only so long, because it burns through your energy. I once turned a keynote talk into an improv, stand-up comedy routine, which I have never done before or since. For whatever reason, the audience loved it and I've never replicated it. I don't understand where it came from.

Big wave surfer Laird Hamilton defined flow for Steven Kotler, for his book *The Rise of Superman*:

When you're in that moment, there's no beginning and no end. It starts off where it left off. When you go to that place, there's no time, and there's definitely no thought. It's just pure. You are and it is and that's why we continually seek it out, and always search for it, and need it.[cxiii]

Surfers like Hamilton ride crazy-sized waves. I'd feel anxious just standing onshore. These waves are five times the size of the double overhead wave that rolled me, and exponentially more powerful; and his waves are often sucking up water from over shallow, jagged reefs. Most of us would not have the guts to do what extreme athletes do. We may like to imagine that their courage stems from extraordinary ego, bordering on narcissism, paired with a death wish. But sometimes a group of these death-defying radical athletes, participating in an individual, nonteam sport, join together to make it safer. For example, several big wave riders started the Big Wave Risk Assessment Group (BWRAG) to teach surfers how to help each other be more safe, how to save each other's lives. "All surfers share an obligation to look out for one another in the lineup," says big wave surfer Brian Keaulana.[cxiv] This sense of responsibility reflects the same stepping out from the micro into the macro I discuss in Chapter 9. It's an act for the betterment of all.

Surfers can marry their highly individual performance flow with an awareness of their broader, mutual responsibility. I'm pretty sure flow in the business world doesn't have quite the same death-defying rush. But flow does exist. McKinsey's study on the topic among business leaders (cited by Kotler) revealed pretty typical desired characteristics of such work: a clear understanding of objectives and having the right resources, collaborative teamwork, a significant challenge, meaningful work.[cxv] Sounds an awful lot like a well-focused agile team.

True flow requires a mixture of focus, intuition based on expertise, and an uncritical mind. Startup gurus and life coaches tell you to do what you're passionate about, but my advice is to be passionate about what you do. That direction brings focus to the less tolerable duties you still must do. Flow requires your mind be thoughtfully engaged in your work, but not in a critical, second-guessing sort of way. One can work through a problem incorrectly without second-guessing the methodology. A dead end can be part of the flow if it's simply allowed to pass by. In Zen, this is releasing the ego. A lemon tree doesn't always produce viable fruit, but it is always in "flow," never second-guessing a bad bud.

Chapters 4 through 8 were, in a sense, about creating an organization that flows. A RAD organization is "in the flow." It's not perfect by any stretch. Every company I've profiled in these pages fails at the Five Elements sometimes. But a RAD organization endures. I'm hopeful that the organization you are a part of is moving forward somewhere on its journey toward being resilient, aware, and dynamic, leveraging the behavior of the Five Elements, in service to a mission that seeks to create value for human beings.

But for now, I hope you will don a different hat for the remaining part of our time together. Please take off your capitalism-first, free market–or-die, innovate-or-bust, efficiency-is-sexy hat. I need you to wear a special hat, one that opens your mind, suspends the critical internal narrator who interrupts flow, and helps you see a better world. For just as I suggested in the previous chapter, the whole of society is undergoing continuous disruption. The educational system, entrepreneurs, and startup ecosystems feel the impact and are responding to it, too—many in novel and remarkable ways that exemplify the 5Es and stem from a deep desire to move the world forward.

We can embellish a bit the dystopian future "The Jetsons versus the Flintstones" we discussed in Chapter 2. The Jetsons protected the well-being of the Flintstones through philanthropy, until they didn't need to anymore. They digitally fabricated their society in the sky, roboticized the service industry until they no longer needed Flintstone labor. Or maybe the Jetsons transported themselves to another planet via the Amazon-Tesla Intergalactic Wormhole Hyperloop™ in search of new plebes to rescue with their wisdom and big hearts.

While change and disruption are inevitable, the outcome we create for people is by choice. It's interesting how new technology seems to benefit both dystopian and utopian alternative story lines. While some believe that the inherent evil nature of capitalism will hurl us down the dystopian path, their procapitalism counterparts ironically and unwittingly hurl us down the exact same path, believing that little to no controls will result in the most optimal outcome. They are both equally daft.

Such thinking quickly allows the outcome to feel as inevitable as the change. But we have an amazing amount of control over the outcome. We get to choose. Corporate leaders get to choose how to shape their companies for the twenty-first century, but we all get to choose how we shape the economy, government, and education, as well as philanthropy, startup ecosystems, Wall Street, labor unions, NGOs, and other institutions we work with and rely on to benefit society.

We need to change these institutions similarly to how corporations must be changed. Thankfully, people are already doing the work. Most are on a track, some faster than others, toward putting to rest twentieth-century conventional wisdom. They are disrupting conformity, and I want to share some of their stories.

MORE BUSINESS, PLEASE

As discussed previously, increasing competition is equal in importance to capitalism as building a wall between business and government. Indeed, I've argued that contrary to the narrative of market efficiency driven through corporate consolidation (in other words, eliminating competition), increasing competition should be the paramount role of government regulation.

To quickly recap, "business efficiency" has been defined narrowly—in fact, arbitrarily—to the benefit of the desired outcome of corporate consolidation. To wit:

- Lower consumer prices are more favorable than better product quality.
- Economies of scale in product manufacturing are more favorable than better customer service or more product differentiation or any other measure that might benefit consumers.
- Efficiency is for the sake of financials only, rather than in accomplishment of the business mission.

On the other hand, healthy competition obviates the need for regulatory micromanagement, since robust competition in itself results in:

- Increased power of workers and consumers
- Better worker wages and working conditions
- Improved corporate sustainability and social-responsibility actions
- Improved products
- Innovation
- Disrupting conformity

The last point, disrupting conformity, is a natural way for new ideas to be brought not only to markets but to business management. In the wake of the last fifty years of "big is best" mentality, we do a very poor job of supporting new businesses. While it would seem that there's nothing hipper under the sun than Silicon Valley–style tech startups, the number of small businesses has plummeted during the same time frame.

Victor Hwang, founder and CEO of Right to Start and the former vice president of entrepreneurship at the Kauffman Foundation, says data shows that "the number of people who spend at least fifteen hours a week on a new business has fallen by over half over the last forty-some years. We also know that the percentage of people employed by smaller firms is much lower than it used to be. It's fallen by roughly a quarter to a third."[cxvi]

While those entrepreneurs who seek to become scalable start-ups may have ecosystems of support that include university and government funding, advisors, mentors, and equity investors, the vast majority of emerging businesses and existing small businesses do not. Programs like the Small Business Administration (SBA) and Service Corps of Retired Executives (SCORE) are well-meaning and provide basic services to small businesses, but they tend to use old-school techniques and lack relevance to the technology, uncertainty, and complexity of the digital age.

Right to Start is an advocacy organization seeking to make the government more active in supporting emerging and small businesses. "We have a theme we call '5% to Start,'" Hwang says, "which proposes on the federal, state, and local levels, 5 percent of new government contracts should go towards entrepreneurs, 5 percent of workforce training should go towards people starting and growing their businesses, and 5 percent of economic development should go towards entrepreneurial development."

While not insignificant, it's tiny in comparison to the massive amounts of government time, money, and resources committed to existing big businesses in their "free market" fantasy. Hwang is attempting to disrupt conformity by providing a coordinated flow of entrepreneurship funds to ensure they're spent on entrepreneurial support.

"What happens with the funds today is like river water flowing down to where it gets dammed up. At the federal level, program people say, 'Go be prosperous and create new businesses.' The river flows to the state and local levels, where it's caught in local politics. They still basically put money into the way the workforce has been done for the last twenty, thirty years. There's virtually zero mention of entrepreneurship or startups in the region. That's what Right to Start really is: syncing up the local, the state, and the federal in support of new and small businesses. We're trying to create a common hymnal for entrepreneurial activism."

The private funding situation is even worse. The Kauffman Foundation found that 83 percent of entrepreneurs don't have access to venture capital or bank loans. Equity funding for most small businesses is inappropriate, while bank financing requires assets most entrepreneurs lack. Sixty-three percent rely on savings, while 10 percent run up credit card debt. Since banks are allowed to charge credit card fees most societies would deem usury, backed by bankruptcy laws that protect the banks, they have no incentive to offer different funding.[cxvii]

On the other hand, with interest rates at record lows and a stock market dominated by speculators, there are a few vehicles to serve the more conservative end of an investment portfolio. Seems like an opportunity.

Alternative funding models are emerging, particularly revenue-based financing (RBF). According to leading alternative financing investor Lighter Capital, RBF is a hybrid debt-and-equity model: structured like a loan, but with returns based on growth. Typically, this financing requires steady revenue, but not necessarily profitability. The best fit are companies that seek to scale but are either not ready for venture capital or perhaps are opposed to venture capital. The companies get to maintain their own growth plans, as opposed to receiving pressure to grow prematurely.

Lack of funding is often exacerbated by gender and race. Kauffman reports that "black entrepreneurs' loan requests are three times less likely to be approved than white entrepreneurs. This difference persists even after accounting for credit scores and the net worth of founders" and that "men were significantly more likely to secure funding than women when pitching the same business content."

The Kauffman Foundation is piloting a program to fund alternative funding experiments, called the Capital Access Lab. It provides money to firms testing new investment models—in other words, not traditional equity or lending models—particularly in support of underserved entrepreneurs. The idea is to create an infrastructure—an industry—for alternative funding models. They call the founders of these businesses "capital entrepreneurs."

One such entrepreneur is Kim Folsom, veteran tech executive and startup founder, and founder and CEO of Founders First Capital Partners. Founders First provides revenue-based investments, as well as a nonprofit accelerator program for underrepresented founders. She is spearheading a growth market.

According to American Express's prepandemic data, women-owned businesses represent 42 percent of all businesses. Further, "as of 2019, women of color account for 50% of all women-owned businesses. An estimated 6.4 million women of color-owned businesses employ nearly 2.4 million people and generate $422.5 billion in revenue." Unfortunately, the systemic financial disadvantages facing these businesses made them more vulnerable to disruption due to the COVID-19 pandemic.[cxviii]

It's management of the system that needs to change in order to get the desired outcome. While diversity in business and on boards has its own benefits, such as being able to create products for the markets that diversity represents, funding and revenue for diverse businesses has its own big impact. Folsom explains that as a business or government, "maybe you don't need to keep your 1 percent, or 2 percent, diversity numbers that you've had for forever. But if you have 5 percent of your business spend go to much more inclusive microbusinesses every year, those diverse-founder businesses will have 90 percent diverse work-forces. If you look at it from the view of the impact of communities, there is a huge multiplier effect."

The same sort of multiplier exists for funding. "In our model," Folsom says, "we provide investors with a one, two, three times return on investment by funding businesses that are service or manufacturing, and create twenty to fifty jobs in a community that is much more inclusive than what you would see by the low-diversity tech company that gets to be nine or ten times ROI."[cxix]

Once again, we all tend to focus our policy debates on looking at the edge where we can see the output of the system, and we try to change the output. We tweak at the margins, which requires massive change because the surface area of the edge is infinite. But if you instead tweak at the center by adjusting the inputs to make the system better, the positive outcomes are potentially massive.

Folsom puts it plainly: "To paraphrase Maya Angelou, I don't want to be the unicorn. I want to be the conduit that helps the thousands of diverse founders currently running their business as a side hustle or a solopreneur, to get them the financial and social capital to become a sustainable job creator." This is where the multiplier effect occurs.

FUNDING SOCIAL IMPACT

Alternatives to banking and equity funding support the new wave of social-impact companies. The last ten years have given rise to for-profit businesses committed to having positive social impact on the world, including startups, "benefit corporations," and "B Corporations." Benefit corporations are legal entities, just like LLCs or C corporations, who commit to maintaining their mission, which includes social responsibilities. The companies are protected from investors who might pressure them to stray from their commitments.

B Corporations can be structured as any company might be—a partnership, LLC, C corporation, and so on. They can be private or listed on a public stock exchange. The difference is that these B Corp companies, like Patagonia or San Diego's Classy, are certified to meet specific standards of social performance, transparency, and accountability to purpose-driven metrics. There are more than 3,500 certified B Corps worldwide, with tens of thousands more that measure their performance using the nonprofit B Lab's impact assessment tool.

Just as with many small businesses, there's a dearth of funding for businesses focused on making social change, even when they create significant and scalable social impact. Most of these businesses are, quite simply, ill-suited for equity investments. Equity investors are generally not interested in interest rate returns or dividends. They look for a liquidity even where their stock shares are sold at ten times or more than the price paid for them.

How, then, to scale these businesses?

Flikshop CEO Marcus Bullock took an unusual journey to a familiar place. "I was an entrepreneur from the time I was selling Blow Pops on the school bus when I was in elementary school. And then I grew to selling Snickers bars. And then later on, I saw the guys who lived in my neighborhood who were selling weed and selling crack. And I was like, 'Oh, snap, they got business.'"[cxx] Which led to incarceration.

Once outside again, Bullock built a successful construction business doing kitchen remodels. Counting the dollars, managing multiple jobs, learning how to build a little margin, a little bit of scale. Building on this success, he created a mobile app, called Flikshop, that delivers postcards from family members to incarcerated loved ones.

"My world changed, then the access changed," he says. "Access is a very interesting thing, because what it did was not only just give me the social capital to learn how to deliver the next-level business, but my vision continued to grow simply because of access. When I got into Techstars, I met these real people that had built, sold, and started again, multi-million-dollar corporations and billion-dollar companies. That gave me permission to dream so much bigger."

Still, scaling this is hard. Is there an acquisition or an IPO in the future that might attract equity investors? That's hard to imagine, unless it's one of the two private equity funds that each owns one of three dominant players in the price-gouging prison phone system.[cxxi] (These companies charge exorbitant rates for phone calls and provide kickbacks to the prisons.)

Corporate responsibility funding arms typically are silos within silos—they are certainly not connected strategically to their needs portfolios, as I outlined in Chapter 8. Foundations and wealthy family donor funds are not well-organized markets. In other words, because they are built around "doing good," they don't fund based on a market style of metrics. Those responsible for distributing funds would rather spend a lot of money on a few big, safe nonprofits than on smaller, growing, revenue-generating social-impact firms.

What's needed is an "impact of investment" dashboard. In other words, a way to promulgate the impact a business has via its work and illustrate how an increase in funding scales that impact. The numbers work for nonprofit or social-impact funders in the same way startup metrics work for startup investors. Data helps drive market decisions. Investors choose which businesses result in greater impact, as well as those that might return interest or dividends.

"I tell these people," Bullock says, "we'll build that dashboard for you! Empathy is not just inside of what we build at Flikshop, but it's also for the entrepreneurs, investors, and business people inside this structure [of incarceration] that's been designed to box people like me out, to not gaining the access point. Because there's no way in the world you can tell me all these amazing ideas aren't out there, or like they're a million miles away. I'm not a unicorn. I'm not an anomaly."

THEY SHOULD ALL BE LIFESTYLE BUSINESSES

While big businesses struggle to reinvent themselves, alternative business management practices can be found in the startup and small-business world. David Heinemeier Hansson and Jason Fried launched Basecamp (as 37 Signals) in 2004, a project management product that scratched their own itch as a web development firm. By 2020, more than 20 million people have worked on a project in Basecamp. One might think this is a pretty good Silicon Valley–style tech startup story. When did they IPO?

Basecamp is different. Their founders are different. Hansson shared with me his take on the Five Elements of disruption. Ethics come first. And by "ethics," Hansson makes clear he means "being willing to make decisions and choices that are in opposition to growth. Lots of companies say they have ethics, as long as they come free. Real ethics are forged in trade-offs and sacrifice. If you're not willing to sacrifice, those aren't ethics."[cxxii]

Basecamp ethics are based on empathy. Hansson and Fried canceled a new product launch in April 2020—forgoing new growth revenue they'd been working on for two years—after COVID-19 hit, not because they couldn't get the work done, but because it was unimportant compared to the needs of their employees. Empathy for colleagues is more important than a date on a calendar. Hansson, following the stories of impacted employees in other companies that lacked empathetic practices, says "in every single one of those cases, whatever the relationship the employees might have had with their company was gone in an instant."

Exploration is also part of Basecamp's DNA. When it's part of the core way of working, patience is essential. There's no sense of the false need to "go disrupt." The launch of their email platform Hey.com took years: "We wandered that exploration journey over seven years, trying three different product approaches that never saw the light of day, just experiments. After that long exploration, we also came to the conclusion that even though we originally had no interest in competing with Google's Gmail, in the end we decided to. The world changed. The market changed. Gmail isn't truly free."

Perhaps most important is Hansson and Fried's take on what equilibrium means to them. The startup world has long loved the mythology of "go big or go home." Where a business that doesn't seek to scale and go public is a "lifestyle" business, and somehow that's a derogatory term.

Hansson explains: "It's heresy to simply say, 'Do you know what? We have enough. We're big enough. We have enough products. We just want to work on those we have and make them the best they can be and serve our customers. We don't need more.' Somehow this is not even within the vocabulary of the American business experience. And I think that's a complete travesty." Basecamp even closed several of its successful products over the years, because growing to properly serve them was not what they wanted to become.

In April 2021, Fried and Hansson saw nearly one-third of their company leave after a change of internal policies, including at least three senior leaders. As an outsider, it's impossible for me to know all that happened at Basecamp. I also do not doubt the sincerity of the ethos Hansson shared with me in our conversation for this book. That being said, I feel it's safe to say that the way this episode transpired doesn't represent well the behavior described by the 5Es. At the very least, there was a significant lack of empathy for workers, and it's hard to see how the previously espoused values were adhered to as discussed. The belief that one can declare "no politics in the office" fundamentally misses the fact that one person's accepted belief is another person's political trigger. *It doesn't work.* Everything has political angles. More than anything, however, I think this episode demonstrates how hard navigating politics and business is, rather than exposing anyone's insincerity.

Moreover, equilibrium extends to the expectation that all employees are able to balance the different parts of their life that make them happy, fulfilled people. A lifestyle business is not one that arbitrarily carves up the day to balance the amount of time spent here or there, doing this or that. But rather one that gives people the space to define what their days look like in service to the business mission they're signed up to tackle and their own personal humanity.

THEY SHOULD ALL BE PAID $70,000—WAIT, WHAT?

In 2015, Dan Price, founder and CEO of Gravity Payments, dropped a bombshell on the world of capitalism when he announced he was taking a significant pay cut so that the minimum wage in his company could be raised to $70,000 per year. Famed, late firebrand personality Rush Limbaugh, who understood no limits to CEO salaries, ironically called the plan "pure, unadulterated socialism." As confused as Limbaugh was on economic systems, the results were not too shabby:

> Processing volume—a key metric used in the payments industry to measure growth—increased by more than 160 percent, and our client base grew by more than 75 percent. Our headcount increased by roughly 70 percent—from 120 to 200 employees— while our employee turnover dropped from an annual average of 40 to 60 percent to 15 to 30 percent.[cxxiii]

What sets Price apart from other business owners is not just the boldness of his action, and how he walks his talk, but his commitment to delegating decision-making; to empowering employees. Five years after the new minimum wage was put in place, the culture at Gravity was characterized by employee autonomy. "There's a lot of healthy skepticism of leadership, skepticism of power that's built into the organization now." Similar to Basecamp's Hansson, Price saw the pandemic as a stress test for the company values.

Early 2020 business planning at Gravity included fifty out of two hundred employees participating, and regular communication with the balance of the organization. "One of the most important parts of that planning session," Price says, "was thinking about the next financial crisis, despite being told by the experts that the 2008 Great Recession was our once-in-a-generation crisis."[cxxiv]

In late 2019, the economy was showing signs of weakness, and Gravity revenue was down 20 percent. Price feared the worst. He and COO Tammi Kroll were adamant about not reducing head count if at all possible, while also committed to not raising rates on their small-business customers, who were suffering in the same way Gravity was. "It hits at the very core," Dan says. "Do we actually care about our mission? Are we actually committed to it?

"We go into 2020 fully prepared for a 20 percent drop in small-business activity and fully expect that that's the worst it's going to get. We were witnessing in real time whether our mission was a core value or a communications strategy. March rolls around, and our processing volume is suddenly dropping 20 percent every couple of weeks. We were losing $1.5 million a month."

Ultimately, Price and Kroll decided to leverage the company culture to help navigate the tough times. Critics will call this socialism again, probably, while at the same time others will say it's democracy or crowdsourcing in an environment not conducive to that. Indeed, a few employees felt the same way—desiring autocracy in the time of crisis. But what Price and Kroll do is not democracy. It's empowering people to solve a problem. It's allowing people to choose how to sacrifice in service to the company's mission and values, which in good times provides them the ability to buy homes, grow their families, and live in healthy and contented ways.

Employees anonymously voted themselves pay cuts that prevented layoffs or gouging suffering customers. "We got this opportunity to come together in a way that I think is unprecedented," Price says. "It was all volunteer, all anonymous, and that was what the team came up with. It allowed me to be in the background, to have this powerful story that showed that ultimately none of this is about me. We really do have wonderful, extraordinary people at Gravity."

BALLOONS, PHISH JAMS, AND DRIVING IMPACT

Zappos is famous for its customer service, as exemplified by former CEO Tony Hsieh's life mission and title of his best-selling book, *Delivering Happiness*. In truth, his mission was to deliver happiness to everyone, not just customers.

Arguably, Hsieh's greatest impact may be not on customers but on the inside of Zappos—the employees. Zappos has historically experimented with organizational structure, perhaps most notably with Holacracy, which is a very specific operating system for employee self-management. Derided by the outside world and seemingly complex in theory, Holacracy is just a particular way of working agile. Zappos still utilizes aspects of Holacracy today; however, it's an evolved version that layers its culture, core values, and focus on people into the system. But most critics don't dive deeper than perceiving it to be some sort of hippie capitalism.

As with both Basecamp and Gravity Payments, the structure and practices at Zappos are in service to its values and mission. Zappos officers are, like in any other company, held accountable to MBOs (Management by Objectives) by its owner, Amazon. Shocking, I know. Holacracy specifically, or self-management generally, is not simply "doing whatever you want." Just as with good, agile organizations, Zappos "circles" belong to a domain, with every domain representing a particular part of the company's mission to serve customers. They must deliver results.

What's even less well understood is the internal economic system implemented in Zappos' version of Holacracy, known as Market-Based Dynamics (MBD). To be honest, if one were to be consistent, this internal capitalism ought to make Zappos the most capitalist company on planet Earth. Circles that wish to work on a new project within their domain, or move to another part of the company, must find an internal financial sponsor. The sponsor is not the manager of that circle in a hierarchical sense, but could choose to sponsor circles that contribute to its mission. Internal accounting mechanisms and service agreements create an economy of sorts for testing new ideas.

Instead of human resources being allocated by a hierarchy, which can lead to all sorts of inefficiencies based on desires and biases not connected to corporate priorities, employees essentially allocate themselves to missions based upon their own desires and *their ability to drive impact*.

To test MBD, Hsieh launched an experimental platform with 1 percent of Zappos' customers (and revenue), allowing anyone to pitch ideas to try and grow the 1 percent.

"For example," says a Zappos employee familiar with the program, "I funded an idea, which by no means was revolutionary, that tested: What if we funded a circle made up of developers and marketers who wanted to show the amount of loyalty rewards points you earn through product purchases on each of the product pages? Customers will see, 'If I buy these $100 shoes, I get ten rewards points' and perhaps respond, 'Oh, this Rewards Program is free. If I'm going to buy the shoes anyway, I might as well join the Rewards Program.' Then we measure the lift."

The MBD program has continued to evolve, becoming more focused on projects that can directly benefit the core e-commerce business. "Investment in the customer experience is one of our main pillars," a Zappos representative told me. A great example of this is the "Voice of the Customer" Circle, which was created for the specific purpose of addressing customer pain points. A cross-functional team reviews customer feedback, designs systematic solutions, and prioritizes the top customer pain points in a constant feedback loop. Other great examples are the curated shopping experiences on Zappos.com, The Style Room and Zappos Adaptive, which were both started by passionate Zapponians.

CREATING A RAD GOVERNMENT

The nature of politics, taxes, and budgets means that government bodies must be leaner. They must improve the delivery of services with less resources. Currently the structure is generally modeled the same way as corporations, for no apparent reason other than the un-killable myth that the government should act like business. There's no reason why government bodies cannot be organized by agile teams that are assigned missions very similarly to the ideas detailed previously. Large amounts of money, time, and effort can be saved through exploring, rather than merely executing like they've always done.

The City of Hayward, across the bay from Silicon Valley, California, has practiced Lean Innovation techniques for six years, under the forward-thinking leadership of City Manager Kelly McAdoo. Unlike most cities, which practice innovation theater just like their corporate counterparts, McAdoo's team of dedicated professionals leave the confines of their downtown office building to interview constituents, design and run experiments to test ideas, and leverage the results to better serve their citizens. Over the years, they've gained the explicit trust of the city council because they save money and respond to citizen needs.

As I've mentioned before, the COVID-19 pandemic drove home the need for RAD systems, and this was true in government, too. When the pandemic hit, McAdoo's people leapt into action because the environment had already been created where people were not scared to take risks. The City of Hayward's fire chief was among those people:

"Garrett Contreras [Hayward's fire chief] came to me," says McAdoo, "and says, 'I have two firefighters who have been exposed to COVID and can't come back to work, because no one will test them.' This is March fifth or sixth, and he says, 'I have this crazy idea.'

"'Okay, what's your crazy idea?' I asked.

"'We should set up our own testing site.'

"'Okay, go figure it out.'

"He literally starts pinging people on LinkedIn and finds a group who helped build one of the first testing operations in South Korea and who had extra lab capacity. Then my fire chief says, 'The county health department don't want us to do this.' And I said, 'I don't care, let's figure it out.'

"Within two weeks he had gotten the entire paramedic scope of practice in the state of California changed so that paramedics could administer COVID tests. Our testing site was up March twenty-third and it was free. I decided we would pay for it, because this is a service that our community needs. We have a ton of service workers in Hayward. We are a lower income community. We're not going to require an ID. We're not going to require insurance.

"Alameda County ended up relying on us for several months as they tried to get their testing program up and running. We had set up a mobile testing unit, with several of our firefighters going to long-term care facilities, for example, and doing mass testing on behalf of the county."[cxxv]

The City of Hayward was also one of the first cities to provide small-business grant relief. "We were clearly not going to do special public events downtown," McAdoo said, "So I thought, 'Let's take that budget and use it for small-business grants.'"

After the George Floyd murder and subsequent protests in the summer of 2020, McAdoo's team, in partnership with local colleges, did close to seven hundred empathy interviews with community members, documenting negative experiences with Hayward police and creating a public interactive map to see themes discussed by residents.[cxxvi] (This was done in addition to a formal, statistically significant community survey.) According to McAdoo, what they found, for instance, went beyond police relationship matters (which were prevalent), but that "one reason people don't feel safe in their neighborhoods is because they don't know each other."[cxxvii] They have now formed teams of community members and city staff who are diving deeper into the problems that have surfaced and are working toward pilot programs or policy changes that the city council can consider as part of the next annual budget process.

The 5Es are all here:

Empathy—needs of service workers and constituents

Exploration—go figure it out

Evidence—see how others are doing it; double down on what drives highest impact

Equilibrium—balance the execution of rules, laws, and best practices with learning how to improve lives

Ethics—do the right thing

The city council specifically pointed out to McAdoo that the organizational culture she and her colleagues developed over the prior six years had positioned the city to respond capably to crisis. McAdoo and her team's work tells the story of why organizational culture and investing in this kind of work are vital, even if you don't immediately see a direct financial benefit. I doubt there's a governmental body on the planet that couldn't benefit from organizing itself and working this way.

LOOKING BEYOND ASSEMBLY-LINE EDUCATION

My dad was a terrible singer. It didn't stop him from loving music, however, nor did it stop him from singing. My mom, on the other hand, was a very good singer, but unfortunately rarely sang. Alas, the genetic mixture I received puts me plum in between the two. In the seventh grade I took a singing class, taught by Ms. Green, who appeared ancient to me. I now suspect she was a chain smoker. She could hit her notes, to be sure, but it was a bit surreal to be taught singing by an old, gravelly-voiced, baritone woman.

My dad was not too shabby as a small point guard, with a mean no-look pass as likely to surprise teammates as defenders. Not sure my mom ever played, but her height wasn't going to help me be a better basketball player. Alas, I was an okay player, too, but not great and not tall. In the seventh grade, I often played basketball during lunch with the PE coaches and other students.

Since I played basketball during lunch, I would often wolf down my meal at the beginning of my next class, which, I'm sure you've surmised by now, was singing. Not a great combo. Likely forewarned a number of times to not stuff my face during choir, I finally was sent to the vice principal's office. The VP is always the enforcer, not the principal—something Hollywood never seems to get right.

The VP was a small, frail man made smaller and frailer by memory's lapse over time, I suppose, as he came to represent to me the ineffectiveness of misused command-and-control tactics. To this day I remember the encounter: a small man in full-on tirade mode, attempting to instill terror in a small seventh-grade boy who had eaten a sandwich in music class, in a small, inconsequential middle school, in a small, rural town, a mere twenty miles as the crow flies but light-years from the epicenter of global democracy, Washington DC.

The primary purpose of the VP was to enforce the secondary purpose of the school, namely: beyond teaching educational fundamentals, create citizens who are subservient to authority.

Human beings are failure machines. It is natural. Unlike foals, we are not born able to stand. We are born able to *learn* to stand. We try, we fail, we try again. "If at first you don't succeed" is taught to all children as they learn to walk, run, and ride a bike. As they get older and move into school age, we systematically undo "try, try again."

The second purpose is what is required to prepare citizens to serve in global efforts to "export democracy," and also to be good, productive workers in the efficiency-for-efficiency's-sake, command-and-control businesses of the twentieth century.

It stands to reason then, that to succeed in the twenty-first century, education will have to reinvent itself. The old system doesn't work in either war or business, so why would we train the next generation in that system?

It turns out that high schools using agile-style learning methods to teach students twenty-first-century skills already exist and thrive. Imagine that. Texas high school principal Steven Zipkes has led an extraordinary effort to build project-based curricula, where students collaborate in teams to accomplish missions resulting in education that includes:

- Knowledge of principles and facts
- Oral and written communication skills
- Applying knowledge and skills to solving problems
- Developing a "growth" mindset where effort builds abilities

The students work together in groups of three to four on teacher-created projects that are based upon state educational standards. But the projects require action, not just memorization. The students research, interpret, analyze, and collaborate, just as you would expect to see among a team of engineers building a bridge. The projects are "authentic," Zipkes says. "They provide autonomy and ownership for the student; they require creativity."[cxxviii]

Zipkes's high schools are part of New Tech Network, a non-profit school model provider that has shown promising results with high attendance and graduation rates. Schools, including those with economically disadvantaged kids, excel.

New Tech Network doesn't operate schools, but rather works deeply with schools or districts to implement a project-based way of learning. Like with corporate Agile implementations, there are many models and many vendors, and anyone can use the jargon. But New Tech's president and CEO, Lydia Dobyns, says its mission is to "fundamentally rethink schools rather than playing around the edges. It's not, 'We've got laptops, therefore we are ready for the twenty-first century.'"[cxxix]

"Unfortunately," Dobyns says, "there's a lot of money in the charter school world, and a lot of people who believe the only way to change public education is to blow it up." That point of view is more about politics than education. In other words, because schools are not adequately preparing students for twenty-first-century work and careers, and are horribly inequitable across economic lines, disrupting education through quasi-market approaches does nothing to actually fix the old-school ways of teaching (no pun intended).

Putting the school system aside for the moment, it's necessary to define what the desired outcome is, and the customer behavior required from student, teacher, and administrator perspectives. If the desired outcome is for businesses to make money from parents, one can take a "blow it up" approach to change. If, however, what you want are students who are prepared to learn, advance, work, and contribute to society, then you must start with the learning that gets them there.

"Deep learning is a way to talk about what a school model like ours is about," says Dobyns. "It's completely reimagining what we want students to know, to demonstrate, to apply, and to create. We want them to have experiences that feel relevant and rigorous, to create thinkers and doers and agile people, people who know how to navigate uncertainty. That means we develop skills that are essential to being functioning humans as well as earning a decent living."

K–12 schools have a tough system to navigate, with a standards-based testing regime that is designed to serve bureaucracy, a schedule to suit working parents, pressure from unions and anti-union forces, universities that are primarily marketing engines, and last, but hopefully not least, students. "Customer experience is exactly the way we think about school and school design. The student is the customer. But the tricky part for us is we only work with the adults in the world, so the adults are the customer, too. Our job as a network and a model provider is to work with the adults as if they were the students, so they themselves experience what we create for the students."

Increasingly, New Tech must take a portfolio-based approach when going into districts, whereby different-style schools can address the differently perceived needs of students (and their parents). It starts with community dialogue, determining how to measure school performance, how to get adults involved in the dialogue. "There are lots of examples of good, data-driven, highly effective research to back these ways of going about change."

NewTech is like the 100 startups in 100 days of corporate change. They are in the acceleration phase. The obstacle is that they depend on a hierarchy that's not necessarily on board. And they depend on change being demanded from parent stakeholders.

WHAT'S YOUR ROLE?

As participants in the global economic system, we each have multiple roles, some combination of consumer, worker, and owner. We also each have a role to play in determining what we want the balance of our economic system to look like, as well as the path to getting there. We need to look at the other roles we play, so that we can shape the disruption that is happening, whether we like it not.

Where to look? It's perhaps beneficial to look back at the effects the COVID-19 pandemic had on any organization you participate in:

- The school your children attend, or you attend yourself
- Organizations you volunteer for
- Your place of worship
- The company you own
- Where you work
- The residence home where a parent lives
- A board you serve on
- A political office or group you're active with

How did they fare? Perhaps they could be made more resilient. Could they benefit from being more aware of outside information and influences, or internal issues? Could they learn to communicate better in ways that allow them to act more quickly when needed?

The Five Elements can be applied to all of these entities with a bit of creativity. And you can be the catalyst. Change in other types of organizations and entities in society can help influence the necessary business changes, too.

Work as an agile team. You don't need to call it this, but the basic structure is one in which ten or fewer people work together as equals. There is no hierarchy within the team, regardless of job titles or organizational responsibilities. You assign roles to ensure the group operates properly. Roles may include timekeeper to keep discussions timeboxed; a scribe to take notes; or a facilitator to keep discussions on point and ensure all voices are heard. It's important that the roles rotate among the members.

The members ultimately choose what work they'll do, the cadence, and the structure of the work. Frequently, agile teams will define their work via sprint planning, perform daily stand-ups to share what they're working on, and have periodic retrospectives to improve their work. In the Alistair Cockburn mode, the team can organize how they see fit to collaborate on the delivery of their mission, and reflect on how they did in order to improve the next iteration.

Capture the mission of the organization. Why does the group exist and who do they primarily serve? What are the beneficiaries' specific needs that the organization addresses? What are the different roles inside the organization? Are people aligned?

Think about how you attach to the organization. What is the mission of the group you belong to (within the greater organization)? How does the mission align with other groups, as well as with the larger entity? Roughly speaking, who does what? How do other groups contribute to the mission? What is your relationship with the other groups?

Think of the ecosystem. Who outside the organization has a stake in what the organization does? Who are the stakeholders other than the beneficiary of the mission? Ask the same questions for your group, where stakeholders might be external or internal to the organization.

Empathy work seeks to understand the beneficiaries and stakeholders. What makes them tick? What keeps them up at night? What are their priorities? What might you learn from them about how they approach their needs? Establishing empathy with colleagues, team members, and leaders is also important.

Exploration work seeks to learn what you don't know. It might be something you simply don't have knowledge of, but others may know. You could simply ask someone who knows or leverage others' expertise. On the other hand, what you don't know might fall in Snowden's quadrant of a complex problem—in other words, one for which there is no one right answer. Several answers likely exist based on multiple variables. You experiment to figure out what works in a specific context.

Evidence-informed decisions mean that you allow results, data, and insights to help you decide issues. The hope is that you cut through biases by looking at objective results that inform you of the right path or that you're making progress on the path. In a team environment, it's useful to determine the tests and data you agree to weigh before the tests or research are conducted.

Equilibrium means that you must balance work you already know must be done in order to deliver on the mission, with work where you must learn first in order to complete the mission.

Finally, Ethics is applied to all the work conducted and results delivered to beneficiaries and stakeholders. Remember that an ethic is not a true value unless you're willing to give up something valuable to keep it intact.

THE NEW NORMAL

The planet is with us or without us. But here we are. The human mind created the technology spawning the digital revolution. Change rolled from the very core of society's largest institutions to the edge, to you and me. Like a tsunami, launched by an explosion in the core of Earth, it traversed from the deepest ocean to our shores.

So what do we do about it?

We do what we always do, eventually. We go to work. We change our responsibilities. We take the bull by the horns. We ride the wave. We just do it. We go read the titles on the self-help shelf at a local bookstore. (Which may be at the nearest airport, by the way.)

But seriously, we know how to bend and not break. We know how to stand strong. We know how to listen. How to pay attention. How to sense far-off change. We intuit. We're quick on our feet when we want to be. We rally the troops. We pull a stranger out of harm's way without thinking twice.

As humans, we are naturally resilient, aware, dynamic. So it follows that we can create systems that are, too.

How do we do it?

Seek expertise. Experts have spent a long time learning, failing, iterating. They've been there, done that. We live in an amazing time, where the positive democratization of knowledge brought on by the digital revolution provides access to amazing minds like never before. We should reward this expertise while making the knowledge available for free, when possible, especially when the creators wish to do so. Why? Because many experts feel as if it doesn't belong to them anyway. They discovered something not because it didn't exist before, but because they had to remove the parts that didn't belong. Business law and copyright law should not prevent knowledge creators from sharing their wisdom.

Beware of pundits. Pundits want your time, money, and adoration. They play to your fears and biases. I'm pretty sure Facebook and YouTube modeled their feed algorithms based on pundits. The tough part, of course, is when aging experts become pundits. These are the purveyors of stale, anachronistic conventional wisdom. You can sense them by their discourse. They wave their hands a lot. They are wittily dismissive. They don't deign to debate. Their credentials speak for themselves, though I've never heard a diploma enunciate words properly.

Be open to new ideas. As much as nostalgia makes us feel great about how things used to be, they never truly were the way they're imagined. "I wish we could go back to when" really means "Sure was great when I (or someone I admire) had all the power."

Greek philosopher Heraclitus wrote, "No man ever steps in the same river twice, for it's not the same river and he's not the same man." Seek people who have new ideas for the world we're living in now. But also seek evidence that the ideas are true. Use empathy to uncover bias.

Be truthful. Be honest to yourself and others. Admit what you don't know. The first sign of ignorance is being positive you're right. Everyone is subject to bias. Don't hide behind *knowing*.

Be kind. No one is perfect, so don't be hard on yourself. But don't work on yourself in isolation, either. The best way to be better to yourself is to be better to someone else.

Do. Taking one small step is better than planning to take a big one.

The new normal comes from ideas that reflect reality. In other words, we create models of the world that we can analyze, tweak, and massage so we can change variables, test scenarios, and more accurately predict how things turn out. Models are wrong when they don't reflect reality. We must reject these models. We're better off trying something new, without fully understanding outcomes, than remaining with models we know are wrong based on existing evidence.

The new normal emerges from within the old. We sculpt the emerging system so that it looks like the system we want. We balance the forces of the economy so the balance results in the society we choose. We have chosen to be where we are. If we want something different, we must choose differently.

REIMAGINING THE OUTCOME OF DISRUPTION

The point is, ladies and gentlemen, that greed, for lack of a better word, is good. Greed is right, greed works. Greed clarifies, cuts through, and captures the essence of the evolutionary spirit. Greed, in all of its forms: greed for life, for money, for love, knowledge, has marked the upward surge of mankind. And greed, you mark my words, will not only save Teldar Paper, but that other malfunctioning corporation called the USA.

Thank you very much.

—Gordon Gekko, *Wall Street* (1987) [cxxx]

The way of life can be free and beautiful, but we have lost the way. Greed has poisoned men's souls, has barricaded the world with hate, has goose-stepped us into misery and bloodshed. We have developed speed, but we have shut ourselves in. Machinery that gives abundance has left us in want. Our knowledge has made us cynical. Our cleverness, hard and unkind. We think too much and feel too little....

The aeroplane and the radio have brought us closer together.

The very nature of these inventions cries out for the goodness in men, cries out for universal brotherhood, for the unity
of us all. Even now my voice is reaching millions throughout the world—millions of despairing men, women and little
children—victims of a system that makes men torture and
imprison innocent people....

Let us all unite! Let us fight for a new world, a decent world
that will give men a chance to work, that will give youth a
future and old age a security....

Let us fight for a world of reason, a world where science and
progress will lead to all men's happiness.

—The Jewish Barber in *The Great Dictator* (1940)[cxxxi]

R ather than pointing out the obvious differences between these
two points of view, we can ask ourselves, what is similar? Underlying both is the potential virtue of capitalism. Gekko says greed
for life, love, and knowledge and their returns, money, results in an
upward surge of humans. The Barber says the very nature of invention
can reflect the goodness of humans and can unite us.

The crux is in the mission of business and how we go about
achieving it. Do the ends justify the means or the means the ends?
Do we define capitalism as we want and let the chips fall where they
may? An unchanging guiding principle, faith in an Invisible Hand,
perhaps, that will bring us to the upward surge? Or do we allow the
systems and management of capitalism to evolve to meet the needs of
a changing world?

And of this invisible hand, is it the same hand that brings pan-
demics? An earthquake? A tsunami? Does its magic wane in the face
of acts of god? Does the invisible hand dole out bailout funds, set
C-suite compensation, manage stock buybacks? Hmmm...

The meme that dominated the last fifty years of the industrial age, illustrated by Uber CEO Dara Khosrowshahi, who announced during the height of the 2020 pandemic:

"I do think we have the system that's optimized...It's called capitalism. It's not called labor-ism. It's not called socialism. It's capitalism and it's a system that's built to maximize shareholder value and capital."[cxxxii]

It's out of his hands. He's helpless—himself a victim of the inflexible system of capitalism. (Rolling-eyes emoji.) In this statement, Khosrowshahi is defining Uber's primary mission, beyond any other, as maximizing shareholder value over some undefined time period. In Uber's quarterly financial reports and press releases, the business is described as such:

"Uber is a technology platform that uses a massive network, leading technology, operational excellence and product expertise to power movement from point A to point B."[cxxxiii]

The filing lists several of the platform's applications, including "connect[ing] consumers [riders] with independent providers of ride services [mobility drivers] for ridesharing services."

I would argue, then, that Uber's true mission must be based on that. The "contract" with shareholders is that Uber officers have a responsibility to maximize shareholder value by means of powering the movement from point A to point B, whatever that means. The time frame over which value is to be maximized would presumably be over the lifetime of Uber as a publicly traded company.

However, in Uber's 2020 Environmental, Social, and Governance Report for investors, Khosrowshahi writes:

"At Uber, we believe that sustainability is integral to our business. We recognize that Uber's financial performance and prosperity can only be built alongside the prosperity of our key stakeholders. This includes investors, employees, cities, and the drivers, delivery people, merchants, and consumers who use our platform to connect with work, food, goods, families, and friends."[cxxxiv]

Which is it? Why is Uber in business? Uber's purpose is stated differently again on its website, where it is so nebulous as to be meaningless: "We ignite opportunity by setting the world in motion."

But what Uber calls its "cultural norms" (in another word, values) are more clear:

"We build globally, we live locally. We harness the power and scale of our global operations to deeply connect with the cities, communities, drivers and riders that we serve, every day."

"We do the right thing. Period."

"We are customer obsessed. We work tirelessly to earn our customers' trust and business by solving their problems, maximizing their earnings or lowering their costs. We surprise and delight them. We make short-term sacrifices for a lifetime of loyalty."

When deciding how to manage the business, which of these takes precedence? What is Khosrowshahi's job? The bigger issue is not that corporate management declares their intentions in ways that people don't like; it's speaking out of both sides of the mouth. If you tell the world that your mission is to improve the world by doing x, while telling shareholders you will maximize their share value beyond anything else, one of these must be true:

- You are promising shareholders that you will maximize value by managing the business creation and delivery of value for customers as best and efficiently as possible; or
- You will maximize value for shareholders over some undefined time period based on a whim and are deceiving customers, drivers, partners, other shareholders—"the world"—about your mission.

Hold my beer for a moment. The perplexing part of option 2 is: Why deceive the world? If deceiving the world has tangible benefits—in other words, declaring a positive mission and values improves the business—doesn't the logic of option 2 fail prima facie? I suppose if you are very efficient at deception, one can keep up the impression of the mission, while purposefully not delivering on it in order to *maybe* increase shareholder value.

Uber spent at least $57 million to pass California's Prop 22 in 2020[cxxxv] in order to extract itself from labor law, as passed by the citizens of California through their representatives. Further, they are fighting numerous lawsuits around the world in order to be allowed to bypass employee safeguards by classifying drivers as contractors. Short-term, this would obviously not maximize shareholder value. Long-term, it might. Does it jibe with considering the prosperity of drivers?

To be honest, I say all this as an Uber early adopter. Back in 2011, it was difficult if not impossible to get a "quality" cab in San Francisco or New York City. The cab experience was uniformly horrible. A government-created monopoly, cab companies exhibited all the hallmarks of their gifted power status with horrible customer service: dirty cabs, rude drivers, no credit cards accepted—and all this only if you could catch a cab in the first place. Uber disrupted that with a black-car service—on-demand Lincoln Town Cars, with professional drivers, prepaid including tip, with clean cars and courteous drivers.

It was a positive disruption of the miserable status quo created by a government-instituted monopoly. Uber, having achieved its own near monopoly, ended up eroding its own black-car experience, by the way. You can bet my beer you're holding, competition is good.

But more fundamentally, among the mixed messages Uber sends investors, consumers, drivers, and regulators, how should we evaluate Khosrowshahi's statements and beliefs? And is it reasonable that a business, which must be legally incorporated to operate, be able to overcome laws created by citizens—a status not belonging to corporations—by financing a ballot initiative?

On the other side, it is worth considering whether "employee versus contractor" is the right way to bestow rights to working people. In thinking of systems, rather than just outcomes, I look to the business owner versus the worker in the economic power equation, because how businesses classify workers doesn't cover all contract possibilities. Part of the promise of the gig economy is worker independence. There's potential economic freedom in being able to negotiate one's own relationship with an owner.

How do we increase their power so the negotiation is on the right plane? Why not simply extend employee rights to contractors? Why not create and empower worker co-op entities? Eliminate the norm that businesses cover health insurance and retirement, which actually serves to decrease worker independence. Government covering those increases worker power, as do full employment guarantees and minimum wage hikes.

To be honest, these are complex questions. And this is where the ability to wear multiple hats becomes critical. In the micro perspective, one looks at interests as an individual: what is right for me and however I define my circle; what's right for me as a business owner or a corporate officer, as a worker, as a consumer. What creates the best outcomes for those I associate with. But we must also be able to separate ourselves from that and look at the macro level: what's right for the economy; what's right for the people; what's right for the planet. And of course we need to consider the increasing complexity of these questions in the digital age. Whether we like it or not, we're all in this together.

Airbnb went public in late 2020, during the height of the pandemic. It's obviously a bit early to make a call about its long-term ethics and its efficiency ethos, but its SEC Form 424B4 Prospectus filing is chock-full of clear statements that align with its public mission statements:

"Airbnb has five stakeholders and is designed with all of them in mind. Along with employees and shareholders, we serve hosts, guests, and the communities in which they live. We intend to make long-term decisions considering all of our stakeholders because their collective success is key for our business to thrive."[cxxxvi]

Extraordinarily, their opening statement even reflects empathy, given the pandemic:

"We are eager to tell you the story of Airbnb. Before we start, we want to acknowledge the serious impact of the COVID-19 pandemic on people's health, safety, and economic well-being. Given this backdrop, we feel incredibly fortunate to be able to tell our story. In it, we will explain how we are addressing today's challenges, as well as how we are focusing on the opportunities ahead. Our goal is to build an enduring business, and we want to tell you about it, starting at the beginning."[cxxxvii]

With respect to the micro view, many of you will have already started the work. By creating more resilient, aware, and dynamic (RAD) organizations, you're able to better deal with the increasing complexity and ongoing disruptions. You apply your version of the 5Es—Empathy, Exploration, Evidence, Equilibrium, and Ethics—to corporations, startups, government, education, nonprofits, and so on.

Human beings are solving problems by working within collaborative, self-organized, autonomous teams focused on an assigned ambition. Leaders are developing new skills, aligning priorities, managing communications, learning where simple efficiency is not the only metric that matters. Further, measuring learning using behavior-based metrics allows management to closer align team work with company priorities, as well as manage ethical behavior.

While some have not yet begun, kickstarting your company's disruption work is not difficult or costly. To those who have begun and perhaps stalled, I encourage you to look for ways to accelerate the positive aspects of the new mindset to other parts of the organization.

You should endeavor to figure out how to make it last and get leaders more involved. Scaling requires putting in place—in a learning, iterative way—systems and processes that reinforce the desired behavior. Structural and organizational design changes, along with eliminating dependence on leadership by personality, are needed in the final phase for the new business to endure.

In the broader economic system, the increased information and knowledge brought to people via the digital revolution helps increase the power for workers and consumers, but it's only the beginning of what's needed. As shareholders, people must advocate for sustainability, diversity, and employee rights; and as consumers they must push for safety, environmentalism, regulation enforcement, and antitrust enforcement. Government must be an extension of the people as a force to check corporate power and malfeasance. We see the results as corporate management has begun thinking about the role of business in society, and how they might be held accountable for adhering to laws and social norms.

Perched on the shoulders of the captains of industry are the angel and the devil. On one shoulder are the incentives: the money, the respect among peers, the power, the accolades, the proverbial seat at the table. This is the path of least resistance. But on the other shoulder, there's the children and grandchildren, bright-eyed and bushy-tailed, full of hope, curiosity, and energy, the huddled masses yearning to breathe free, like our own ancestors, perhaps.

The heart versus the mind. The deep, gnawing sense of what's right versus the rationality of conventional wisdom. The clenched mind is caught between the risk of failure in the future and the very real consequences born out of yesterday's behavior. The clenched heart sees only red, a constricted vision aware only of its own struggle, untrusting of its very lifeline. It seeks the familiarity of conventional wisdom, the ease of stereotypes that stick like buzzwords, that reek of decay like anachronistic clichés, blind to the original builders, the multicolored backbone of progress and growth.

The unclenched heart frees creativity to solve problems, to seek a diversity of experiences to paint the bigger picture, to understand a larger context. The unclenched mind explores the edge, is additive, uncensored, observant; it flows.

For many years I managed and grew a company feeding off the nebulous concept of "innovation." We taught "lean innovation," a concept embracing human-centered design, rapid experimentation, and agile working methods, to large companies. This was our version of the RAD mindset, based primarily on a startup mentality, iterated upon and tailored for the complexities of large organizations. We were hired primarily by innovation groups, which were rationally thought to have the most similar issues to startups.

Until I swore off the word. Minutes before going up onstage at a packed innovation conference, I went through my presentation deck and crossed the word "innovation" off of virtually every slide. I was so tired of the word and the self-inflicted frustrations innovation executives faced in their companies. The word: ill-defined, unaligned, misapplied, its practitioners ironically lacking empathy, exploration, or equilibrium.

Onstage, I declared that I wouldn't use the word and the members of the audience should stop, too. "If I use the word," I said, "I want you to boo me." I did well. I went a solid twenty minutes without using the word. As I was closing, wrapped up in the flow of the talk, I used the word five times in twenty seconds. Seemingly out of nowhere, the audience was a cacophony of "BOOO! BOOO! BOOO! BOO!"

For a moment, I was absolutely shocked. And I deserved it.

Creating value. That's what this is all about. We optimize what we measure. If you measure innovation by "number of patents," you get a dump truck full of patent certifications. If you assign an agile team the metric number of Uber rides per user per month, you will see an increase. If you incentivize people to increase the seconds of engagement users spend on Facebook, you get radical, off-the-wall, conspiracy-theory videos. You've likely seen more than one, perhaps dozens. We all have.

Chris Arnade, photographer, and author of *Dignity: Seeking Respect in Back Row America*, worked as a bond trader on Wall Street for twenty years before embarking on a soul-searching tour of America's dead or dying cities and the forgotten people who live there. It turns out, he spent a lot of time in McDonald's restaurants, which had become local meeting points virtually everywhere he went.

"I look at McDonald's as an example of a company that actually does a lot in the communities, more than it's given credit for. And I think they really do care about creating an environment where the customer can sit there and be part of the community. I can talk about the unfair labor practices, I can talk about all these things they aren't great about. But I think they understand value in a broader sense than I think a lot of people get. And it's not just about delivering and making money off their food. Their value is being a communal center, and I think they know that."[cxxxviii]

Most of the people inside our economic and social institutions want to contribute positively to the world. Most wish to be a part of community. Refocusing business on creating value for customers helps with that. Altering inputs to the system can correct incentives that misalign business practices with the intent of their people. It's a subtle shift that is tough to implement but drives enormous gains.

I am fortunate and extremely privileged that I get to live close to a world-class surfing peak, called Swami's. When a two-foot swell laps against the reef, you'll still find 137 surfers positioning themselves for the four-foot rogue. In case you haven't caught on yet, I'm not one of them. Not by a mile.

I am an individual, floating on my back, eyes closed, out past the break, rolling with the swell, sun dipping its toes. The wind changes as if the sun going down creates a vacuum.

I am part of the marine ecosystem—the sea life, reef organisms, intertidal systems, and a coastal lagoon; ripples, waves, moving sand, cutting cliffs, and rolling tides; surfers, swimmers, and sunset worshippers.

What is the economic system where its output is something of value to human beings? And where whoever is successful at delivering that value shares in their own value creation—for example, wealth? It's proven that wealth does not trickle down, but value does flow up. Again: Value, rather than wealth, flows upward.

It's not a zero-sum game. A system that creates value for humans creates value for everyone. But it requires a deliberate choice. I have to be aware of my existence in the ecosystem in addition to the awareness of my individual needs and wants. I must do what I can to collaborate with others, to practice empathy, explore what I don't know, use evidence to shape my thinking, consider what equilibrium among competing forces should look like, to maintain my ethics in the face of alternative pressures.

Disruption is happening, has happened, will happen. I choose to bring my creativity and inspiration to creating resilient, aware, and dynamic systems that create value for our wide diversity of human beings. To help build institutions—be they businesses or otherwise—constructed to be a part of the ecosystem, feeding and being fed, flowing with the current, able to withstand the crashing waves. That's the opportunity available to you, too. To us all, for us all. Being disruption proof is a deliberate choice to protect us all from forces beyond our control, to make them work for us as best we can. It's not just innovation disrupting—it's innovating disruption.

ACKNOWLEDGMENTS

Does anyone read acknowledgments? Those looking for their names, I suppose. In the spirit of disrupting conformity, I'm going in a different direction with this section, and I invite you to read on. In our needlessly binary world, where we believe the endpoints of two-dimensional continuums—black and white, zeroes and ones, right and wrong—make the world easier to understand, people wrestle with whether we as individuals are more heavily influenced by the nature of what we're born with or the nurturing we receive upon entering this world.

The answer, of course, is a pretty good balance between the two.

When it comes to change—changing our mindset, ourselves, our institutions—allow me to riff on an idea I've come to recognize as self-fulfilling: Lasting change must happen from within, but the outcome is influenced and shaped by external factors.

Did you know that most cells in your body continually replace themselves? The core part of eye lenses is an interesting exception. You periodically create a new you, emerging from within the old, but how you see the world lasts a lifetime.

That's the physical part. But what about personality—about what makes you, you? Seems for most, normal living is avoiding change in the core "you." But that seems incredibly dull to me. I wish to forever change; to continuously improve, but also to change radically to become a better human—at least every once in a while.

People change me.

Writing *Disruption Proof* took me on a completely unpredictable journey that included the global pandemic and a cancer diagnosis. Radically unfrickinforeseeable. A situation I simply would not have endured without my friend and book consigliere, Jonas Koffler. This book would not have been completed without him. Period. The same goes to friend and communications strategy advisor and a bunch of other things, including a thorn, Peter Loehfelm—with me the whole way.

My Hachette team, of course, led by editors Gretchen Young and Haley Weaver, expertly navigated the uncertainty of a disrupted publishing process, as well as the idiosyncrasies of an addled author. My agent, Jim Levine, was the steady, sage guide throughout, and Kevin Anderson, who helped get this all started. Thank you.

My team at Moves the Needle kept the engine running and on track, including my right-hand woman, Emily McNair, stalwarts Mike Kendall and Kavita Appachu, as well as my growth team Carol Tran and Rachael Halpert. I so appreciate your commitment to the cause.

It's interesting to be able to look back on your life and see a thread that runs through it that you were unaware of when living it. I studied economics in college, not because I wanted to be an economist, but because it had the fewest required number of units. I minored in English and took courses in creative writing, history, calculus, sociology, astronomy, electrical and computer engineering, chemistry, and so on. I wanted to explore it all. And to avoid actually joining the "real" world. This is the thread.

Great innovation is rarely born of unique, stand-alone invention, but rather a new combination of things already existent. In "my" thinking I "borrow" heavily from amazing humans. I get "awareness" from human-centered design experts like Janice Fraser, Ben Blank, Kate Rudder, Giff Constable, and Lane Goldstone; and "dynamism" from the agile thinkers, including Alistair Cockburn, Sonja Blignaut, Kent Beck, Dave Snowden, and Jason Yip.

Those who taught me resiliency are the change agents working within large corporations, fighting the good fight and sharing their incredible leadership stories: Pinar Abay, Troy Barnes, Scott Case, John Chambers, Marleen Dekker, Payam Djavdan, Ria Escher, Melanie Evans, Chuck Gitkin, Elizabeth Gutschenritter, Moritz Hartmann, Tim Hebrink, Dan Kaiser, Sonja Kresojevic, Bruce McGoogan, John Morrow, Dan Murray, Laura Nereng, Pete Richter, Brad Smith, Florian Schattenmann, Van Tran, and Ignacio Juliá Vilar.

For reasons I explore deeper in the book, I seek diversity: diversity of backgrounds, viewpoints, histories, experiences. This not only provides me opportunity to better myself, but makes me more aware of alternative ways of looking at problems and increases the possibility of finding better solutions. I like connecting the dots. I don't connect these without the perspective and shared histories of others.

I am heavily influenced by smart women, starting with the three generations closest to me: my mom, of course, Cynthia Larrabee Cooper; my cardiologist sister, Stephanie Galbraith Cooper; and my crazy-bright activist daughter, Riva Malena Cooper. Also, the world is being changed by leading, powerful female voices, a small subset of whom you will find in this book or hear their influence: Stephanie Kelton, Brené Brown, Zephyr Teachout, Sonja Kresojevic, and Mariana Mazzucato. Black Americans with whom I get to go deep in conversation: Simeon Sessley, Hugh Molotsi, Kim Folsom, Marcus Bullock, Christopher Brummer, and a random, brave woman entrepreneur who correctly called me out in a Zoom workshop for using too many male pronouns in my examples! Spiritual angles it took me too long to consider, led by my brilliant, eyes-of-the-world daughter, Eliza Jacqueline Cooper, and my youngest brother, who died way too young, Todd Churchill Cooper.

Other influencers I owe a debt of gratitude to are those who simply put disrupting conformity into their ongoing, day-to-day work. In this list, I include my creative, problem-solving brother, Craig Larrabee Cooper, who was a "gig economy" worker back in dial-up days, and Chris Arnade, Dean Baker, David Cohen, Lydia Dobyns, David Heinemeier Hansson, Victor Hwang, Kelly McAdoo, Raj Raghunathan, Dan Price, and Steven Zipkes, among others.

I could go on and probably should. I've been blessed by the people whom I have crossed paths with, including, significantly, Daniella Zucker and her mom, Jacqueline Zucker, as well as many others helping me along: Etienne de Bruin, Amber Brandner, Jacqueline Krain, Judy Berlfein, Dadla Ponizil, and Nik Souris. I am surely better for them and not as good as I should be. And hence, that remains the journey. I like to quip, beyond the waves, "I don't want to die when I peak, but I hope I am peaking when I die."

ABOUT THE AUTHOR

Brant Cooper is the *New York Times* bestselling author of *The Lean Entrepreneur* and CEO and founder of Moves the Needle. He is a trusted advisor to startups and large enterprises around the world. With more than twenty-five years of expertise in changing industrial-age mindset into digital-age opportunity, he blends agile, human-centered design and lean methodologies to ignite entrepreneurial action from the front lines to the C-suite. As a sought-after keynote speaker, startup mentor, and executive advisor, he travels the globe sharing his vision for reimagining twenty-first-century organizations. Bringing agility, digital transformation, and a focus on creating value for customers, he helps leaders navigate the uncertainty brought on by increased complexity and endless disruption.

NOTES

i   U.S. Small Business Administration Office of Advocacy, "2019 Small Business Profile," accessed March 12, 2021, https://cdn .advocacy.sba.gov/wp-content/uploads/2019/04/23142719/2019 -Small-Business-Profiles-US.pdf.

ii   Peter Thiel, "Competition Is for Losers," *Wall Street Journal*, September 12, 2014, https://www.wsj.com/articles/peter-thiel -competition-is-for-losers-1410535536.

iii   "Business Roundtable Pledges, Business Roundtable," accessed March 29, 2021, https://opportunity.businessroundtable .org/ourcommitment.

iv   "Timeline of Computer History, Computer History," accessed March 29, 2021, https://www.computerhistory.org/timeline /computers/.

v   Ryan Singel, "Oct. 27, 1994: Web Gives Birth to Banner Ads," *Wired*, October 27, 2010, https://www.wired.com/2010/10/1027 hotwired-banner-ads/.

vi   Rebecca Greenfield, "The Trailblazing, Candy-Colored History of the Online Banner Ad," *Fast Company*, October 27, 2014, https://www.fastcompany.com/3037484/the-trailblazing-candy -colored-history-of-the-online-banner-ad.

vii   The Editors, "After the Crash: How Software Models Doomed the Market," *Scientific American*, December 1, 2008, https://www .scientificamerican.com/article/after-the-crash.

viii IAB Internet Advertising Revenue Report 2016, Interactive Advertising Bureau, last modified April 26, 2017, https://www.iab .com/news/internet-advertising-revenue-first-time-ever-total -digital-ad-spend-hits-landmark-72-5-billion-2016/.

ix Laura Silver, "Smartphone Ownership Is Growing Rapidly Around the World, but Not Always Equally," Pew Research Center, February 5, 2019, https://www.pewresearch.org/global/2019/0 2/05/smartphone-ownership-is-growing-rapidly-around-the -world-but-not-always-equally.

x Mark Andreessen, "The Pmarca Guide to Startups, Part 4: The Only Thing That Matters," June 25, 2007, https://pmarchive .com/guide_to_startups_part4.html.

xi Google's English dictionary provided by Oxford Languages, accessed March 12, 2021, https://languages.oup.com/google -dictionary-en/.

xii Investopedia Staff, Reviewed by Gordon Scott, "Black Swan," updated March 22, 2021, https://www.investopedia.com/terms/b /blackswan.asp.

xiii Aviva Aron-Dine, Richard Kogan, and Chad Stone, "How Robust Was the 2001–2007 Expansion?" Center on Budget and Policy Priorities, updated August 29, 2008, https://www.cbpp.org /research/how-robust-was-the-2001-2007-economic-expansion.

xiv Ira Glass, Alex Blumberg, and Adam Davidson, "The Giant Pool of Money," *This American Life*, May 9, 2008, https://www .thisamericanlife.org/355/the-giant-pool-of -money.

xv Emmanuel Saez, "Striking It Richer: The Evolution of Top Incomes in the United States," Econometrics Laboratory, University of California, Berkeley, June 30, 2016, https://eml .berkeley.edu/~saez/saez-UStopincomes-2015.pdf.

xvi   Federal Reserve Bank of St. Louis, "Economic Research," up-
       dated January 28, 2021, https://fred.stlouisfed.org/graph/?g=oM2u.

xvii   Jeffry Bartash, "The U.S. Has Only Regained 42% of the 22
       Million Jobs Lost in the Pandemic. Here's Where They Are,"
       MarketWatch, August 7, 2020, https://www.marketwatch.com
       /story/restaurants-and-retailers-have-regained-the-most-jobs
       -since-the-coronavirus-crisis-but-theres-a-catch-2020-08-07.

xviii Paul R. La Monica, "Zoom Is Now Worth More Than Nearly
       85% of the S&P 500 Stocks," CNN Business, June 16, 2020,
       https://edition.cnn.com/2020/06/16/investing/zoom-market
       -value/index.html.

xix   Merritt Hawkins in Collaboration with the Physicians Foun-
       dation, "Physicians and COVID-19," April 2020, https://www
       .merritthawkins.com/uploadedFiles/Corona_Physician_Survey
       _Merritt_Hawkins_Report.pdf.

xx   Prashant Gopal and Alex Wittenberg, "Housing Prices Are
       Booming in U.S. Cities—Just Not San Francisco or New York,"
       Bloomberg, February 9, 2021, https://www.bloomberg.com/news
       /articles/2021-02-09/housing-boom-sweeps-u-s-cities-that-aren-t
       -nyc-san-francisco.

xxi   Sarah Anderson and Brian Wakamo, "Inequality and Covid-19 in
       13 Charts," Inequality.org, September 24, 2020, https://inequality
       .org/great-divide/inequality-covid-charts.

xxii   Dion Rabouin, "The Inequality Is Getting Harder to Ignore,"
       Axios, December 15, 2020, https://www.axios.com/inequality
       -harder-ignore-a37be900-c8d3-474d-93fb-943b8a0da345.html.

xxiii Tommy Beer, "Top 1% of U.S. Households Hold 15 Times
       More Wealth Than Bottom 50% Combined," Forbes, updated
       October 8, 2020, https://www.forbes.com/sites/tommybeer/2020
       /10/08/top-1-of-us-households-hold-15-times-more-wealth-than
       -bottom-50-combined/?sh=4f76d4b35179.

xxiv   Stefan Lembo Stolba, "Debt Reaches New Highs in 2019, but Credit Scores Stay Strong," March 9, 2020, Experian, https://www.experian.com/blogs/ask-experian/research/consumer-debt-study/#s1).

xxv   Peter R. Orszag, "Covid Is Killing People in More Ways Than One," *Bloomberg*, December 14, 2020, https://www.bloomberg.com/opinion/articles/2020-12-14/covid-is-killing-people-in-more-ways-than-one.

xxvi   Liz Moughon, "The People Left Behind in a Broadband World," *Wall Street Journal*, November 11, 2019, https://www.wsj.com/articles/the-people-left-behind-in-a-broadband-world-11573501015.

xxvii   Douglas MacMillan, Peter Whoriskey, and Jonathan O'Connell, "America's Biggest Companies Are Flourishing During the Pandemic and Putting Thousands of People Out of Work," *Washington Post*, December 16, 2020, https://www.washingtonpost.com/graphics/2020/business/50-biggest-companies-coronavirus-layoffs/.

xxviii   Congressional Research Service, "US Healthcare Coverage and Spending," Federation of American Scientists, updated January 26, 2021, https://fas.org/sgp/crs/misc/IF10830.pdf.

xxix   Rob Wile, "Detroit Files Largest Municipal Bankruptcy in US History," *INSIDER*, July 18, 2013, https://www.businessinsider.com/detroit-likely-to-file-for-bankruptcy-2013-7?r=MX&IR=T.

xxx   Matt Cooper, "How to Unlock Your Team's Creative Potential," *Advertising Week*, accessed March 12, 2021, https://www.advertisingweek360.com/how-to-unlock-your-teams-creative-potential.

xxxi   Phil Lewis, "Where Businesses Go Wrong with Digital Transformation," *Forbes*, July 31, 2019, https://www.forbes.com/sites/phillewis1/2019/07/31/where-businesses-go-wrong-with-digital-transformation/?sh=26817e2870bb.

xxxii   Amy Greenshields, "Talent and Corporate Responsibility Top List of CEO Concerns in Wake of the COVID-19 Crisis," KPMG 2020 CEO Outlook, August 25, 2020, https://home .kpmg/xx/en/home/media/press-releases/2020/08/ceo-outlook -press-release.html.

xxxiii   Damian J. Troise, "Companies Struggle to Grow Profits, Look Ahead to 2020," *U.S. News and World Report*, November 27, 2019, https://www.usnews.com/news/us/articles/2019-11-27/companies -struggle-to-grow-profits-look-ahead-to-2020.

xxxiv   Robert G. Eccles and Svetlana Klimenko, "The Investor Revolution," *Harvard Business Review*, May–June 2019, https://hbr.org /2019/05/the-investor-revolution.

xxxv   Darrick Hamilton and Trevon Logan, "Here's Why Black Families Have Struggled for Decades to Gain Wealth," MarketWatch, March 4, 2019, https://www.marketwatch.com/story/heres-why -black-families-have-struggled-for-decades-to-gain-wealth-2019 -02-28.

xxxvi   McKinsey Global Institute, "COVID-19 and Gender Equality: Countering the Regressive Effects," July 15, 2020, https://www .mckinsey.com/featured-insights/future-of-work/covid-19-and -gender-equality-countering-the-regressive-effects.

xxxvii   Robin Bleiweis, "Quick Facts About the Gender Wage Gap," Center for American Progress, March 24, 2020, https://www .americanprogress.org/issues/women/reports/2020/03/24/482141 /quick-facts-gender-wage-gap/.

xxxviii   Deepa Mahajan, Olivia White, Anu Madgavkar, and Mekala Krishnan, "Don't Let the Pandemic Set Back Gender Equality," *Harvard Business Review*, September 16, 2020, https://hbr .org/2020/09/dont-let-the-pandemic-set-back-gender-equality.

xxxix   Ravi N. Shah and Obianuju O. Berry, "Venture Capitalists Are Moving into Mental Health," Physicians for a National Health Program,

JAMA Psychiatry, September 16, 2020 (online first), https://pnhp.org /news/venture-capitalists-are-moving-into-mental-health/.

xl Reid Hoffman and Tristan Walker, "Learn from Every No," Masters of Scale, https://mastersofscale.com/tristan-walker-beauty -of-a-bad-idea/.

xli John Kenneth Galbraith, *The Affluent Society* (New York: Houghton Mifflin Harcourt, October 15, 1998), p. 7. Kindle.

xlii Ibid.

xliii *Moneyball*, directed by Bennett Miller (2011; Culver City, CA: Sony Pictures, 2012), DVD.

xliv Gen. Stanley McChrystal with Tantum Collins, David Silverman, and Chris Fussell, *Team of Teams* (New York: Penguin Publishing Group, 2015), p. 2. Kindle.

xlv David Packard, *The HP Way* (New York: Harper Business, 2013). Kindle.

xlvi Matt Stoller, *Goliath: The 100-Year War Between Monopoly Power and Democracy* (New York: Simon & Schuster, 2019), p. 237. Kindle.

xlvii William Kolasky and Andrew Dick, "The Merger of Guidelines and the Integration of Efficiencies into Antitrust Review of Horizontal Mergers" (October 2003), Wilmer Cutler Pickering Hale and Dorr Antitrust Series, Working Paper 31, https://law.bepress .com/wilmer/art31.

xlviii Moritz Hartmann (Roche, Lifecycle Leader Software), in discussion with the author, November 2020.

xlix Brené Brown, *Dare to Lead* (New York: Random House, 2018), p. xviii. Kindle.

l John Chambers (Cisco Systems, Former Executive Chairman and CEO), in discussion with the author, February 2021.

li Mehrdad Baghai, Stephen Coley, and David White, *The Alchemy of Growth: Kickstarting and Sustaining Growth in Your Company* (London: Orion Business Books, 1999).

lii   Abay Pinar (ING, Member of the Management Board, Head of Market Leaders), in discussion with the author, January 2021.

liii Van Tran (formerly with Malaysian financial services company), in discussion with the author, December 2020.

liv   Brené Brown, *Dare to Lead* (New York: Random House, 2018), p. 7. Kindle.

lv   Gen. Stanley McChrystal with Tantum Collins, David Silverman, and Chris Fussell, *Team of Teams* (New York: Penguin Publishing Group, 2015), p. 20. Kindle.

lvi   Troy Barnes (formerly with Malaysian financial services company), in discussion with the author, October 2020.

lvii Gen. Stanley McChrystal with Tantum Collins, David Silverman, and Chris Fussell, *Team of Teams* (New York: Penguin Publishing Group, 2015), p. 128. Kindle.

lviii U.S. Department of Labor, Bureau of Labor Statistics, "Employment Characteristics of Families," April 21, 2020, https://www.bls.gov/news.release/pdf/famee.pdf.

lix   Adi Gaskell, "Productivity in Times of Covid," *Forbes*, December 8, 2020, https://www.forbes.com/sites/adigaskell/2020/12/08/productivity-in-times-of-covid/?sh=7a0abbc21fa1.

lx   "How Many Productive Hours in a Work Day? Just 2 Hours, 23 Minutes," Voucher Cloud, accessed March 21, 2021, https://www.vouchercloud.com/resources/office-worker-productivity.

lxi   U.S. Securities and Exchange Commission, "How to Read a 10-K/10-Q," accessed March 12, 2021, https://www.sec.gov/fast-answers/answersreada10khtm.html.

lxii Facebook, last accessed March 29, 2021, https://about.fb.com/company-info/.

lxiii Gilad Edelman, "The 14 Juiciest Quotes from the House Antitrust Report," *Wired*, October 8, 2020, https://www.wired.com/story/14-juiciest-quotes-house-antitrust-report/.

lxiv   Pete Richter (Cargill, Chief Customer Officer), Chuck Gitkin (Cargill, Chief Marketing Officer), and Marleen Dekker (Cargill, Global CoE Lead—Market Insights & Innovation), in discussion between Cargill and the author, December 2020.

lxv   ESPN, "Allen Iverson's Legendary Practice Rant," YouTube, accessed March 1, 2021, https://www.youtube.com/watch?v=K9ZQhyOZCNE.

lxvi   Brad Smith (Intuit, Chairman and Former CEO), in discussion with the author, August 2020.

lxvii   Ben Blank (Intuit, Innovation & Transformational Change Leader), in discussion with the author, September 2020.

lxviii   Erin McCann, "United's Apologies: A Timeline," *New York Times*, April 14, 2017, https://www.nytimes.com/2017/04/14/business/united-airlines-passenger-doctor.html.

lxix   David Dayen, *Monopolized: Life in the Age of Corporate Power* (New York: The New Press, 2020), p. 35.

lxx   Ibid., p. 20.

lxxi   Peter Eavis, "As the Pandemic Forced Layoffs, C.E.O.s Gave Up Little," *New York Times*, July 29, 2020, https://www.nytimes.com/2020/07/29/business/economy/ceo-pay-pandemic-layoffs.html.

lxxii   Gen. Stanley McChrystal with Tantum Collins, David Silverman, and Chris Fussell, *Team of Teams* (New York: Penguin Publishing Group, 2015), p. 128. Kindle.

lxxiii   "Ud 6:4 Sectarians (1) (Tittha Sutta)," dhammatalks.org, accessed March 12, 2021, https://www.dhammatalks.org/suttas/KN/Ud/ud6_4.html.

lxxiv   "Spotify Engineering Culture Video (Agile Enterprise Transition with Scrum and Kanban)," YouTube, accessed March 29, 2021, https://www.youtube.com/watch?v=R2o-Xm3UVjs.

lxxv   "Mr. Snuffleupagus," Wikipedia, accessed March 12, 2021, https://en.wikipedia.org/wiki/Mr._Snuffleupagus.

lxxvi Jason Yip, "A Few Answers on 'Guilds' (or Communities of Practice /Interest)," *Medium*, February 14, 2021, https://jchyip.medium.com/a -few-answers-on-guilds-or-communities-of-practice-interest-28d9d 5bfacf4.

lxxvii Elizabeth Gutschenritter (Cargill, Managing Director of Global Alternative Protein), Florian Schattenmann (Cargill, Chief Technology Officer and VP of R&D and Innovation), and Bruce McGoogan (Cargill, Director of Strategy and Business Development), in discussion with the author, January 2021.

lxxviii L. David Marquet, *Turn the Ship Around!* (New York: Penguin, 2012), pp. 103–4. Kindle.

lxxix Gen. Stanley McChrystal with Tantum Collins, David Silverman, and Chris Fussell, *Team of Teams* (New York: Penguin Publishing Group, 2015), p. 171. Kindle.

lxxx Peter F. Drucker, *Innovation and Entrepreneurship* (New York: HarperCollins, 2006), p. 92. Kindle.

lxxxi Tim Hebrink (3M Staff Scientist), Laura Nereng (3M, New Business Development Director), and John Morrow (3M, Insights Lead, Corporate R&D), in discussion between 3M and the author, December 2020.

lxxxii Ignacio Juliá Vilar (ING, CEO of ING Spain and Portugal), in discussion with the author, October 2020.

lxxxiii Ria Escher (ING, Former Global Head of Innovation Transformation), in discussion with the author, October 2020.

lxxxiv Payam Djavdan (ING, Former Program Director, Former Global Head Operating Model and Way of Working), in discussion with the author, October 2020.

lxxxv Stephen Heidari-Robinson and Suzanne Heywood, "Getting Reorgs Right: A Practical Guide to a Misunderstood—and Often Mismanaged—Process," *Harvard Business Review*, November 2016, https://hbr.org/2016/11/getting-reorgs-right.

lxxxvi   *Office Space*, directed by Mike Judge (1999; Beverly Hills: 20th Century Fox, 2002), DVD.

lxxxvii   Sidney Fussell, "Why Can't This Soap Dispenser Identify Dark Skin?" Gizmodo, August 17, 2017, https://gizmodo.com/why-cant-this-soap-dispenser-identify-dark-skin-1797931773.

lxxxviii Liz Fuller-Wright, "How a Chemist and a Physicist Solved a 50-Year-Old Puzzle—with Help from the Princeton Catalysis Initiative," Princeton University, March 4, 2020, https://www.princeton.edu/news/2020/03/04/how-chemist-and-physicist-solved-50-year-old-puzzle-help-princeton-catalysis.

lxxxix   Clifton Mark, "A Belief in Meritocracy Is Not Only False: It's Bad for You," Big Think, March 13, 2019, https://bigthink.com/politics-current-affairs/a-belief-in-meritocracy-is-not-only-false-its-bad-for-you.

xc   Melanie Evans (ING, CEO at ING Australia), in discussion with the author, December 2020.

xci   Michael Krigsman, "Nokia Reinvented: Decline, Resurrection, and How CEOs Get Trapped," ZDNet, November 26, 2018, https://www.zdnet.com/article/nokia-reinvented-decline-resurrection-and-how-ceos-get-trapped/.

xcii   "Texas Weather: Deaths Mount as Winter Storm Leaves Millions Without Power," February 17, 2021, *BBC News*, https://www.bbc.com/news/world-us-canada-56095479.

xciii   James Osborne, "Perry Says Texans Willing to Suffer Blackouts to Keep Feds out of Power Market," *Houston Chronicle*, February 17, 2021, https://www.houstonchronicle.com/business/energy/article/Perry-says-Texans-wiling-to-suffer-blackouts-to-15956705.php.

xciv   Adam Shapiro, "Capitalism 'Will Collapse on Itself' Without More Empathy and Love: Scott Galloway," Yahoo Finance, December 1, 2020, https://finance.yahoo.com/news/capitalism

-will-collapse-on-itself-without-empathy-love-scott-galloway
-120642769.html.

xcv   OpenSecrets.org, "2020 Election to Cost $14 Billion, Blowing
Away Spending Records," Center for Responsive Politics,
October 28, 2020, https://www.opensecrets.org/news/2020/10
/cost-of-2020-election-14billion-update.

xcvi   Nina Totenberg, "When Did Companies Become People?
Excavating the Legal Evolution," *Morning Edition*, NPR, July
28, 2014, https://www.npr.org/2014/07/28/335288388/when-did
-companies-become-people-excavating-the-legal-evolution.

xcvii   Osita Nwanevu, "The Corporations Funding the End of Democracy," *New Republic*, January 6, 2021, https://newrepublic.com
/article/160800/corporate-money-trump-gop-coup.

xcviii   "Nasdaq to Advance Diversity Through New Proposed Listing Requirements," Nasdaq, press release, December 1, 2015, https://www
.nasdaq.com/press-release/nasdaq-to-advance-diversity-through-new
-proposed-listing-requirements-2020-12-01.

xcix   Chris Mills Rodrigo, "Civil Rights Groups Call for Facebook
Ad Boycott," *The Hill*, June 17, 2020, https://thehill.com/policy
/technology/503189-civil-rights-groups-call-for-facebook-ad
-boycott.

c   Allen Kim and Brian Fung, "Facebook Boycott: View the List
of Companies Pulling Ads," *CNN Business*, July 2, 2020, https://
edition.cnn.com/2020/06/28/business/facebook-ad-boycott-list
/index.html.

ci   Paul R. Gregory and Robert C. Stuart, *Comparative Economic Systems* (Boston: Houghton Mifflin, 1980), p. 185.

cii   Ibid.

ciii   Samuel Bagenstos, "Lochner Lives On: Lochner Presumption
of Equal Power Lives in Labor Law and Undermines Constitutional, Statutory, and Common Law Workplace Protections,"

Economic Policy Institute, October 7, 2020, https://www.epi.org/unequalpower/publications/lochner-undermines-constitution-law-workplace-protections/.

civ   Drew DeSilver, "For Most U.S. Workers, Real Wages Have Barely Budged in Decades," Pew Research Center, August 7, 2018, https://www.pewresearch.org/fact-tank/2018/08/07/for-most-us-workers-real-wages-have-barely-budged-for-decades.

cv   Stephanie Kelton, *The Deficit Myth: Modern Monetary Theory and the Birth of the People's Economy* (New York: PublicAffairs, 2020), p. 246.

cvi   Dean Baker (Senior Economist at Center for Economic and Policy Research), in discussion with the author, December 2020.

cvii   "Key Findings of the Pentagon," *Guardian*, February 22, 2004, https://www.theguardian.com/environment/2004/feb/22/usnews.theobserver1?CMP=share_btn_link.

cviii   AJ Willingham, "Um, Where Did Fall Go? 162 Heat Records Could Be Broken Across the US This Week," CNN, October 2, 2019, https://www.cnn.com/2019/10/01/us/weather-why-hot-fall-heat-trnd/index.html.

cix   Shannon Hall, "Exxon Knew About Climate Change Almost 40 Years Ago," *Scientific American*, October 26, 2015, https://www.scientificamerican.com/article/exxon-knew-about-climate-change-almost-40-years-ago/.

cx   Raj Raghunathan (University of Texas at Austin, McCombs School of Business, Professor of Business, and Author), in discussion with the author, September 2020.

cxi   Stephanie Kelton, *The Deficit Myth: Modern Monetary Theory and the Birth of the People's Economy* (New York: PublicAffairs, 2020), p. 66.

cxii   Isabel V. Sawhill and Christopher Pulliam, "Six Facts About Wealth in the United States," Brookings Institution, June 25, 2019, https://www.brookings.edu/blog/up-front/2019/06/25/six-facts-about-wealth-in-the-united-states/#:~:text=1.

cxiii Steven Kotler, *The Rise of Superman: Decoding the Science of Ultimate Human Performance* (Boston: New Harvest, 2014), p. 29. Kindle.

cxiv "How Safety Transformed Big-Wave Surfing," Patagonia, accessed March 12, 2021, https://www.surfline.com/surf-news/safety-transformed-big-wave-surfing/105003.

cxv Susie Cranston and Scott Keller, "Increasing the 'Meaning Quotient' of Work," *McKinsey Quarterly*, January 1, 2013, https://www.mckinsey.com/business-functions/organization/our-insights/increasing-the-meaning-quotient-of-work.

cxvi Victor Hwang (Right to Start, Founder and CEO), in discussion with the author, December 2020.

cxvii "The State of Access to Capital for Entrepreneurs: From Barriers to Potential," Ewing Marion Kauffman Foundation, February 5, 2019, https://www.kauffman.org/wp-content/uploads/2019/12/capital_access_lab_exec_summary_FINAL.pdf.

cxviii "Woman-Owned Businesses Are Growing 2X Faster on Average Than All Businesses Nationwide," American Express, U.S. Research & Insights, September 23, 2019, https://about.americanexpress.com/all-news/news-details/2019/Woman-Owned-Businesses-Are-Growing-2X-Faster-On-Average-Than-All-Businesses-Nationwide/default.aspx.

cxix Kim Folsom (Founders First, Founder, Chairperson, and CEO), in discussion with the author, December 2020.

cxx Marcus Bullock (Flikshop, Founder and CEO), in discussion with the author, February 2021.

cxxi Matt Stoller, "A Land of Monopolists: From Portable Toilets to Mixed Martial Arts," BIG, July 10, 2020, https://mattstoller.substack.com/p/a-land-of-monopolists-from-portable.

cxxii David Heinemeier Hansson (37 Signals, Cofounder), in discussion with the author, November 2020.

cxxiii Dan Price, *Worth It: How a Million-Dollar Pay Cut and a $70,000 Minimum Wage Revealed a Better Way of Doing Business* (Seattle: Gravity Payments, 2020), p. 144. Kindle.

cxxiv Dan Price (Gravity Payments, Founder and CEO), in discussion with the author, November 2020.

cxxv Kelly McAdoo (City of Hayward, City Manager), in discussion with the author, December 2020.

cxxvi City of Hayward, California, "Public Safety Community Outreach Project," accessed March 12, 2021, https://www.hayward-ca.gov/content/public-safety-community-outreach.

cxxvii City of Hayward, California, "Hayward Community Conversations on Safety Results: 2020," ArcGIS Experience Builder, accessed March 12, 2021, https://experience.arcgis.com/experience/8106672de32946e5acfa69527c50f260/?data_id=dataSource_1-Hayward_Community_Safety_Survey_Results_3260%3A1.

cxxviii Steven Zipkes (Cedars International Next Generation High School, Founding Principal), in discussion with the author, December 2020.

cxxix Lydia Dobyns (New Tech Network, President and CEO), in discussion with the author, December 2020.

cxxx *Wall Street*, directed by Oliver Stone (1987; Beverly Hills: 20th Century Fox, 2000), DVD.

cxxxi *The Great Dictator*, directed by Charlie Chaplin (1940; New York, Criterion Collection, 2011), DVD.

cxxxii Andrew D. Hawkins, "Uber CEO on the Fight in California: 'We Can't Go Out and Hire 50,000 People Overnight,'" *Verge*, August 19, 2020, https://www.theverge.com/2020/8/19/21376009/uber-ceo-interivew-california-ab5-drivers-khosrowshahi.

cxxxiii Uber Technologies, Inc., "Uber Announces Analyst Call," March 18, 2020, https://investor.uber.com/news-events/news/press-release-details/2020/Uber-Announces-Analyst-Call/default.aspx.

cxxxiv Uber Technologies, Inc., "ESG Report 2020," accessed March 29, 2021, https://s23.q4cdn.com/407969754/files/design /Uber-2020-ESG-Report-Final.pdf.

cxxxv George Skelton, "It's No Wonder Hundreds of Millions Have Been Spent on Prop. 22. A Lot Is at Stake," *Los Angeles Times*, October 16, 2020, https://www.latimes.com/california/story/2020-10-16 /skelton-proposition-22-uber-lyft-independent-contractors.

cxxxvi U.S. Securities and Exchange Commission, Airbnb, Inc. Prospectus, December 9, 2020, https://www.sec.gov/Archives/edgar/data /1559720/000119312520315318/d81668d424b4.htm.

cxxxvii Ibid.

cxxxviii Chris Arnade (Author and Photographer), in discussion with the author, February 2021.

INDEX